W9-AAT-951

AMERICAPEDIA
TAKING THE DUMB OUT OF FREEDOM

JODI LYNN ANDERSON ★ DANIEL EHRENHAFT ★ ANDISHEH NOURAEE

WALKER & COMPANY ✳ NEW YORK

NO LONGER LIBRARY PROPERTY

NO LONGER LIBRARY PROPERTY

Tazewell County Public Library
Tazewell Branch

B&T 24.99

4A
320.60973
AN
T

For our first and best teachers, our parents, Jo-An and Dave Anderson,
Charlotte and Peter Ehrenhaft, and Mahin and Mack Nouraee

Text copyright © 2011 by Jodi Lynn Anderson, Daniel Ehrenhaft, and Andisheh Nouraee
All rights reserved. No part of this book may be reproduced or transmitted in any form or by any means, electronic or mechanical,
including photocopying, recording, or by any information storage and retrieval system, without permission in writing from the publisher.

First published in the United States of America in July 2011 by Walker Publishing Company, Inc., a division of Bloomsbury Publishing, Inc.
www.bloomsburyteens.com

For information about permission to reproduce selections from this book, write to
Permissions, Walker & Company, 175 Fifth Avenue, New York, New York 10010

Photo credits can be found on page 234. Every effort has been made to trace the copyright holders; the publisher apologizes for
any unintentional omission. Please contact us if this has occurred and we will place an acknowledgment in future editions.

Library of Congress Cataloging-in-Publication Data
Anderson, Jodi Lynn.
Americapedia : taking the dumb out of freedom / Jodi Lynn Anderson, Daniel Ehrenhaft, and Andisheh Nouraee.
p.   cm.
ISBN 978-0-8027-9793-3 (paperback) • ISBN 978-0-8027-9792-6 (hardcover)
1. United States—Politics and government—Juvenile literature. 2. Civics—Juvenile literature.
I. Ehrenhaft, Daniel. II. Nouraee, Andisheh. III. Title.
JK40.A53 2011   320.60973—dc22   2010038028

Book design by Jane Archer (www.psbella.com)
Printed in China by Toppan Leefung Printing, Ltd., Dongguan, Guangdong
1 3 5 7 9 10 8 6 4 2 (paperback)
1 3 5 7 9 10 8 6 4 2 (hardcover)

All papers used by Bloomsbury Publishing, Inc., are natural, recyclable products made from wood grown in well-managed forests.
The manufacturing processes conform to the environmental regulations of the country of origin.

As much as it may surprise you—despite being devastatingly brilliant, attractive, and witty—the authors, Andy (more formally known as Andisheh), Jodi, and Dan, are not always correct. In fact, we can occasionally be downright stupid. That's why we rely on readers like you to set us straight. If you notice any factual errors in this book, if you are offended by our biases, or if you disagree with anything we've written, by all means "BARK BACK." (Keep it tasteful, of course.) Please register your complaints in 100 words or fewer here: **www.americapediathebook.com/feedback.**

TABLE OF CONTENTS

AMERICAPEDIA
(File under Vampires and/or Weight Loss)

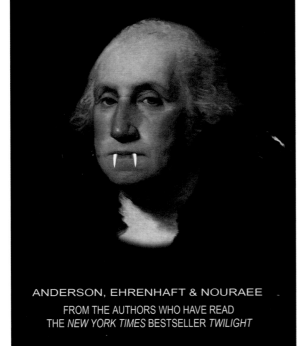

americapedia

ANDERSON, EHRENHAFT & NOURAEE
FROM THE AUTHORS WHO HAVE READ
THE *NEW YORK TIMES* BESTSELLER *TWILIGHT*

Welcome to *Americapedia*, or, as we're hoping book retailers will start calling it, the next installment of the Twilight Saga. It's a fun, vivid, at-a-glance guide—a sort of citizen's manual—to understanding why critical events unfold the way they do, how important decisions are made, and what you can do to get involved. Need to brush up on how Congress works? Go to page 25. Wondering where states and the Supreme Court stand on issues like stem cells, abortion, and gay marriage? Read about it in Hot Buttons on page 177. Confused about relations with Cuba? Flip to pages 105–109. Want to take an active role on the local, national, or international level on specific issues—in this book or elsewhere—that have you fired up? Go to page 223.

This is a new kind of resource—not a textbook and not a parody but a primer that combines the best elements of both: entertaining, but most important, informative and empowering. This is a civics book that will make you laugh and make you think—one that is user-friendly, interactive (check out www.americapediathebook.com), berry-scented, and, most of all, engaging—aimed at anyone who wants to know more about the world and the day-to-day workings of the U.S. government.

The U.S. has been at war for the past decade. Before it's over, it'll cost hundreds of thousands of lives and several trillion dollars. Yet for some reason, Americans are weirdly resistant to examining or understanding the root causes and historical context.

In fact, part of the reason this book exists is because "root causes and historical context" is a five-word American synonym for Ambien. It doesn't need to be that way. Stiff, heavy topics like religious strife, the rise of China, the War on Terror™, the health care debate, and even the workings of our constitution are actually loaded with comedy and irony. That's not to say this book takes its subject matter lightly. On the contrary, we sat down

Do you think a lobbyist is someone who hangs out on the first floor? Do you think Iran is the past tense of "I run"? Do you think stem cells are jails for criminal flowers?

It's okay. We did, too.

We were confused about how the government really works. Why is the electoral system worth paying attention to (and actually fascinating)? How did certain countries become our allies and others our enemies? What, exactly, does the Fed do, and how does it do it? How can you, I, or anyone else who cares influence what's happening?

And shouldn't somebody write a book about it?

and crafted a history of terrorism, the United Nations, Israel-Palestine, and global climate change because we take the subjects very seriously. We think writing about U.S. and foreign affairs should be at least half as interesting as actually having an affair with a foreigner.

We started working on this book in the summer of 2006. To give you some idea of how much the world has changed since then:

★ The Tea Party was not a political movement. Those words were either accompanied by the word "Boston" in reference to an event in 1773, or used in the context of a social event involving your grandma, preferably to be avoided.

★ MySpace was the social network of choice for most teens. Facebook was a relative novelty. Twitter hadn't even been launched.

★ Bernie Madoff was a respected investor. Rod Blagojevich was a respected governor. Ted Haggard was a respected minister. (Don't even get us started on all the other businessmen, politicians, and members of the clergy who have been disgraced since 2006 by mistresses, corruption, or "rentboys.")

★ You probably would have gotten some laughs—or offended people—if you'd joked, "The next president of the United States will be a black man who smokes cigarettes and has admitted using cocaine."

Yes, back in 2006 Barack Obama was still an Illinois senator most famous for writing a book and for a speech he gave at the 2004 Democratic National Convention. Little did he know that Hillary Clinton, the presumed 2008 Democratic presidential nominee at the time, would soon be working for him. Or, for that matter, that she would hire two young men—Jared Cohen and Alec Ross—whose primary jobs at the State Department are to tweet. Not kidding. Their Twitter posts represent the face of "21st Century Statecraft" (Hillary's term): diplomacy conducted in 140-character microblogs. LOLBD (laughing out loud, but diplomatically).

Mind-blowing, isn't it? A social network that nobody had heard of five years ago is not only reporting important news in real time, it is shaping policy that affects the entire world—even sparking revolutions in the Middle East! All of which is to say that the world will probably change a lot more in the months after these words are typeset. But don't worry. New entries of *Americapedia* will be available online, with updates and lots of interactive features. Readers will be able to get the latest on the topics we cover . . . plus blog, debate, call us out on our biases by "barking back," and connect on topics where there's a common interest.

After all, another part of the reason we wrote this book and created the accompanying website is because we have a hunch: even though history is changing faster than we can tweet about it, we (and that mostly means you, the reader) are in a better position than ever to help influence that change. That's why we end the book with a section on getting involved in the topics we cover. From immigration issues to media protection to gay marriage and voters' rights, we offer tools and tips to get active about what strikes a chord with you, plus online forums to help you connect with like-minded people who want to help influence the course of current events.

We hope you'll find a lot here that you didn't know, a lot that you want to know more about, and a lot that you feel passionate enough about to join the debate. We've aimed to give you a book that's not only an authoritative reference (and a good item to put under the short leg of your coffee table) but also a resource that inspires you to start shaping the issues and the world you live in. We hope you learn as much from it as we have.

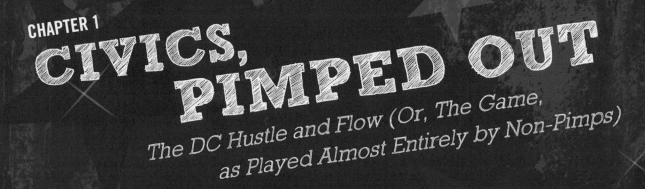

CHAPTER 1

CIVICS, PIMPED OUT

The DC Hustle and Flow (Or, The Game, as Played Almost Entirely by Non-Pimps)

INTRODUCTION
The Birth of a Nation, in Case You Missed It

THE DECLARATION OF INDEPENDENCE
America Unfriends Great Britain

★ **GEORGIA ON MY MIND**
The First Continental Congress

★ **TAXATION WITHOUT REPRESENTATION**
The Inspirational Call to Independence That Endures Today as an Angry Slogan on Washington DC License Plates

★ **SLAVERY** *Affectionately Known as "Our Peculiar Institution"*

THE CONSTITUTION
Understanding the Document Our Leaders Ignore

★ **THE GENIUS OF OUR CONSTITUTION AT WORK** *How George W. Bush Defeated Al Gore in the 2000 Presidential Election, Even Though He Didn't Receive a Majority of the Votes*

★ **WHY ARE THERE TWO HOUSES OF CONGRESS? IN CASE ONE IS FORECLOSED?**

★ **WHAT DOES IT MEAN WHEN PEOPLE SAY THE REPUBLICANS OR THE DEMOCRATS "TOOK" THE HOUSE OR THE SENATE?**

★ **WHO'S THE SPEAKER OF THE HOUSE AND WHAT DOES HE OR SHE DO?**

★ **WHAT'S A WHIP?**

FEDERALISM
The Only Word That Makes Us Yawn More Than "Civics"

THE AMERICAN ELECTORAL PROCESS
One Person, One Vote—Sort Of

★ **WHERE DO CANDIDATES COME FROM?**

★ **WHAT'S THE DIFFERENCE BETWEEN A PRIMARY AND A CAUCUS?**

★ **WHY DO PEOPLE TALK SO MUCH ABOUT IOWA AND NEW HAMPSHIRE?**

CAMPAIGN FINANCE
How Do People Fund Their Campaigns? Why Is It Controversial? And How Can I Get In on the Action?

★ **WHAT'S A PAC?**

★ **WHAT'S A NATIONAL CONVENTION?**

THE ELECTORAL COLLEGE
What Is It, Anyway? Can I Get In Even if My SAT Scores Stink?

★ **SO WHY DO WE EVEN HAVE THE ELECTORAL COLLEGE? SHOULD WE DROP OUT?**

★ **WITH SO MANY PEOPLE THINKING IT'S UNFAIR, WILL IT CHANGE?**

THE TWO-PARTY SYSTEM
Democrats, Republicans, and Why No One Else Is Invited

★ **SO HOW DOES HAVING A TWO-PARTY SYSTEM SERVE US?**

★ **IS THERE A REASONABLE ALTERNATIVE?**

★ **WHERE DID DEMOCRATS AND REPUBLICANS COME FROM? AND WHY ALL THE NAME-CALLING?**

GERRYMANDERING
The Single Greatest Threat to Your Vote That Sounds Like a Word British People Would Use

INTRODUCTION
The Birth of a Nation, in Case You Missed It

Holy *Scheisse*! Did you know that this chapter could very well have been written in German, Dutch, French, or Spanish?[1] No joke. As far as our current common language goes, history's iffy winds just happened to blow in favor of English.

For a while, before the Great Migration (see chapter five, page 140), there were more German and Dutch speakers in America than there were English. So, say the Dutch had triumphed over the British during the seventeenth-century Anglo-Dutch wars. New York might still be called New Amsterdam and, at this very moment, you might be wearing wooden shoes instead of Crocs.

A typical New Yorker, had the Dutch triumphed during the seventeenth-century Anglo-Dutch wars

And if the British hadn't won the French and Indian War[2] in 1763? There's a good chance we'd all be eating crepes and escargots instead of hamburgers, Jell-O, and the other delicious American fare that is served in our school cafeterias.

A typical American public school lunch, had the British lost the French and Indian War in 1763

Along these lines, if Spain hadn't squandered its own claims to the heartland at the turn of the eighteenth century, North America might still include a big fat country called New Spain—perhaps with fewer Walmarts but more bullrings—stretching from Florida, throughout the South and West, all the way to Wyoming. That means you could probably say *vaya con Dios* to California, too.

A typical American pastime, had Spain held on to its North American land

---

1. And we hope it will be, if we can sell the foreign rights and get it translated.
2. For some reason, the French and Indian War was also known as the Seven Years' War, even though it was fought by the British against either the French or the Indians for most of the early eighteenth century. The French and Indians weren't natural allies, but they banded together for self-protection. This is only one of many ill-fated historical examples of the "the enemy of my enemy is my friend" strategy.

Indeed, given all the early territorial confusion, the United States might have wound up divided in any number of ways. Credit is due to the Founding Fathers for impressing upon their fellow citizens the need to stay united at all costs. Their relentless sloganeering helped: "United we stand, divided we fall" . . . "If we don't hang together, we'll all hang separately" . . . and the no-nonsense "Join, or die"—care of Benjamin Franklin, and later adopted by Samuel Adams and his Sons of Liberty militia, who could always be counted on for their creepy lack of humor.

Today we tend to think of the United States as a single, massive, awesome entity. U.S.A.! U.S.A.! (Well, depending on our mood.) Sure, there are red states and blue states, the tree huggers and gas-guzzlers, the "liberal elite" and Beck University[3] graduates, and of course, team Edward versus team Jacob. But we're all *Americans*.

That wasn't always the case.

In the beginning, the country wasn't much more than a loose rabble of former colonies. The founders had the foresight to know that our fledgling nation would succeed

JOIN, or DIE.

only as a whole, with a common language and a strong central government. By emphasizing the "United" over the "States" part of the country's name, they planted in our collective brain the seed of knowing that we'd all be better off as one.[4]

HISTORY'S IFFY WINDS AND THE BATTLE OF BROOKLYN

If it weren't for lousy weather, the Americans would have probably lost the Revolutionary War in late August 1776. At the time, most of the Continental Army was based in New York City. (Even then it was a hot spot.) The British, under the command of General William Howe, had taken nearly all of Brooklyn in a frenzied onslaught, stopping only to booze up at a Flatbush-area bar called the Rising Sun Tavern. Howe's force was ready to advance on Brooklyn Heights, where George Washington and half his troops were holed up. But three days of pounding rain had given way to a dense fog. Howe decided to wait for improved visibility before the final assault, taking the downtime to write a letter back to England proclaiming "total victory in Brooklyn."

The letter turned out to be a little premature. Using the fog as cover, George Washington was able to sneak his soldiers to the safety of Manhattan—via rowboats—where the rest of his troops stood strong. (Or relatively strong, anyway. Their cannons faced in the wrong direction.) Luckily, the rain had prevented British warships from sailing up the East River, which would have split Washington's army and blocked his escape. When Howe finally made it to Brooklyn Heights, all he found were rusted buckets. Psych! It remains unclear whether he and his troops returned to the Rising Sun Tavern to drown their sorrows.

3. It's true: Glenn Beck has his own online univesity, where you can learn "real American history." (His words.)
4. Um . . . well, technically, it would take another hundred years of growing pains, internal strife, and finally the Civil War—the bloodiest war in U.S. history—for the majority of U.S. citizens to agree that common national interests should trump individual states' rights (see Federalism, page 28).

THE DECLARATION OF INDEPENDENCE

America Unfriends Great Britain

The history of . . . Great Britain is a history of repeated injuries . . . all having in direct object the establishment of an absolute tyranny over [America].
> *—Thomas Jefferson, the Declaration of Independence*

America has no truer friend than Great Britain.
> *—George W. Bush, 2001*

History is kind of funny, isn't it? It's pretty tough to argue with George W. Bush's 2001 pronouncement, especially given Great Britain's steadfast support of even our most unpopular policies. But try to put yourself in the shoes of an American, circa 1776.

For starters, you would stink to high heaven. Those shoes would most likely be shabbily cobbled from cheap rawhide—and unless you were very wealthy, you'd wear them without socks. They wouldn't be very comfortable, either.

Now, to add insult to injury, imagine if British soldiers invited themselves over while you were taking off said shoes. (*Ah, relief.*) The Quartering Act of 1774 would give them the right to spend the night. Furthermore, they could eat your food, hog your blankets, and use your chamber pots. If they wanted to sing annoying songs like "Rule, Britannia," they could do that, too. You'd be obliged to provide all of this for them at no charge.

If you refused? These same British soldiers—or worse, Hessian mercenaries acting on their behalf[5]—could force you to surrender all your weapons. Or they could take you prisoner. Or they could just shoot you, whichever was easiest.

Keep in mind: your feet ache; you're tired; it's late; you have no Wi-Fi, no iPod, no TiVo, no light other than candles and oil lamps, no source of entertainment other than the King James Bible . . . You'd probably be pretty pissed off.

Thomas Jefferson and the rest of the free white men behind the Declaration of Independence were pissed off, too. If you actually study the document[6]—at its heart a bullet-point presentation of bitter but gorgeously written complaints—you almost get the sense that King George III was screwing with the American colonies for no other purpose than his own maniacal kicks. In addition to the Quartering Act of 1774, King George III (to paraphrase Jefferson) "plundered seas, ravaged coasts, burnt towns, destroyed lives." He also forced colonial representatives to meet in "unusual, uncomfortable, and distant places . . . for the sole purposes of fatiguing them."

Fatigued and fed up, the Founding Fathers decided to meet on their own—and ultimately to break free of Britain's tyrannical rule. Well, on paper, at least.[7]

---

5. Hessians were from the principality of Hesse (in what is now Germany), a place known for almost nothing except providing mercenaries to the British Army during the Revolutionary War.

6. For a full transcript, go here: www.archives.gov/exhibits/charters/declaration.html.

7. It would take another five years of fighting before the British finally surrendered at Yorktown in 1781, and another two years before the British officially granted independence to the American Colonies upon signing the Treaty of Paris in 1783. And even then, the British were such sore losers that they refused to pose for a portrait commemorating the event.

THOMAS JEFFERSON, OUR NATION'S FAVORITE SMARTY-PANTS

I think this is the most extraordinary collection of talent, of human knowledge, that has ever been gathered together at the White House, with the possible exception of when Thomas Jefferson dined alone.

—*John F. Kennedy, remarks at a dinner honoring Nobel Prize winners*

You gotta give Jefferson props; it was no wonder he was chosen among all the delegates at the Second Continental Congress to author the Declaration of Independence. Nobody else could have packed words like "consanguinity" with the same liberating punch. In fact, few people know what "consanguinity" means, including the authors of this book. (We looked it up. It means "kinship.")

GEORGIA ON MY MIND
The First Continental Congress

At Benjamin Franklin's urging, the First Continental Congress convened mostly as a symbolic slap in the face to King George III, to prove to him that such a congress *could* meet. Until 1775, disgruntled bigwigs from the thirteen colonies weren't all that interested in hanging out together. For the most part, guys from Georgia (like Button Gwinnett and Lyman Hall[8]) didn't consider the problems of guys from Massachusetts (like John and Samuel Adams; see chapter two, pages 44–46) to be their problems—except when it came to taxes.

Yes, in the mid-1770s, trendy outrage was "all about the Benjamins."[9] (Again, see chapter two, page 44.) British taxes were the one peeve that united almost every free white male in the colonies—regardless of their other peeves, such as opposing views on slavery. And yet, because traveling in eighteenth-century America was such a huge pain in the butt, they rarely did more than grumble about it from their own hometowns.

All that changed in December 1773. The British sent three boatloads of tea to Massachusetts with the expectation that the Americans would pay taxes on it and drink up, as they always had. (Who doesn't love a cup of hot tea during winter in New England, even if it is overpriced?) Instead, some of those Americans dumped the tea into Boston Harbor. LOL!

The intolerable King George III

---

8. Their actual names, not aliases, we swear. You can see for yourself on the Declaration of Independence.
9. Benjamin Franklin would not appear on a $100 bill until 1914, long after his death—lending credence to his famous quote: "In this world nothing is certain except death and taxes." (See box, page 45.)

PATRIOTS GONE WILD! TOMAHAWKS, FACE PAINT, AND OFFENSIVE WHOOPING

George Hewes, one of the two hundred men who participated in the famous Boston Tea Party, offers this shockingly boring eyewitness account: "I immediately dressed myself in the costume of an Indian, equipped with a small hatchet . . . and a club, [with which,] after having painted my face and hands with coal dust in the shop of a blacksmith, I repaired to Griffin's wharf, where the ships lay that contained the tea . . . In about three hours [we had] broken and thrown overboard every tea chest to be found . . . We were surrounded by British armed ships, but no attempt was made to resist us."

In response, King George III immediately imposed a series of laws that came to be known as the "Intolerable Acts."

THE INTOLERABLE LAWS THAT SENT AMERICA OVER THE EDGE

★ The Quartering Act of 1774
★ The Boston Port Act, which closed the Boston Harbor
★ The Impartial Administration of Justice Act. This may deserve the Best Oxymoron[10] prize in that its title meant the exact opposite of what it enforced. This law allowed the royal governors of the American colonies to move all trials to England to ensure "fair judgment." So, say, for example, you were a Boston ship owner, and you were arrested for illegally taking your boat for a spin in the recently closed Boston Harbor. You could be extradited to England to face trial in front of a British jury.
★ The Massachusetts Government Act, which put the state of Massachusetts under complete British control
★ The Quebec Act, which made life nice for Canadians but was perceived as a slap in the face to Americans

King George III, once again proving he was out of his gourd, figured that most Americans would be angrier at Bostonians than they would be at him for the crackdown—and would turn against the colony of Massachusetts. (Nobody would want *their* ports closed, too, right?) Not surprisingly, his plan backfired. Instead of blaming Massachusetts, representatives from all the other colonies finally agreed to heed Benjamin Franklin's call to meet—and to turn words into action.

Well . . . except for Georgia. At the time, Georgians felt they needed the British more than they needed to commiserate with their fellow Americans—mostly because British soldiers were the only ones who were any good at fighting the Creek Indians.[11] Besides, arms-bearing Georgian citizens had their hands full keeping their slaves in line.

So on September 5, 1774, fifty-six delegates from twelve colonies gathered for the first time at Carpenter's Hall in Philadelphia. Their original intention was not to declare independence from Britain. In fact, the First Continental Congress was little more than a schmooze fest. The roots of the old boy network (see chapter two once more) can be traced to its frequent lunch breaks, banquets, and cocktail parties, where the delegates bickered and bantered, often while drunk.[12]

---

10. Other oxymorons include "boneless ribs," "friendly fire," and our favorite, "military intelligence."
11. The Creek Indians were a confederation of southeastern tribes who bravely banded together to protect their lands from the growing plantation society. As you might have guessed, they didn't succeed.
12. The one notable exception is Sam Adams, who made a point of showing off his sober ways by not participating. Funny that his face would eventually appear not on currency but on beer bottles.

The First Continental Congress's To-Do List

☆ Whine, complain, and bloviate
☆ Toast one another
☆ Stop paying taxes
☆ Powder wigs and noses
☆ Mail a nasty letter off to England
☆ Boycott all British imports
☆ Make a date to meet again the following spring for more fun (Woo-hoo!)

TAXATION WITHOUT REPRESENTATION
The Inspirational Call to Independence That Endures Today as an Angry Slogan on Washington DC License Plates

PAMPHLETEERING: THE BLOGGING OF DAYS OF YORE

Just as politicians today are wise to heed the blogosphere, the Founding Fathers were wise to heed the pamphleteers, who inspired the same kind of DIY political movement at the grassroots level. The first real cry for independence didn't come from the Second Continental Congress but from Thomas Paine's *Common Sense*—the overnight colonial sensation of early 1776. Taking a cue from firebrands like Patrick Henry (who had the brains to rally working-class Americans by painting the British as a common enemy of both rich and poor), its mass appeal lay in its down-home folksiness and blunt language: "Everything that is right or reasonable pleads for separation. The blood of the slain, the weeping voice of nature cries, 'TIS TIME TO PART!" Come on: who *doesn't* want to get up and form their own nation after reading that?

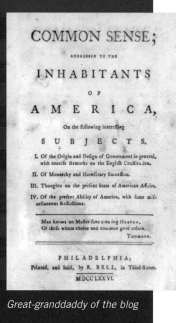

Great-granddaddy of the blog

The Second Continental Congress turned out to be a much more sober affair than the first. King George III responded to the First Congress's shenanigans not by lowering taxes but by sending more troops. Tensions came to a boil at Lexington and Concord on April 19, 1775. During what was essentially a staring contest between British soldiers and American minutemen, somebody blinked. Worse, somebody fired a musket. Nobody knows who from which side started it, but the Revolutionary War had begun.

The bloodshed made clear that boycotting and complaining would never be enough to lower taxes. It also made clear that Britain wouldn't let America go without a fight.

The following year, the Founding Fathers forcefully turned action back into words. By this time, even Georgia was on board with the plan to secede and form a new nation. Thomas Jefferson, charged with the task of breaking the news to King George III, spent most of June 1776 in seclusion, playing his violin and drafting a formal declaration of independence. What emerged eventually became the mottled yellow parchment now enshrined in the National Archives. Incidentally, it's not two-sided. In spite of what's suggested in the 2004 box-office smash *National Treasure*, the only message on the back reads: "Original Declaration of Independence / dated 4th July 1776."[13]

---

13. In the movie, Nicolas Cage discovers that the back of the Declaration of Independence is inscribed with the clues to finding a secret stockpile of fabulous riches. Coincidentally, the film and its sequel grossed several hundred million dollars—a stockpile of fabulous riches by anyone's standards.

IS THE DECLARATION OF INDEPENDENCE IN THE NATIONAL ARCHIVES REALLY THE DECLARATION OF INDEPENDENCE?

Sort of. The copy on display at the National Archives is the handwritten draft signed by all fifty-six delegates. But on July 4, 1776, a guy named John Dunlap printed twenty-five copies—now known as "Dunlap Broadsides"—which were much easier to read, and which made the rounds among the colonies. Today, two remain in the Library of Congress. George Washington owned one of them. Maybe that one should be considered the real one, instead of the chicken-scratch behind the glass.

Speaking of which, have you ever tried to read the Magna Carta? Written in 1215 by frustrated English barons, this nearly illegible document is modern democracy's baby-daddy. It wrested absolute power from the British monarchy, subjected the king for the first time to the rule of law, and granted the nobility the right of habeas corpus (see The Constitution, page 17). Jefferson and the other Founding Fathers were profoundly influenced by both the Magna Carta's revolutionary philosophy and terrible penmanship.

The copy of the Magna Carta ("Great Charter") that sits in Britain's Royal Archives. Even without the holes, there's no point in trying to decipher it.

While Jefferson's powerful words celebrate the inalienable right of all men to "life, liberty, and the pursuit of happiness," the Declaration of Independence's practical purpose still lay in getting Americans off the hook for the British taxes they owed. As a matter of fact, an earlier draft read that all men were entitled to "life, liberty, and property." But since not all American men—namely slaves—could own property, the wording didn't quite ring true. In the end, Jefferson and the others decided that for appearances' sake it was best to celebrate what *couldn't* be owned (and therefore taxed), not even by the British.

THEM'S FIGHTIN' WORDS

Ever been to Washington DC? Not only is it the seat of our government, it's also a kindred spirit of the original thirteen colonies. Since its citizens don't live in a state, they have no vote in the Senate, and therefore no say about their taxes. Oh, the irony!

And you think modern advertising is evil?

SLAVERY
Affectionately Known as "Our Peculiar Institution"

What's more American than hot dogs and apple pie? You guessed it: spin. Love us or hate us, you can't deny the lunatic marketing genius it took to make slavery seem, for nearly two hundred and fifty years, not only palatable but also *good*.

The first African slaves, twenty in all, arrived in Jamestown, Virginia, in 1619. They were sent to aid desperate colonists, some of whom had resorted to cannibalism in order to survive. The British, craving American tobacco, were willing to do whatever it took to ensure a steady supply. If slaves could provide the colonists with free farm labor, the colonists figured they could concentrate on more important things: fending off Native Americans, feeding themselves, and meeting tobacco quotas—with the added bonus of saving money.

This simple strategy set the precedent for two centuries of robust slave trade. By 1763, there were 170,000 slaves in Virginia, nearly half the colony's population.

James Madison, one of many Founding Fathers who owned slaves, boasted that each slave earned him $257 a year and cost only $13 to keep. The profits no doubt went a long way to easing any guilt he may have had about preaching liberty while owning other human beings. The trick, of course, was not to view slaves as human. Sure, they were status symbols and proof of financial success, but they were also *meant* to be owned, like his wife Dolley's exotic pet parrot.

Dolley Madison

To promote this idea, America generated mountains of pro-slavery literature with catchy titles such as *Slavery Ordained of God* and *Cannibals All!* (Referring to slaves, not the actual cannibals of Jamestown who became slave owners.) The Bible was a big help, too. Many slave owners believed that black Africans were the descendants of Ham, the cursed son of Noah. Besides, ancient Israel was a slave-owning society; it's all there in the book of Leviticus. Ancient Greece was a slave-owning society, too, for that matter—birthplace of democracy, America's philosophical forefather, and the "classical civilization" Madison and the other Founding Fathers claimed to be re-creating in the New World.

As time went on, however, championing slavery became increasingly difficult. The abolitionist movement, spearheaded largely by white Christian males (three traits slave owners cited as proof of their own superiority), started to gain momentum. It didn't help that the abolitionists' black leaders, former slaves such as Frederick Douglass, tended to be brilliant and charismatic—thereby making slave owners look like idiots.

Former slave Frederick Douglass versus former slave owner President James Madison

THE ANCIENT GREEKS AND FOUNDING FATHERS: COMPARE WHAT THEY HAVE IN COMMON!		
	ANCIENT GREEKS	FOUNDING FATHERS
Slave Ownership	✓	✓
A Taste for Pretty Marble Columns	✓	✓
The Belief That Men Are Superior to Women	✓	✓
Capital Punishment	✓	✓
Togas	✓	
Knickers		✓
Government by Representative Democracy	✓	✓

By the 1830s, even using the word "slavery" was considered in poor taste in the etiquette-obsessed South. Pro-slavery advocates had to resort to clever euphemisms such as "our peculiar institution," made famous by Senator John C. Calhoun in an 1837 speech on the Senate floor. He also called slavery "a positive good." Twenty-four years later the country was at war over it.

THE CONSTITUTION
Understanding the Document Our Leaders Ignore

It has been said that Democracy is the worst form of government, except for all the others that have been tried.

—Winston Churchill

If you're like most people—and by "most people," we mean the kind who zone out at the mere mention of the word "constitution"—don't worry: many of our elected officials do, too.

Anything written in eighteenth-century legalese is bound to seem more complicated than it actually is. The U.S. Constitution is no exception. But don't fret. The trick is to remember that the people who wrote it—those free white men we've been lovingly calling the Founding Fathers—had a simple agenda. They wanted to make sure that the power to govern could never fall into the hands of a single person or entity. (Say, a colorful psychopath like King George III.) To borrow the rallying cry of the Black Panthers,[14] the Founding Fathers' philosophy was "All power to all the people!"

---

14. The Black Panthers were a group of 1960s radicals who fought for the rights of African Americans, and who tended to scare a lot of people while doing so. Like the Founding Fathers, they believed that armed revolution was the only means to achieve justice and defeat their oppressors. It's somewhat ironic that those oppressors happened to be the U.S. government, the inheritors of the Founding Fathers.

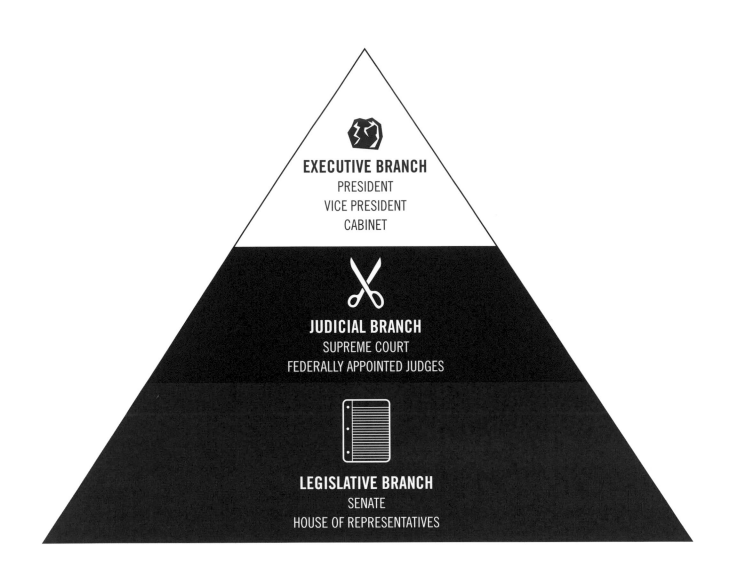

EXECUTIVE BRANCH
PRESIDENT
VICE PRESIDENT
CABINET

JUDICIAL BRANCH
SUPREME COURT
FEDERALLY APPOINTED JUDGES

LEGISLATIVE BRANCH
SENATE
HOUSE OF REPRESENTATIVES

The Constitution's genius lies in its masterful system of checks and balances. One branch of government can never acquire too much power, because the other two branches can gang up on it if it starts acting dictatorial.

Think of it as a game of Rock, Paper, Scissors. The paper, the legislative branch (all those laws have to be written *somewhere*, right?), appears flimsiest, but it can smother the rock—the executive branch—with its impeachment powers. The executive branch appears strongest; after all, it has the power to appoint the judicial branch: the scissors. Moreover, it can smash those scissors with its executive decisions. Of course, the judiciary can slice up the laws of the legislature with its rulings.

In the end, nobody wins. And then again, *everybody* wins.

THE GENIUS OF OUR CONSTITUTION AT WORK
How George W. Bush Defeated Al Gore in the 2000 Presidential Election, Even Though He Didn't Receive a Majority of the Votes

Given how dull a regular old civics textbook can be, we decided it was best to introduce the U.S. Constitution with a gripping anecdote, to show rather than tell. By showing you how George W. Bush defeated Al Gore to become the forty-third president of the United States, we'll take you on a wacky trip through all three branches of government as laid out in the Constitution. You'll laugh, you'll cry, you won't believe what you read!

PART ONE: THE LEGISLATIVE BRANCH
(Paper)

At the time of the 2000 election, Al Gore was vice president of the United States. As such, he was also president of the Senate. One of the Senate's primary jobs is to ratify laws proposed and passed by the House of Representatives. Most of these laws don't make history.[15] But occasionally the two houses of Congress will ratify a law so bold that it can actually change the Constitution permanently. These are known as constitutional amendments. (To keep our gripping anecdote humming along, we'll explore how constitutional amendments get made and passed a little later on.)

In the case of *Bush v. Gore*, 2000, the constitutional amendment that would eventually seal George W. Bush's victory was the Fourteenth.

Proposed on June 13, 1866, and ratified by the Senate on July 9, 1868, the Fourteenth Amendment entitles every citizen of the U.S. to "due process" and "equal protection" under the law. It was written mostly to protect the rights of the nation's newest citizens at the time—its former slaves—and to reaffirm the writ of habeas corpus. Until the passage of the Fourteenth Amendment, killing a former slave was considered bad, but not all *that* bad.

The late commentator Tim Russert, preoccupied with the goings-on in Florida on election night 2000, with his famous "whiteboard," which is now part of the Smithsonian collection

At first glance, the Fourteenth Amendment may not look like it would have much to do with a presidential election 132 years down the road. And it certainly wasn't first and foremost in people's minds on November 7, 2000, as they watched the election results pour in on NBC, CNN,

WHAT IS HABEAS CORPUS, ANYWAY? CAN I GET IT FROM KISSING?

No, habeas corpus is not contagious. It's a Latin command, which translated means "Produce the body." This command is directed to any authority figure who has arrested or detained a suspected criminal. The "body" actually refers to the suspect, who has the right to appear before a court to hear whatever charges have been brought against him or her. Without the writ of habeas corpus, suspected criminals could be detained and locked up indefinitely without ever being charged with a crime. This is such an affront to our unalienable rights of "life, liberty, and the pursuit of happiness" that the writ of habeas corpus has only been suspended once, during the Civil War. Well, unless you count what went on at Guantánamo Bay, Cuba, otherwise known as "Gitmo," during the Bush Administration's War on Terror. But that isn't even part of the United States, so it *shouldn't* count. Or so say those who are in favor of keeping it open (see the Unconstitutional Hall of Shame, page 27).

FOXNews, or *The Daily Show*. No, everybody was far too preoccupied with what was going on in Florida.

As the clock ticked, it became clear that the entire presidential election hinged on Florida's twenty-five electoral votes (see the Electoral College, page 34). Every other state's electoral votes had been officially tallied. Gore was in the lead with 266 to Bush's 246, four shy of the 270 electoral votes needed to win. Plus, Gore had already won the popular vote by a margin of almost 336,000—at the time of the 2000 census, roughly the population of Pittsburgh.[16]

---

15. An example of a less-than-newsworthy law passed by Congress: It is illegal to shoot a hole in a penny. Shooting a penny can carry a jail sentence of up to five years. Seriously.
16. Home of the Steelers, birthplace of Modern Reform Judaism, and brewer of Iron City beer.

Thanks to Article II, Section 1, of the Constitution, the people who have the ultimate say over who is elected president and vice president of the United States are not you, the people, but "electors." That means, technically speaking, that we U.S. citizens do not live in a democracy. We don't even live in a republic. We live in our own freakish invention.

As we'll see later in this chapter, electors aren't even *elected*. They're appointed by governors. At the time of *Bush v. Gore*, 2000, Governor Jeb Bush was responsible for appointing the twenty-five Florida electors who ultimately elected his brother, George W. Bush. Which might make you wonder: could Florida's electors have been biased in any way? Well, yes, but it wouldn't even matter if they were. They were obligated by law to vote for the candidate who received the most votes, Democrat or Republican. In Florida, it's a winner-takes-all electoral scenario.

At first, Gore was the projected winner.[17] But by nightfall, Bush had squeaked by with a victory of less than 2,000 popular votes, which meant all of Florida's 25 electoral votes were his.

A baffled Floridian, with chad

In any close election, Florida state law requires an automatic recount of the popular vote. The recount shrunk Bush's victory to a margin of only 347 popular votes.

But even that number wasn't 100 percent reliable, due to Florida's outdated voting machines.[18] (Strangely, it was senior citizens who had the most trouble figuring out the old-fangled technology.) Gore demanded a second recount and an investigation into Florida's entire voting process.

Bush wasn't about to sit back and let Gore snatch victory from his grasp. He hired his dad's former secretary of state, James Baker, as his lawyer—and filed suit against Gore in the state of Florida, demanding that Gore halt the recount.

On November 13, a federal judge in Miami tossed out Bush's lawsuit. Bush immediately appealed, which brought the case before the United States Supreme Court.

And that brings us to the judicial branch.

✂ PART TWO: THE JUDICIAL BRANCH (Scissors)

Question: Before we go any further, is it true that some of the justices go naked under their robes?

TMI!!! Besides, that question is disrespectful of the sanctity of the office. For one thing, Supreme Court justices are the only members of government who wear robes. (At least publicly.) Plus, everybody has to call them "Your Honor." And, like electors, they aren't elected. They're appointed by the president and must be approved by both houses of Congress—by a 60 percent majority vote in the Senate, no less. Finally, they serve for life or until they resign. Being a Supreme Court justice is truly "the gig of a lifetime."

But why *are* Supreme Court justices worthy of such respect? Because, thanks to Article III of the Constitution, they must decide vital historic cases that—in the government's own words—"challenge or require interpretation of the legislation passed by Congress and signed by the president."

---

17. Or so claimed former CBS news anchorman Dan Rather, who was never able to live down the gaffe.
18. The scandal has given us lots of flowery and baffling phrases such as "butterfly ballots" and "hanging chads"—all of which speak to the absurdity of trying to use ineffective punch cards to determine the leader of the free world. A "chad" is the small piece of cardboard punched out by a hole punch. Not all the chads were fully punched out (hence the "hanging" part), which screwed up the votes.

SIX GROUNDBREAKING SUPREME COURT DECISIONS THAT EITHER CHANGED HISTORY, PISSED PEOPLE OFF, OR BOTH

MARBURY v. MADISON

This 1803 case ensured that the Supreme Court would never be bound by an act of Congress that it found "repugnant." In the immediate aftermath of the case, members of the judiciary and legislature often flipped each other the eighteenth-century equivalent of "the bird."

Today's happier Supreme Court

DRED SCOTT v. SANFORD

Dred Scott, injustice's poster child

In 1857, the Supreme Court ruled 7–2 that any person of African descent, whether slave or free, could never be a U.S. citizen because—and this is not a joke—of what was written in the Declaration of Independence. Nobody found the ruling very funny, not even the winning side. It infuriated the northern states and helped set the stage for the Civil War.

PLESSY v. FERGUSON

This 1896 case ruled that segregation was perfectly fine, so long as everybody had "separate but equal" rights. Here's a telling exercise: compare the drinking fountains in the photo below, then decide where *you'd* most want to quench your thirst.

Mmm . . . this sucks.

BROWN v. BOARD OF EDUCATION

In 1954, the Supreme Court finally decided that "separate but equal" was bogus. Needless to say, a lot of racists weren't very happy.

From now on, when I say, "Be careful walking to school," please pay attention, okay?

MIRANDA v. ARIZONA

Fans of the *Law & Order* franchise will no doubt recognize this 1966 ruling, which guarantees any person accused of a crime the right to a free lawyer, and protects the accused against self-incrimination. It is also a rare historic case in which one of the participants' names morphed into a verb. Even Bill Gates (right) has been "Mirandized."

No, really; I am going to have the last laugh.

ROE v. WADE

This 1973 Supreme Court decision is one of the few that directly involves the human body. And here's something you may not know: the plaintiff, Norma L. "Jane Roe" McCorvey, is now an outspoken

As you can see, the Freedom to Change One's Mind and Shout about It is also guaranteed under the Constitution.

antiabortion activist. Here she can be seen exercising her First Amendment rights by burning six "wicked" (her word) Supreme Court decisions (including the one named after her), a gay pride flag, and a copy of the Koran.

In the case of *Bush v. Gore*, 2000, the Supreme Court was asked to interpret the Fourteenth Amendment, thanks to some ingenious legal maneuvering on Bush's part.

According to Bush (or, more accurately, his lawyers), a recount in Florida would mean that Gore had better protection under the law than Bush. At the time, there was no universally accepted method for recounting votes by hand. Bush wanted to know: Who would do the counting? Gore's people? Not so fast. That would skew justice in Gore's favor. And there wasn't enough time to find someone both sides could agree on. Federal law decreed that the next president had to be chosen by December 13. There was no way to extend the deadline without passing a brand-new law, and that would have taken too long, as well. So the only way for justice to be served, constitutionally, was to stick with the first count—even though it was probably wrong.

This is not a joke. This was Bush's actual argument, based on the Constitution, and it won.

The Supreme Court is made up of nine justices: an odd number, so there can't be any tie votes. On December 13, 2000, in deference to the hallowed Fourteenth Amendment, the court voted 5–4 in Bush's favor and decreed him president of the United States.

In a final and somewhat cruel twist of fate, Gore was forced to preside over the official counting of the electoral votes on January 6, 2001. To make matters worse for him, the Constitution specifies that the president of the Senate must perform this duty in front of a joint session of Congress. So poor Gore had to get up in front of the entire legislative branch and hand Bush the presidency that could have been his, counting the votes out loud: 271 for Bush, 266 for him.

Which brings us to the executive branch.

PART THREE: THE EXECUTIVE BRANCH (Rock)

Question: Um . . . so President Bush wasn't really elected president in 2000?

Long answer: yes and no. He did lose the nationwide popular vote. But the Supreme Court upheld the ruling of the Florida State Legislature, which determined that he'd won the popular vote *in the state of Florida*. That gave him those crucial twenty-

President Bush, wielding his executive authority

five electoral votes that put him over the top. And what's done can't be undone, so there's no point harping on it or complaining about it. Besides, who cares anymore? He's back home in Crawford, clearing brush and tending to his beloved dog, Barney.

Thanks to the Supreme Court decision, George W. Bush took office on January 20, 2001. There he made the traditional solemn oath to "preserve, protect and defend the Constitution of the United States." His duties also included fund-raising, pardoning a turkey every Thanksgiving, and controlling a massive nuclear arsenal. Oh, and he was also obliged to veto any bill or law passed by Congress that could be unconstitutional.

In his first five years as president, George W. Bush vetoed only one bill: a bill to fund stem-cell research (see chapter six, pages 183–184). To give you some context, in less than three years in office, thirty-eighth president Gerald Ford vetoed sixty-six bills—owing to their potential to subvert the economy, empower criminals, and allow the country to engage in dubious business with dictators. Incidentally, President Ford was also often lampooned as a "dumb" president, owing to his unfortunate tendency to fall down in public.

President Ford, tumbling down the stairs of Air Force One

NO, REALLY: WHAT DOES THE CONSTITUTION SAY?

Excellent question—though grammatically incorrect: as a document, the Constitution doesn't *say* anything; it *reads*. Now let us never read or speak of grammar again.

The Constitution is made up of three parts.

★ The Preamble: This is the inspirational "We-the-People" bit, which explains, to anyone who cares, what the Constitution is.

★ The Articles: Seven in all, these lay out the structure of the U.S. government. Think of the articles as a how-to guide for forming a country. (They could be applicable to *your* country if you wanted to secede from this one.) The first three articles cover how the three branches of government are formed and what they do: legislative, executive, and judicial, in that order. The fourth establishes states' powers and limits. The fifth, sixth, and seventh basically inform you how to amend and protect the Constitution. They also urge states to ratify the Constitution.

★ The Bill of Rights (aka the First Ten Amendments): Yes, people, *this* is why we are entitled to assemble without fear, to call our leaders jerks in public, to own guns if we want to, to worship Satan if we're so inclined . . . my goodness, there are far too many rights to list here. In short, the Bill of Rights exists to ensure and protect *your* rights, otherwise known as the rights of the individual. The Founding Fathers wouldn't even ratify the Constitution without the first ten amendments, which include the oft-forgotten Eighth: bail should never be set too high. (The Eighth also forbids "cruel and unusual punishments.")

But that's not all. The Bill of Rights continues to grow and grow, amendment by amendment, which is why the Constitution is known as a "living document." (Like many living things, it also has the power to turn around and bite people in the rear, like its public servant Al Gore.) As of this writing, the most recent is the Twenty-seventh Amendment, first proposed in 1789 and ratified in 1992. No, that's not a typo. *1789*! It reads: "No law, varying the compensation for the services of the Senators and Representatives, shall take effect, until an election of representatives shall have intervened." In other words, the most recent amendment ensures that Congress can keep giving itself raises for all eternity. The Founding Fathers were smart, weren't they? It took only two hundred years for two-thirds of the Senate to catch up and agree: "Let's get *paid*."

If you want more information about the Constitution and the Bill of Rights, you can either visit the National Archives in Washington DC or go here: www.archives.gov/exhibits/charters/constitution.html.

THE CURIOUS CASE OF MOHAMMED AL-QAHTANI

"The United States does not torture," said former President George W. Bush. Well, um . . . except when it does. A week before Bush left office, Justice Susan J. Crawford—the top Pentagon official in charge of choosing which Guantánamo Bay detainees get sent to trial—told *The Washington Post* that she had been unable to prosecute suspected 9/11 "twentieth hijacker" Mohammed al-Qahtani because he had been tortured.

A 2008 military report shows that not only had al-Qahtani been subjected to extreme cold, isolation, and physical abuse, he had also been threatened with a violent military dog named Zeus (we leave to your imagination what Zeus looked like). In addition, he was "forced to wear a woman's bra and had a thong placed on his head" and was told repeatedly that "his mother and sister were whores." Twice his heart rate dropped so dangerously low that he had to be hospitalized. Crawford stated that all of this evidence obligated her to dismiss the charges against al-Qahtani.

In other words, the United States was unable by law to bring a terrorist to justice because we broke our own laws regarding torture. Moreover, by doing so, we were guilty of what we swore we would never do to other human beings—one of the very things that separates the United States from the "evildoers." (Bush's word, though in the case of al-Qahtani, very accurate.)

Crawford has said that there was "no doubt" in her mind that al-Qahtani was a "muscle hijacker" who was supposed to be the fifth member of the Al-Qaeda cell on Flight 93, which crashed in rural Pennsylvania. As of this writing, he remains detained at Guantánamo Bay—at least until President Barack Obama closes the prison. Now that the United States has legally tied its own hands and is unable to prosecute, it remains unclear what will happen to him.

None of this is very ha-ha funny, obviously, especially in light of the so-called torture memos, which were made public in April 2009. The memos were drafted in 2002 and 2005 by some very creative officials in the Bush administration who decided that slamming a person's head against a wall or convincing a person that he was drowning did not qualify as torture. Barack Obama pledged not to prosecute any of these higher-ups, saying that it was important to "look forwards, not backwards." Some see Obama's refusal to act as a miscarriage of justice on par with President Ford's exoneration of Richard Nixon after Watergate (see Hot Buttons, page 212). Which is apt, seeing as many of the Bush officials who *could* be prosecuted got their starts in the Nixon administration, Donald Rumsfeld and Dick Cheney among them.

I'm a very, very, very bad man. Lock me up, please!

"MIDNIGHT REGULATIONS": BUT WAIT! IT AIN'T OVER TILL IT'S OVER

As it turns out, the president of the United States doesn't need either the Constitution or the legislative branch to make all sorts of zany new rules—particularly if the clock is ticking on his or her presidency. Federal law requires a sixty-day waiting period before any major regulatory changes become law. ("Major regulatory changes" are defined as those that will have more than a $100 million effect on the economy or might otherwise significantly freak people out.) This has compelled most recent presidents, from Jimmy Carter to George W. Bush, to make a bunch of laws at the last minute that they might have otherwise been unable to get through Congress. For example, George W. Bush's midnight regulations included:

★ making it legal for "factory farms" to dump animal urine and feces into waterways
★ opening up protected public land for the extraction of oil shale
★ removing the gray wolf from the Endangered Species list

"Why me?"

WHY ARE THERE TWO HOUSES OF CONGRESS? IN CASE ONE IS FORECLOSED?

People often wonder what the difference is between the House and the Senate. As with almost every other painstaking decision that went into crafting the Constitution, the Founding Fathers established two houses of Congress for the purpose of compromise and the promise of dissatisfaction. Think of the two houses of Congress like renting a DVD with your significant other: One of you wants a romance, the other wants a horror movie, so you end up renting that Adam Sandler movie again. Neither of you gets exactly what you want, but you both go home with something.

Compromise—the eternal struggle

When creating Congress, the Constitution sought to establish a balance between big states and small states. When it was being drafted, the bigger states (New York, Pennsylvania, and Massachusetts) naturally wanted more power. The smaller states, not surprisingly, wanted all states to have *equal* power. Two houses of Congress exist so that every state, regardless of its size or population, is represented equally in at least some way. Each state gets two senators, no matter what its size. But each state also gets a number of House representatives proportional to its population.

Another big difference? The House of Representatives (whose members are elected every two years) represents current public opinion, while the Senate, which has to worry about elections only every six years, is—in theory at least—more removed from current trends. So while the Senate can afford to "kick it old school," the House must "keep it real."

WHAT DOES IT MEAN WHEN PEOPLE SAY THE REPUBLICANS OR THE DEMOCRATS "TOOK" THE HOUSE OR THE SENATE?

Short answer: it means "They won! Yippee!" Long answer: within the House and the Senate there are majority and minority positions. As expected, the majority is the party that won the most votes. Once the new Congress is established, members vote for positions in the party like leader, whip, and, in the case of the majority party, Speaker of the House.

WHO'S THE SPEAKER OF THE HOUSE AND WHAT DOES HE OR SHE DO?

The Speaker is the highest-ranking member in the House of Representatives, and he or she always belongs to the majority party.  If the president and vice president were to die, the Speaker would become president. She or he is the party's leader, presiding over debates in chamber, plus deciding which committees will consider certain bills and who belongs to most of those committees. Normally, the

John Boehner, the current Speaker, is considered a bit of a crybaby.

Speaker votes only when his or her vote would be decisive, and only on really important stuff like constitutional amendments. Otherwise, he or she mugs for the camera and attends glamorous and crucial fund-raisers.

WHAT'S A WHIP?

According to C-SPAN: "The Whip is a member elected by his or her party to count potential votes and promote party unity in voting. The Majority Whip is the third-ranking leadership position in his or her party and the Minority Whip ranks second."

THE UNCONSTITUTIONAL HALL OF SHAME

THREE FAMOUS BILLS OR ORDERS THAT, ON SECOND THOUGHT, PROBABLY SHOULDN'T HAVE BEEN PASSED

THE USA PATRIOT ACT

Signed into law on October 26, 2001. The acronym stands for Uniting and Strengthening America by Providing Appropriate Tools Required to Intercept and Obstruct Terrorism. These "tools" include but are not limited to:

- *Warrantless wiretapping and eavesdropping*
  The government can listen in on citizens' phone calls, read their e-mail, and check out their medical and financial records—so long as those citizens are suspected of being terrorists.

- *Extraordinary rendition*
  The government can transfer suspected terrorists to countries where torture is permitted and interrogate them there.

- *Suspension of habeas corpus*
  "Enemy combatants" can be held indefinitely in places such as Guantánamo Bay without charges brought against them.

- *Expansion of executive powers*
  Um, the president can get away with a lot more than he used to in terms of using military force without having to tell Congress.

- *Expansion of the secretary of the treasury's powers*
  Sketchy financial transactions—particularly those involving foreign banks—are much, much easier these days.

EXECUTIVE ORDER 9066

Issued by President Franklin Delano Roosevelt on February 19, 1942, this order called for the imprisonment of anyone with "foreign enemy ancestry." Thousands of Japanese Americans were rounded up and forced into internment camps for the duration of World War II. It wasn't until 1988 that the government formally apologized, when President Ronald Reagan authorized the payment of roughly $1.6 billion to the surviving prisoners or their heirs.

Give us your tired, your poor, your huddled masses yearning to be free—unless, of course, they have Japanese ancestry.

THE INDIAN APPROPRIATIONS ACT

Passed by Congress in 1851, this established the first Indian reservation, in Oklahoma, and subsequently forced all surviving Native Americans to live in places where no right-minded human being would ever want to settle. At least they can build casinos, right?

Home, sweet home, before the liquor and gambling licenses turn this wasteland into the next Vegas

FEDERALISM
The Only Word That Makes Us Yawn More Than "Civics"

In addition to creating a system of checks and balances within the federal government, the Constitution also establishes a system of power-sharing between the federal and state governments. This is known by the dull and somewhat misleading name "federalism." (Suggested alternatives: "State Govts Are Govts, Too," "Stay Out of My State Bid-ness," or "Another Fifty Constitutions: Read 'Em and Weep.")

In order to prevent too much power from ever falling into the hands of the elected officials in Washington, individual states enjoy a certain degree of autonomy, as well as their own special privileges. No, they don't have the right to declare war, print their own money, or handle postal services. But they *can* issue licenses of all kinds—from driving to hunting to marriage to *gay* marriage if the state's majority feels like it (see Hot Buttons, pages 184–186). Take that, federal government!

States also have the power to enact their own laws, provided they don't conflict with federal laws or the U.S. Constitution. So while some activities—say, regulated prostitution and gambling—may be perfectly legal in one state, they can be punishable by hard time in another state's correctional facilities. (Note to former New York governor Eliot Spitzer: You should have gone to Vegas, baby. What happens in Vegas . . . aw, you know the rest.)

Each state provides its own colorful examples of federalism at work. Take Alabama, our first state, alphabetically. Alabama law prohibits any citizen from wearing a fake mustache that causes laughter in church. In addition, it's illegal to flick boogers in the wind, impersonate a member of the clergy, or maim oneself to escape civic duty. Putting salt on a railroad track may be punishable by death. Incestuous marriage, on the other hand, is perfectly legal. So if you've married your first cousin but can't stop dressing up like a nun in public, you'd better file for divorce and move out of Alabama.

This is all true. You can look it up in the Alabama State Law Library: www.alalinc.net/library.

Our point? By empowering the states, federalism truly makes and keeps us a nation of laws—some more ridiculous than others. And while flicking boogers may not have been on the Founding Fathers' minds when they hashed out these principles in the Federalist Papers (though who's to say?), the system ensures that all U.S. citizens can govern themselves and protect their oddball values at the most local level.

THE NOT-SO-MYSTERIOUS FEDERALIST PAPERS: YES, WE KNOW WHO WROTE THEM

THE
FEDERALIST:
A COLLECTION OF
ESSAYS,
WRITTEN IN FAVOUR OF THE
NEW CONSTITUTION,
AS AGREED UPON BY THE
FEDERAL CONVENTION,
SEPTEMBER 17, 1787.

IN TWO VOLUMES.
VOL. I.

NEW-YORK:
PRINTED AND SOLD BY JOHN TIEBOUT,
No. 358 PEARL-STREET.
1799.

The Federalist Papers are a series of anonymous newspaper articles published in 1787 and 1788, urging the ratification of the U.S. Constitution in the state of New York. Why they were written anonymously is unclear, as everybody knew that the authors were John Jay, Alexander Hamilton, and James Madison— and in fact, the three boasted of their authorship in public. At their core, the Federalist Papers attempt to reassure average citizens that the government (made up almost entirely of a wealthy elite) will protect but never infringe upon the basic rights of the governed (mostly people with little wealth). The unspoken message: the rich still rule the poor, but now the rich are on the poor's side.

A SMATTERING OF ★ ★ ★ FAVORITE STATE LAWS

ARKANSAS	Schoolteachers who bob their hair cannot be given raises.	Alligators cannot be kept in bathtubs.
HAWAII	Citizens are subject to fines for not owning boats.	Coins may not be kept in one's ears.
UTAH	Alcohol cannot be sold during an emergency.	Birds have the right-of-way on highways.
ALASKA	Pushing a live moose out of a moving airplane is illegal.	Viewing a moose from an airplane—moving or not—is illegal.
OHIO	It is illegal to arrest anyone on Sunday or on the Fourth of July.	It is illegal to get a fish drunk.

THE AMERICAN ELECTORAL PROCESS
One Person, One Vote—Sort Of

So let's say you're voting for the leadership of one of the most powerful countries in the world. Not to brag or anything, but the leaders you choose have the power to affect the lives of almost everyone in the world. Your vote is, well, kinda important. Sometimes it needs to be protected. We thought that—and the electoral process that surrounds it—was worth dedicating a section to.

WHERE DO CANDIDATES COME FROM?

Okay. First, a candidate for president in the U.S. has got to be at least thirty-five years old and a natural citizen of the U.S. Not so fast, Ahh-nold!

Once those requirements are met, a candidate has a couple ways to get on the ballot.

★ Simply get nominated by the Democratic or the Republican party (like Obama and McCain were nominated in 2008).

★ Satisfy the requirements for a minor party or independent candidate. These requirements—which differ from state to state—range from getting a certain number of signatures on a petition to winning a certain number of votes in the most recent state election.

THE "TEFLON" VEEP AND THE DUEL THAT KILLED THE FEDERALIST PARTY. LITERALLY.

If any Founding Father deserves the title of Original Gangsta Patriot, it's Aaron Burr. After kicking butt during the Revolutionary War, he went on to serve as third vice president under Thomas Jefferson. In 1804, his longtime political foe, Federalist leader Alexander Hamilton, dissed Burr at a dinner party. Burr promptly challenged Hamilton to a duel—and on July 11, fatally capped him on the cliffs of Weehawken, New Jersey.

Burr served out the rest of his term as vice president even though he was indicted for murder in both New York and New Jersey. (No one could make the charges stick.) In 1805, he split for the West, where he allegedly committed treason by attempting to steal the entire Louisiana Purchase from the United States. (Again, he was acquitted. Suckas!) He formed his own two-hundred-man army but eventually grew tired of all the beefs, choosing to lay low and chill for a while in Europe.

Give him his props: Burr is the only vice president ever to make quail hunting with Dick Cheney seem safe.

While a major-party candidate gets on the ballot in all states, a minor-party or independent candidate may make it onto some ballots and not onto others, simply because of the difference in state requirements. You can go to your state's board of elections website to find out what the requirements are. And then, if you want, and if you qualify, you can run for office.

ANDY 2000

Andy ran for president in 2000. His platform was "straight talk, honesty, and integrity; ceasing encroachments on personal freedom; and ensuring that the United States abide by international law." Incidentally, he auctioned a "Night of Passion with a Presidential Candidate" on eBay and earned a cool $21.

WHAT'S THE DIFFERENCE BETWEEN A PRIMARY AND A CAUCUS?

Primaries and caucuses allow people to vote for the person they think will be the strongest contender in the race for president.

In a primary, people vote by ballot box. Primaries can be "open" or "closed." "Open" means voters can cast a ballot for either party, no matter which one they're registered with. "Closed" means that people can vote only for their party's candidate: Democrats for Democrats, Republicans for Republicans.

In a caucus, people don't vote by ballot. They vote for "delegates" pledged to certain candidates by gathering around the delegate they want, then signing in on that candidate's register.

Some states hold a primary, some states hold a caucus, and some hold a spicy primary-caucus combo. It's up to the

OPEN AND UNFAIR

Open primaries can be controversial because a group of, say, Democrats can gang up and decide to vote for a weak Republican candidate they know their candidate can beat, stacking the odds in their favor. Once the general elections come around in November, that "weak" Republican candidate doesn't stand a chance.

Some claim this kind of sabotage voting happened in the case of Cynthia McKinney, a representative of Georgia, when Republican voters grouped together to vote for a weaker Democratic candidate in the primaries—thereby ruling out the possibility that a strong Democrat like McKinney would win the election.

state legislature to decide which system to use. Where both are used, the primaries act as a gauge of general public opinion while the caucuses—which attract more political types—reflect the views of more intensely involved, grassroots voters.

Primaries and caucuses begin after the candidates have been

nominated. They start in Iowa, in January of an election year, and go on forever and ever, or until the last primary, in Nebraska, in July. They are generally held only by the major parties and a few of the bigger minor parties, like the Green Party.

Another kind of caucus race can be found in Alice in Wonderland.

WHAT'S SO SUPER ABOUT SUPERDELEGATES?

Unlike regular delegates, superdelegates don't have to be selected by voters in a primary or caucus. They're already so established in their political party that they're "seated" at the national convention automatically. In addition, they are able to vote for any candidate they choose to support, unlike regular delegates, who have pledged to support a particular candidate.

WHY DO PEOPLE TALK SO MUCH ABOUT IOWA AND NEW HAMPSHIRE?

Short answer is, it's all about media and momentum. New Hampshire is the first primary in the country, and Iowa is the first caucus. Since they're first (and well-covered by the media because of it), how candidates do in New Hampshire and Iowa gains them a certain status in the eyes of the nation. If they do better than expected, they're "scrappy underdogs." If they were well-favored going in and they do poorly, they might be thought of as "fallen giants." That affects how people in the rest of the primaries and caucuses vote. In fact, rarely does a candidate win New Hampshire without going on to win his or her party's nomination. Which makes the voters in New Hampshire and Iowa pretty powerful.[19]

Do the other states feel left out? Why, yes, thanks for asking. Some states are trying to get primaries to go on a rotating basis, so that every state has a turn to go first. (And by the way, neither New Hampshire nor Iowa is terribly representative of the country as a whole. For example, New Hampshire's number of minority voters is about one-fifth the national average, according to the U.S. Census Bureau.)

CAMPAIGN FINANCE
How Do People Fund Their Campaigns? Why Is It Controversial? And How Can I Get In on the Action?

"You be president first."

"No, old chap, you go first."

Back when our country was new, it was a given that the people running everything were the wealthy elite, and they tended to serve the interests of their good friends, the wealthy elite.

It wasn't until 1905, when President Teddy Roosevelt called for a ban on corporate contributions (and, in 1907, *for* public financing for candidates), that we started having serious attempts to level the playing field of American elections. In 1925, the Federal Corrupt Practices Act established spending limits on presidential campaigns. Candidates pretty much ignored that until 1971, when they started ignoring a new act, called the Federal Election Campaign Act (FECA).

Thanks largely to Watergate (see page 212), the Federal Election Commission (FEC) was added to monitor and enforce FECA's laws. This means politicians these days have to do their shiftier campaign financing more shiftily. There are all sorts of rules about how much money candidates can spend on campaigns, where they can get that money, and how much their contributors can offer them. Feel free to look them up at www.campaignfinance.org.

Candidates can choose to fund their campaigns privately or to use public funds. Public money comes from the government, kindly donated by Joe Taxpayer, who checks a box on his tax return saying whether or not he'd like to give $3 to the public campaign fund.

---

19. New Hampshire actually has a state law that says it must be first in the country to hold a primary.

Public funds are supposed to make it possible for anyone, a minor-party candidate or even your cousin Tom, to run for president. But it doesn't really work. Why not? Because major-party candidates are likely to raise three to four times as much privately. Public funding just hasn't kept up with the astronomical (and astronomically growing) amounts major-party candidates spend on campaigns.

OBAMA: $730 million spent
McCAIN: $333 milion spent

WHAT'S A PAC?

When you hear the phrase "special interest group," it's often referring to a PAC. PACs, or Political Action Committees, are private groups made up of contributors who share a common interest in electing a candidate or defeating or supporting a new law. In a PAC, people bundle their money to give to a candidate they feel will best represent their interests. There are corporate, union, and independent PACs. The FEC has different rules for each of them.

PACs are formed for all sort of reasons and by people all along the political spectrum. They started in the 1970s, when labor unions began to organize them to raise money for their favorite candidates who were likely to stand up for them against big business. But the tables were turned when corporations started to do the same thing: the Sun oil corporation (Sun Company, Inc.) was the first to set up its own group, called SUN PAC, likely to support its oil interests in elections. How's that for irony?

These days, there are many, many more corporate PACs than labor PACs. And hundreds of millions of dollars are spent by those PACs on elections every year. There's no solid proof that the money PACs spend on candidates is directly connected to the laws candidates make once they're in office. But it's pretty clear that donating a huge pile of money gets you a candidate's ear. And, since our presidential election process is the longest and most expensive in the world, PAC money can be crucial to whether a candidate sinks or swims.

Critics say PACs put government up for sale to the highest bidder. PAC supporters argue that people should have the right to group together with others who share their points of view to make it more likely that their views get heard. Either way, there's no doubt that PACs have and—without intervention—will continue to have a big influence on American politics.

President Obama has banned his campaign and the Democratic National Committee from accepting contributions from PACs.

BIG SETBACK ON CAMPAIGN FINANCE

In 2010, the Supreme Court made a crucial and controversial decision to overrule a ban on political spending. We can't overemphasize how important the ruling is. Essentially, it removes the legal limit on the amount of money companies can contribute to campaigns.

What does that really mean? Well, presumably the more money a company spends on a candidate's campaign, the more influence that company has on that candidate. So if that candidate is elected, that company has more influence over the laws that affect you and me. A company's interests may often be at odds with the interests of you, me, your uncle Frank, or the environment. Ruh-roh.

The removal of a political spending limit, in a nutshell, means corporations having more influence on our government than most of us would like. Not a great setup for a democracy, huh?

So how'd the Supreme Court let it happen? Basically, they decided that banning companies' ability to spend their dollars on campaigns was akin to encroaching upon their right to free speech. Incidentally, the only person who seemed excited about the ruling was Mr. Burns from *The Simpsons*.

FOLLOW THE MONEY

All campaign donations are officially public information. Which means if you want to find out who your next-door neighbor is sending money to, or what you need to do to get public funding to run for president, go to www.fec.gov or www.opensecrets.org.

WHAT'S A NATIONAL CONVENTION?

National political conventions are not to be confused with *Star Trek* conventions. Here is how they differ.

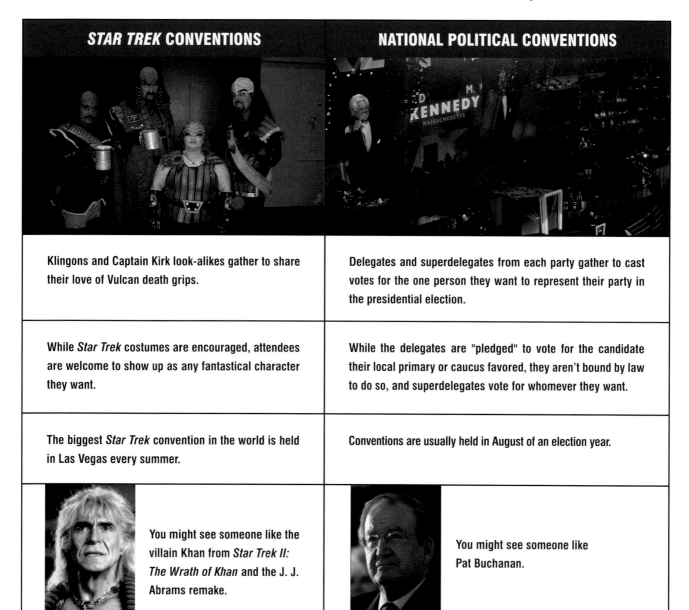

STAR TREK CONVENTIONS	NATIONAL POLITICAL CONVENTIONS
Klingons and Captain Kirk look-alikes gather to share their love of Vulcan death grips.	Delegates and superdelegates from each party gather to cast votes for the one person they want to represent their party in the presidential election.
While *Star Trek* costumes are encouraged, attendees are welcome to show up as any fantastical character they want.	While the delegates are "pledged" to vote for the candidate their local primary or caucus favored, they aren't bound by law to do so, and superdelegates vote for whomever they want.
The biggest *Star Trek* convention in the world is held in Las Vegas every summer.	Conventions are usually held in August of an election year.
You might see someone like the villain Khan from *Star Trek II: The Wrath of Khan* and the J. J. Abrams remake.	You might see someone like Pat Buchanan.

THE ELECTORAL COLLEGE
What Is It, Anyway? Can I Get In Even if My SAT Scores Stink?

Don't worry: the Electoral College is not an accredited university. Frankly, we don't know why it's called a college. But if you know and you want to tell us, go to www.americapediathebook.com and give us the info. We'll send $1 to the first five people who respond. Hubba hubba.

The Electoral College is a system that, many say, jeopardizes your most fundamental right as an American citizen—your right to vote. Here's how it works.

First, when you select one of the candidates on an election ballot, you aren't actually casting a vote for that person but for an "elector" who's pledged to represent that candidate.

Every state gets a number of electors equal to the total number of senators and representatives it has in the United States Congress. The number of representatives per state is based on population. However, each state gets two senators to start with, automatically. Still with us? So, for instance, New York, which, based on its population has twenty-seven representatives, plus the standard two senators, has twenty-nine electors. South Dakota, which is sparsely populated, has three electors (the lowest possible number).

Here's the kicker: in all but two states, the party that wins the *most* votes gets *all* of the electoral votes. In other words, if just over half the people in New York vote for a certain candidate, that candidate gets all twenty-nine of New York's electoral votes. (Nebraska and Maine are the exceptions. They split electoral votes among their districts.) Whoever wins the most electoral votes in the country as a whole (there are 538 out there, so they've got to win at least 270) becomes president. So, a candidate can win the popular vote (that is, the most votes cast by real live people) but not win the election, because they haven't won the most electoral votes. Still confused? Here's a handy chart showing the presidential election of 2008 versus the controversial Bush-Gore defeat of 2000:

In each state, electoral votes are sealed and sent to the president of the Senate (aka, the vice president) to be counted.

ELECTION YEAR	CANDIDATE	ELECTORAL VOTES	POPULAR VOTES	PERCENT OF ALL VOTES CAST
2008	Barack Obama	365	66,882,230	53%
	John McCain	173	58,343,671	46%
2000	George W. Bush	271	50,460,110	47.87%
	Al Gore	266	51,003,926	48.38%

HE WON BUT HE DIDN'T WIN

Al Gore won the popular vote for president in 2000 but lost the electoral vote and, therefore, the election (see pages 19–22). This made the people who voted for him (the majority of Americans) sort of mad.

Unfair, you say? You're not alone. Over the past two hundred years, more than seven hundred proposals have been introduced in Congress to reform or eliminate the Electoral College. The unfairness of the Electoral College has prompted more proposals for constitutional amendments than any other subject.

But wait, there's more.

To go a little deeper and look at it another way . . . The Electoral College causes the value of people's votes to depend on which state they live in. For starters, thanks to the fact that each state gets two "freebie" electors (the electors that correspond to each state's senators), highly populated states' electors are spread more thinly, giving them less representation. Second, under the Electoral College system, the battle for the presidency is mostly fought in a few "swing" states. Instead of trying to get the most votes everywhere, candidates have to focus on getting the electoral vote of these few states, making those voters (and their interests) especially powerful.

Finally, the Electoral College tends to smother any political parties beyond the major two. How? For example, a small party, such as the Green Party, is not likely to carry most of the votes in any given state. But thanks to the winner-takes-all system for electoral votes in most states, the party gets *none* of the vote. So even if 15 percent of Americans want the Green Party to play some part in government, the party actually ends up playing zero part. (More on the two-party system on page 36.)

Despite his charming drawl and hefty fortune, independent candidate Ross Perot (who won 19 percent of the popular vote nationwide in 1992) did not win any electoral votes.

SO WHY DO WE EVEN HAVE THE ELECTORAL COLLEGE? SHOULD WE DROP OUT?

Supporters say the system makes elections more fair for rural voters. If it were up to popular vote, they argue, the concerns of the more populated urban areas would always win out over rural ones. Opponents of the Electoral College say that reason's outdated, since its purpose was to support the less populated states back when our country revolved around agriculture.

If you know other reasons to love the Electoral College, please come to the website and Bark Back!

WITH SO MANY PEOPLE THINKING IT'S UNFAIR, WILL IT CHANGE?

There are a couple of ways the Electoral College could change.

★ *Constitutionally.* As we said, there have been serious calls for constitutional amendments to create a more straightforward one-person, one-vote system. But it's not likely to happen. Why? Because a constitutional amendment requires three-quarters of the states to agree.

SWING STATES

Swing states are states in which the presidential race could go either way. Unlike states where there's a heavy leaning toward one political party or another, swing states are up for grabs. If you live in one—in recent years they've included Nevada, New Mexico, Colorado, Iowa, Ohio, Missouri, Michigan, Florida, Virginia, West Virginia, and Arkansas—get ready to be bombarded by campaign ads and visits from the candidates.

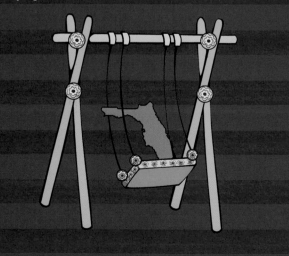

And more than a quarter of the states (the less populated ones) benefit from things the way they are.

★ *State by state*. States can change how they count and report their electoral votes. They can move from a winner-takes-all system (where *all* the state's electoral votes go to the candidate with the most votes statewide—even if the candidate wins only by one percentage point) to a system that divides up the state's electoral votes by congressional district (giving each district's vote to the winning candidate in that area). For example, if one part of a state is more Republican and another is more Democrat, each part of the state could contribute electoral votes toward the candidate of its choice. How likely are these changes? In some places, like Maine and Nebraska, they're already happening. And several more states are making changes along these lines.

THE TWO-PARTY SYSTEM
Democrats, Republicans, and Why No One Else Is Invited

Under today's system, we take it for granted that the presidency and Congress belong to either the Republicans or the Democrats. But it hasn't always been this way (and in many other countries, it still isn't). In fact, George Washington claimed that the constant alternation of only two parties in the federal government would lead to a "frightful despotism."

Back in the nineteenth century, it was harder to find a clean bathroom or live past the age of fifty, but it was much easier for third parties to get on the ballot. Smaller parties were constantly challenging the major parties by using big reforms—

Two parties

like abolition, workers' rights, and women's suffrage—as their platforms. Though these specialized parties didn't win the presidency, their focus on these issues forced the major parties to tackle the issues, too.

Today, minor parties have much less influence than they had in the past. Why? For one thing, each state has its own standards for getting on its ballot. It's time consuming and costly to jump through every hoop, so it's rare that any minor party gets on all fifty. That, of course, makes it pretty hard to win a national election.

Plus—as we mentioned before—thanks to the winner-takes-all Electoral College, it's almost impossible for a minor party candidate to carry any electoral votes. And that means minor parties end up acting as "spoilers." Unable to win themselves, they draw votes away from the major party that people would have voted for instead.

SO HOW DOES HAVING A TWO-PARTY SYSTEM SERVE US?

There *are* major pluses to the two-party system, the most notable being that since each side has to get such a large percentage of votes to win, neither side can become too extreme in its position. Parties have to lean toward the middle of the road to win enough voters, ruling out a possible Pat Robertson or Michael Moore presidency.

IS THERE A REASONABLE ALTERNATIVE?

Yep. It's called proportional voting. It's a system that better matches what voters actually prefer and how those preferences are represented. One example of proportional voting is called "instant run-off voting," where, instead of choosing just one person on a ballot, voters rank candidates in order of preference.

In countries that use proportional representation, the number of votes received for a party relates directly to the number of representative seats they get. So, for instance, if the Prohibition Party got 15 percent of the vote, that party would have a 15 percent representation in Congress.

Proportional voting is becoming the international norm. Most developed countries use it. Some local governments in the U.S. have tried it, though it has yet to catch on nationally, possibly due to the resistance of the two parties in power.

WHERE DID DEMOCRATS AND REPUBLICANS COME FROM? AND WHY ALL THE NAME-CALLING?

In 1792, a political party called the Democratic Party was formed to oppose the Federalist Party. In 1798, it was renamed the Democratic-Republican Party, or the "dream team" if you will. Today's Democrats rose from the ashes of the Democratic-Republican Party when it fractured in the 1820s. The Republican Party was founded about twenty years later, in 1854, by antislavery activists (who elected Abraham Lincoln). Since their creation, these parties have changed and evolved significantly.

Today, Democrats and Republicans can be defined differently depending on who you ask, but here is a general rundown.

DEMOCRATS	REPUBLICANS
★ Associated with farmers, laborers, labor unions, and religious and ethnic minorities.	★ Associated with old money, economic liberalism, fiscal conservatism, a strong military, and conservative social values.
★ They oppose unregulated business and finance.	★ The party generally supports lower taxes and less government intervention in social programs and commerce.
★ The party generally believes that government should play a bigger role in alleviating poverty and social injustice, even if that means higher taxes.	

CHANGES

The party's popularity with Southern conservatives began to erode after Democratic president Lyndon B. Johnson supported the Civil Rights Act of 1964, which is when the party's popularity with African American voters began to grow. In recent decades, it's been linked with environmentalism.

CHANGES

Since the early 1980s, the Republican Party has become strongly identified with evangelical and fundamentalist Christianity, including its stance on moral issues like abortion and same-sex marriage.

WHAT'S THE GOP?

It stands for Grand Old Party and refers to the Republican Party.

Democrats are often accused of being impractical "bleeding-heart liberals," and Republicans are often associated with greedy, evil overlords. Why all the animosity? Maybe because it makes people on TV a lot of money. See pages 200–204 to read about a free and fair media, and why it's crucial to the way you view political parties . . . and to the way you vote.

WHAT'S WITH THE ANIMALS?

When Democratic president Andrew Jackson was called a jackass by his opponents, he decided to make lemons into lemonade and started using the image of a donkey in his campaign. A cartoonist of the time, Thomas Nast, made the symbol famous and then went on to create the Republican elephant.

GERRYMANDERING
The Single Greatest Threat to Your Vote That Sounds Like a Word British People Would Use

As a mapmaker, I can have more of an impact on an election than a campaign . . . more of an impact than a candidate . . . When I, as a mapmaker, have more of an impact on an election than the voters . . . the system is out of whack.
—Consultant David Winston, who drew House districts for the GOP after the 1990 U.S. Census
(from www.redistrictinggame.org)

If you think this man looks like he's about to go for a wee gerrymander about town, you are mistaken.

Though it sounds like something Englishmen in the 1890s might do on a Sunday, gerrymandering is actually the rearranging of voting districts for the gain of a particular party or candidate.

When states lose or gain population, they lose or gain seats in Congress (in the House of Representatives, to be specific), and whenever you add or subtract a congressional seat, you have to redistrict: redraw the lines of the voting districts into which the population falls, using information from the U.S. Census.

Gerrymandering is when political parties use redistricting for their own political gain. How? By shuffling voters who don't support them into districts where their votes are overruled by a majority that does, or by locking them into as few districts as possible. Said another way, gerrymandering lets political parties in power choose their voters, instead of their voters choosing them.

There's even something called minority gerrymandering. If a party knows they will not get, for example, the African American vote in certain districts, they can redraw district lines so that these voters are either squeezed into as few districts as possible (making the other districts clear for the taking) or spread thinly enough that they'll be overruled in each district. Once these voters are maneuvered around in this way, their votes are powerless, and representatives don't have much of an incentive to stand up for their interests and needs in Congress.

COMMANDER GERRYMANDER

One of the most infamous instances of gerrymandering in recent years: in 2003, then–House Majority Leader Tom DeLay successfully unseated multiple Democratic House seats in Texas through redistricting.

When all is said and done, redistricting is probably the most powerful political maneuver available in our electoral system today, and it's used by both parties. It's truly one of the biggest threats we have to a fair and free vote.

Why is gerrymandering so easy to get away with? Because in most states, the public plays little role in redistricting. Most often, districts are redrawn by the party in power, which generally wants to stay in charge.

How can this change? Each state can appoint independent, bipartisan commissions to do the redistricting. Five states have done this already: Arizona, Hawaii, Idaho, New Jersey, and Washington. Want to know how you can get your state to jump on board? Go to Activism on page 226. Wanna gerrymander some districts for fun and see how it all works? Go to www.redistrictinggame.org and play.

DISCUSSION QUESTIONS
(OPTIONAL)

1. We're thinking of doing away with the term "Founding Fathers" and renaming the brilliant white men who drafted the Constitution the "Mothers of Invention." Would you be willing to start a revolution to back us up?[20]

2. Why do you think Al Gore gained so much weight and grew a beard after he lost the 2000 election?

3. According to some, President Obama has "Marxists" and "followers of Chairman Mao" in his inner circle. Can you define either of those terms?[21]

4. Discussion questions sort of suck. Do you agree?

20. We plagiarized the term "Mothers of Invention" from Frank Zappa, a revolutionary in his own right. Go here: www.zappa.com/flash/lumpymoney/index.html.
21. We can't, which is why we're asking. Go to www.americapediathebook.com for further discussion.

CHAPTER 2

DYNASTY
The Closest You'll Get to Royalty in the USA
(Except When Actual Royalty Visits Us)

INTRODUCTION
The Six Secrets of Highly Dynastic People

dy·nas·ty dy-nas-ty \\'dī-nə-stē *also* –,nas-tē, *esp.*
Brit. 'di-nə-stē\ *n, pl* **-ties** (14c)

 a succession of rulers of the same line of descent

 a powerful group or family that maintains its position for a considerable time

—From *Merriam-Webster's Collegiate Dictionary*, 11th Edition

If you've ever been on a field trip to any renowned metropolitan art museum, you've no doubt passed enormous vases bearing the enigmatic placard: "Vase, Ming dynasty." This does not refer to an ancient Chinese brand, or to a kick-ass Chinese designer, or even to an actual vase maker (vasist?). Rather, it refers to the ruling family in China circa 1368–1644 CE.

Sadly, vase makers who lived under the Ming toiled and died in anonymity. Imagine if every episode of *Gossip Girl* had simply been credited: "TV show, Bush and Obama administrations." Yikes! Four hundred years from now, we'd have no idea who Josh Schwartz[1] was, and maybe not even Blake Lively[2] or Wallace Shawn.[3]

The very word "dynasty" implies power of such magnitude that it can define an entire era. All other names stand in its shadow or are completely obscured by it. What's a dynasty? Dynasties are most often associated with mighty emperors and their mighty empires. Think Ming, the Tudors, the Chicago Bulls in the 1990s.

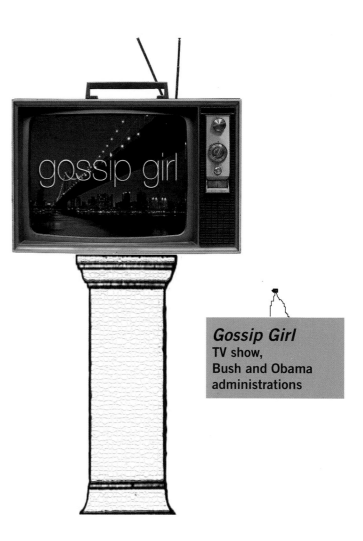

Gossip Girl
**TV show,
Bush and Obama
administrations**

Outside of having Michael Jordan on your team, there are six paths to dynastic success in the U.S. (i.e., the six secrets of highly dynastic people): wealth, real estate, nepotism, luck, an abundance of family portraits hung outside the family compound,[4] and having two or more rich, white, male family members named George or John. Sorry, Ringo.

---

1. Actually, we had to look him up. He's the producer of *Gossip Girl*.
2. Though she'd probably like us to forget *Accepted*.
3. Wallace Who?
4. If people you've never met refer to your family's home as a compound, there's a good chance your family qualifies as a dynasty.

WEALTH. Tony Montana, the ruthless drug kingpin played by actor Al Pacino in 1983's *Scarface*, said it best: "In this country, you gotta make the money first. Then when you get the money, you get the power." (One of the few lines in *Scarface* delivered without an expletive, which is why we chose to include it.) Money does indeed make America go round, with the added bonus of more legroom.

REAL ESTATE. To wield influence in the U.S., property ownership has always been vital. Members of a U.S. dynasty seldom rent. The more land you own, the more powerful you seem to become. Real estate mogul Donald Trump was able to finagle his way into becoming a reality TV mogul for this very reason.

NEPOTISM. It never hurts to be the son, daughter, or grandchild of someone with lots of money and real estate. You know that stupid senior with straight Cs and zero extracurricular activities and who always picks his nose, but who got into Yale because his father and grandfather went there? Be nice to him, because he'll probably be president one day.

LUCK. Being the right person in the right place at the right time never hurts, either. Once a dynasty is established, however, its inheritors don't have to be the right people (see Nepotism). They can simply reap the rewards sown by preceding generations. Luck comes to them like proverbial flies to figurative poop.

AN ABUNDANCE OF FAMILY PORTRAITS HUNG OUTSIDE THE FAMILY COMPOUND. They might be found in public schools and libraries. This proves that a dynasty is worthy of respect and can claim a place in history. It also demonstrates political leverage and a reputation for civic duty. Note: the most arresting portraits tend to be paintings. Photo-booth portraits, while fun and goofy, are best kept private.

TWO OR MORE RICH, WHITE, MALE FAMILY MEMBERS NAMED GEORGE OR JOHN. It's ironic that this trait is unique to American dynasties because it owes its origin to a seminal British rock quartet. Then again, The Beatles' origins can be traced directly to American blues, soul, country—even Tin Pan Alley. The Beatles copied *us*, not the other way around.

As you can imagine, given these criteria—and given our nation's self-proclaimed status as the greatest on earth—American history is bursting with dynasties of all sorts. It would be impossible to list or categorize them all here, which is why we took the default top-five approach: a smattering of illustrative examples. But by all means, if you feel other dynasties are worthy of inclusion, let us know! Better yet, start your own dynasty and enforce your will.

OUR TOP FIVE AMERICAN PRESIDENTIAL DYNASTIES
Oil, Guns, and Money

In America any boy may become President, and I suppose it's just one of the risks he takes.

—Adlai Stevenson, losing Democratic presidential candidate, 1952 and 1956

With only one exception, each of our top five American presidential dynasties includes at least two presidents. This is quite a feat, considering that there have been only forty-four U.S. presidents to date. Three of our top five dynasties are represented on some form of U.S. coin or currency—another remarkable feat, considering that there are only sixteen different types of coin or currency in circulation.[5] Two of our top five boast members with major international airports named after them . . . really not so impressive, considering there are dozens of major international airports all over the country.

John Adams, Franklin Roosevelt, and John Kennedy were all honored on U.S. coins.

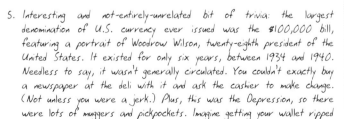

5. Interesting and not-entirely-unrelated bit of trivia: the largest denomination of U.S. currency ever issued was the $100,000 bill, featuring a portrait of Woodrow Wilson, twenty-eighth president of the United States. It existed for only six years, between 1934 and 1940. Needless to say, it wasn't generally circulated. You couldn't exactly buy a newspaper at the deli with it and ask the cashier to make change. (Not unless you were a jerk.) Plus, this was the Depression, so there were lots of muggers and pickpockets. Imagine getting your wallet ripped off! Incidentally, Woodrow Wilson did not belong to any dynasty, though he did get married while in office—to Edith Galt, his second wife. This, and the fact that his face graced the largest bill in U.S. history, makes him an unofficial "Mac Daddy" or "Player."

DYNASTY #1
The Adams Family[6]
(Duh-Nuh-Nuh-Nuh. Snap-Snap.)

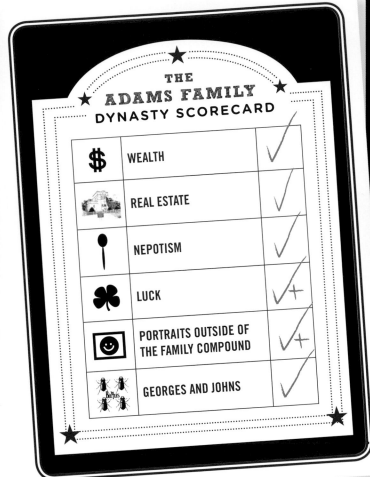

THE
ADAMS FAMILY
DYNASTY SCORECARD

$	WEALTH	✓
	REAL ESTATE	✓
	NEPOTISM	✓
♣	LUCK	✓+
	PORTRAITS OUTSIDE OF THE FAMILY COMPOUND	✓+
	GEORGES AND JOHNS	✓

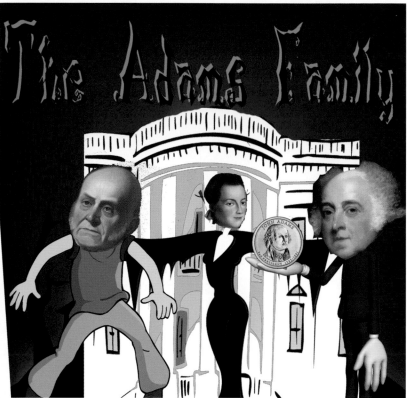

John Adams, second president of the United States, was the first president ever to sleep in the White House. It had a leaky roof at the time. Long before that, however, he attended Harvard (class of 1755, go Crimson!) and became a lawyer. Even in the 1700s, Harvard-educated lawyers were overpaid. Mr. Adams used the exorbitant legal fees he charged to buy several homes, all with quality roofs. Our point? He had wealth and real estate even before there *was* a U.S.A. Plus, his first name was John. The rhetorical answer to your unspoken question? Yes, sirree. Mr. Adams was primed to start a dynasty.

There was only one problem. Wealth + Real Estate = Taxes. Lots of taxes. Back then Mr. Adams even got taxed for buying playing cards.[7] Worst of all, the taxes weren't levied by a government of Mr. Adams's choosing or forming. As we learned in chapter one, the taxes were levied by the British Empire, ruled by King George III,[8] a certifiable lunatic.

---

6. We tried not to go for the obvious gag here: "Not to be confused with The Addams Family." We respect your intelligence too much. Also, many of you may not be familiar with this wacky 1960s TV series or the recent Broadway play.

7. The Stamp Act of 1765 was responsible for the playing-card tax. It also taxed legal documents, which was doubly annoying to Mr. Adams, as he was a lawyer.

8. Even British dynasties are George-prone.

"I want you . . . to pay your taxes!"

In this world nothing is certain except death and taxes.

BENJAMIN FRANKLIN

This has been true for as long as civilizations have flourished on Planet Earth, which helps explain why UFO enthusiasts so fervently believe that there *must* be intelligent life elsewhere in the universe. The peaceful, bubble-eyed waifs on faraway planets are too advanced to tax one another, so naturally they're less irritable and have lots more money to spend on fabulous physics-defying spacecraft.

King George III couldn't care less that Mr. Adams and his rich buddies over in the American Colonies were ticked off. He even *raised* their taxes. And on a gross side note, this blue blood also had bright blue pee. No joke. Doctors theorize that this was a result of porphyria—a rare enzyme disorder that can also cause dementia—but that's for the medical community to debate; and besides, this inappropriate digression has gone on long enough.

Having an enfeebled adversary was a lucky break for Mr. Adams. Other instances of Mr. Adams's luck, in no particular order:

★ Back in chapter one, we read about how his rich, white, male friends were as pissed off about British taxes as he was, and they were all very smart. And there were *dozens* of them, dressed in wigs and frills—except on December 16, 1773, when some of them (though not Mr. Adams) disguised themselves as Native Americans ("Indians") and threw taxed British tea into the Boston Harbor.[9]

---

9. Inspired by the original Boston Tea Party, hundreds of thousands of self-proclaimed Tea-Party Patriots (or "tea-baggers," as their opponents call them) threw their own tea parties in various locales around the country on April 15, 2009: the deadline for filing 2008 taxes. They were protesting . . . well, nobody could quite agree on one single atrocity. But most of it had something to do with tax hikes, enforced by a thuggish, jackbooted federal government. Odd, since jackboots have long gone out of style (even among the government's most thuggish members), and Obama's fiscal plan calls for reducing taxes for over 97 percent of the population.

The more dour John Adams said of his rival, "Jefferson ran away with the stage effect and all the glory."

★ In spite of the taxes, Adams and friends had lots of money, so they could afford to take time off work to secede from the British Empire, form various congresses (First and Second Continental), draft those mind-blowing documents (the Declaration of Independence, the Constitution, and the Federalist Papers, to name a few), and even brew untaxed beer.[10]

★ As the right person in the right place at the right time, Mr. Adams became the first vice president of the United States. He had this to say about it: "My country has in its wisdom contrived for me the most insignificant office that ever the invention of man contrived or his imagination conceived." So as you can see, being lucky also entitles you to be a bitter know-it-all. (Okay, not really, but Adams did often feel as if he got the short end of the stick.)

★ His wife, Abigail (proto-feminist and Mr. Adams's long-suffering champion, critic, and muse), often felt that she, too, got the short end of the stick. Here's what she had to say about it: "Do not put such unlimited power into the hands of the husbands. Remember all men would be tyrants if they could." Adams agreed, and felt very lucky to have her—particularly when he was the second president of the United States. "May none but honest and wise Men ever rule under this roof," he wrote to her from the White House. (He didn't mention the roof was leaky.)

★ He died exactly fifty years to the day after signing the Declaration of Independence, on July 4, 1826—which happens to have been exactly the same day Thomas Jefferson, the author of the Declaration of Independence, died.[11] Well, maybe this isn't *lucky*, per se, but it is sort of a freakish coincidence.

Which leaves us with nepotism and portraits. As far as nepotism goes, John Adams's son, John Quincy Adams, became the sixth president of the United States. If that's not nepotism, we don't know *what* is. Do you think he would have been elected president if he weren't part of the Adams dynasty? True, he had many fine qualities, including a sharp wit. He also promoted government-subsidized education (i.e., public schools) and objected to slavery, positions that were unfashionable at the time. And here's his portrait. You tell us.

A flaccid, unfashionable John Quincy Adams

---

10. Samuel Adams, part of the Adams family dynasty, was John's second cousin. Today his beer is taxed.

11. Thomas Jefferson and John Adams rarely agreed on much while they held elected office, but in their old age, they struck up a deep friendship. Other one-time foes turned old pals include presidents Jimmy Carter (#39) and Gerald Ford (#38), who bonded over corruption at home and human rights issues abroad, and presidents Bill Clinton (#42) and George H. W. Bush (#41) who bonded over tsunami relief. "Time heals all wounds," or so the cliché goes.

If William Henry Harrison were alive today, he'd probably drive a Scion, as befits the scion of a tobacco empire.

DYNASTY #2
The Harrison Family
(They Electrified the White House. Literally.)

If you haven't heard of the Harrisons, don't worry. Their story is seldom told. Yet it is often tragic, occasionally brutal, and sometimes downright kooky.

THE HARRISON FAMILY
DYNASTY SCORECARD

💲	WEALTH	✓
🏠	REAL ESTATE	✓
	NEPOTISM	✓
☘	LUCK	?
🙂	PORTRAITS OUTSIDE OF THE FAMILY COMPOUND	✓+
🪲🪲🪲 Beatles	GEORGES AND JOHNS	✱

✱ Well, okay, if you go by full names, then the last name "Harrison" certainly belongs to The Beatles as well—which is really the whole point of the "Georges and Johns" category anyway.

By far the most famous member of the Harrison dynasty was William Henry Harrison, ninth president of the United States. According to the official White House website, he was a "scion of Virginia planter aristocracy."[12] This is a sunny euphemism for "heir to rich slave-owning tobacco farmers." Back then, of course, smoking was considered a harmless pastime. Nobody knew that tobacco contained an addictive carcinogen. Tobacco chewing was also popular, turning a disgusting, messy habit into a massive opportunity for the spittoon industry.

In an ironic twist of fate, health issues proved central to William Henry Harrison's tobacco-stained legacy. He holds the U.S. records for both longest inaugural address and briefest presidency: he died only thirty-one days after taking office,

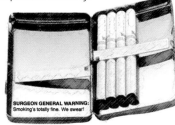

SURGEON GENERAL WARNING:
Smoking's totally fine. We swear!

"Totally fine. We swear!"

having caught a fatal cold while delivering the aforementioned address in freezing wind and sleet. The speech lasted over two hours. His original draft was even longer, but fellow Whig and all-around wordsmith Daniel Webster edited it for length.[13]

Before he made it to the inaugural podium, Mr. Harrison spent his life as a soldier, earning a fearsome reputation for invading and conquering Native American lands in the Northwest. His most decisive victory was the defeat of the

---

12. The website www.whitehouse.gov/about/presidents is a great resource for learning about all forty-four U.S. presidents through the biased lens of whoever currently holds office.
13. No, not the same Webster who gave us Webster's dictionary, but one of the last great Whig leaders (see page 49). And no, he didn't wear a wig, at least not to our knowledge.

Shawnee warlord Tecumseh at the Battle of the Thames in 1813. Legend has it that Tecumseh placed a curse on Harrison, dooming him and every subsequent president elected in a year ending in zero to die while in office.

So far, the curse of Tecumseh—true or not—has proven remarkably effective, claiming the lives of every president elected in a zero year up until Ronald Reagan (1980), who was shot by an assassin but survived. Apropos of neither dynasties nor the Harrison family, Reagan's would-be assassin, John Hinckley Jr., was obsessed with actress Jodie Foster and committed this crime as an insane bid for her attention. And hats off to George W. Bush (2000), who managed to retire from his tumultuous presidency completely unscathed. It's as if he never left his ranch in Crawford!

CURSES! | TECUMSEH'S REVENGE FROM BEYOND THE GRAVE, IN CHRONOLOGICAL ORDER

PRESIDENT	YEAR ELECTED	CAUSE OF DEATH
ABRAHAM LINCOLN	1860	Assassinated by John Wilkes Booth on April 14, 1865
JAMES A. GARFIELD	1880	Shot by Charles Guiteau on July 2, 1881; died of complications from the wound on September 19, 1881
WILLIAM McKINLEY	1900	Shot by Leon Czolgosz on September 6, 1901; died of complications from the wound on September 14, 1901
WARREN G. HARDING	1920	Died of a stroke on August 2, 1923
FRANKLIN D. ROOSEVELT	1940	Died of a cerebral hemorrhage on April 12, 1945
JOHN F. KENNEDY	1960	Assassinated by Lee Harvey Oswald (or so says the Warren Commission) on November 22, 1963

Dynasty-wise, the Harrisons seem to be lacking only in the number of well-known Georges and Johns in their family. (And luck, perhaps; they did have their share of hard knocks.) But they do, at least, have a Beatles connection with the name Harrison.

William Henry Harrison's grandson Benjamin was elected twenty-third president of the United States. He is the only president ever to serve a term sandwiched between the presidencies of the same man: Grover Cleveland, who was both twenty-second and twenty-fourth president. As of this writing, Benjamin Harrison was also the last U.S. president to sport a full beard. Like his grandfather, Benjamin Harrison is best known for slaughtering Native Americans. His presidency, however, is known for little other than the installation of electricity in the White House—electricity he reputedly refused to use, for fear of electrocution.

WHIGGED OUT!

The Whigs were the shortest-lived major political party ever. Founded in 1834 in protest of seventh president Andrew Jackson's authoritarian rule, the Whigs took their name from a British party of the same name, who opposed royal tyranny. (The name comes from a seventeenth-century British slur for "country bumpkin.") The Whigs split in 1856: the antislavery "Conscience Whigs" became Lincoln Republicans; the pro-slavery "Cotton Whigs," Southern Democrats. Wig wearing, at least by men, stopped being fashionable long before the party was established.

Famous Whigs (left to right) Daniel Webster, William Henry Harrison, and John C. Calhoun (sporting his own impressive wig)

DYNASTY #3
The Roosevelt Family
(The Only Thing They Had to Fear Was Fear Itself.)

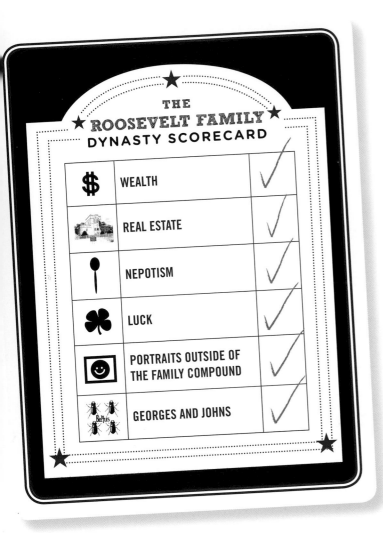

THE ROOSEVELT FAMILY
DYNASTY SCORECARD

$	WEALTH	✓
	REAL ESTATE	✓
	NEPOTISM	✓
☘	LUCK	✓
☺	PORTRAITS OUTSIDE OF THE FAMILY COMPOUND	✓
	GEORGES AND JOHNS	✓

DISCLAIMER: if you're at all offended by tales of kissing cousins, you might want to skip ahead a few pages. Be forewarned that Franklin Delano Roosevelt, thirty-second president of the United States, not only married his fifth cousin (once removed) Eleanor—but somehow also managed to be related to ten other U.S. presidents,[14] including his wife's uncle, twenty-sixth president Theodore Roosevelt. This dynasty is an example of nepotism at its finest.

Theodore Roosevelt galloped into office at only forty-two, following the assassination of President William McKinley by a deranged anarchist named Leon Czolgosz.[15] Roosevelt didn't literally gallop, obviously—but his youth and loud mouth brought the energy and vigor worthy of such a verb. To this day, he remains the youngest president ever to serve in the White House. He *did* literally gallop up San Juan Hill in 1898 with the Rough Riders, demonstrating near-delusional courage. (Seventy-six percent of his troops suffered casualties.) Yet he was also a man of peace, winning the Nobel Peace Prize in 1906 for brokering the treaty to end the Russo-Japanese War.[16]

In terms of dynasties, of course, he was a man of wealth, with the real estate to back it up. His ancestors, seventeenth-century Dutch shipping magnates, were among the first to settle New York City. (Ever wonder why so many New York City landmarks have unpronounceable spellings such as Spuyten Duyvil, why Manhattan was once called New Amsterdam, or why Dutch Masters cigars once carried a certain cachet? Thank the Dutch.)

---

14. Coincidentally, these include the Adams- and Harrison-dynasty presidents—as well as George Washington, James Madison, Martin Van Buren, Zachary Taylor, Ulysses S. Grant, and William Howard Taft.
15. If "Czolgosz" were a legit Scrabble word, it'd be worth twenty-nine points.
16. America wasn't even directly involved in this war. Why bring this up? Because even in 1906, at the tender age of 130, America was eager to boss other countries around. Roosevelt was among the first presidents to assert that the U.S. was the greatest country in the world. Now *that's* a dynasty talking.

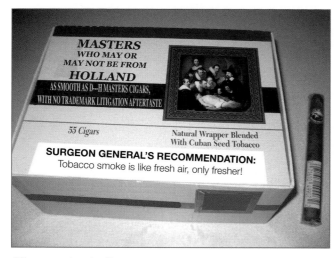

"These are okay, too!"

Although Teddy was a pampered city boy, his heart lay in the great outdoors. Following the tragic deaths of both his mother and his first wife on Valentine's Day 1884, Roosevelt spent the next two years at a vast ranch in the Dakota Badlands. There he consoled himself by hunting big game, rustling cattle, and even capturing three outlaws—mysteriously unnamed in the April 25, 1886, *New York Times* article reporting the event. Roosevelt himself, however, was named several times and referred to as "quite prominent in New York politics and society." Bully for him.

The teddy bear was so named after a political cartoon was published recounting a story about a bear Roosevelt refused to shoot on a hunting trip.

Roosevelt was famous for his colorful and unusual sayings. Among his favorites were "Bully for you" and "Speak softly and carry a big stick." When he was shot—campaigning in Milwaukee for the twenty-eighth presidency—he proclaimed, "No man has had a happier life than I have led; a happier life in every way." Of course, he survived the attempt on his life—perhaps because he wasn't subject to the curse of Tecumseh?

Theodore Roosevelt spouting clichés, big stick not pictured

His distant cousin Franklin Delano Roosevelt (FDR) was also a survivor: specifically of polio, which he contracted at the age of thirty-nine and which confined him to a wheelchair for the rest of his life. Not only couldn't he gallop into the White House when elected as thirty-second president, he also couldn't walk. Undeterred by physical setbacks, however, Roosevelt yanked America out of the Great Depression. More dynastically, he sought to reestablish America's reputation as a first-rate power by reinterpreting the Monroe Doctrine.

The 1823 Monroe Doctrine proclaimed that if a European power waged war against a former colony in North or South

America, the United States would view this as an act of war against the United States—and fight back. Roosevelt officially updated this in 1935 with his "good neighbor" policy, which allowed the United States to view any act of war against an ally anywhere on the globe as an act of war against the United States, period. Not that he really *wanted* to fight. When Nazi Germany invaded France and attacked Britain in 1940, he sent lots of war "materiel"[17] and warm wishes, but no troops. It wasn't until Japan bombed our own Pacific fleet in Pearl Harbor on December 7, 1941, that FDR declared it "a date which will live in infamy" and plunged the nation into World War II.

But you probably know all this. We're here to talk dynasty in this chapter. And FDR's most dynastic accomplishment by far was the sheer length of his presidency—at four consecutive terms, it remains the longest in history. Coincidentally, Adolf Hitler's reign over Germany's "One-Thousand-Year Reich" lasted during exactly the same period, 1933–1945. This put Hitler 988 years shy of his dynastic prediction. But as far as misstatements go, he'd done a lot worse.

Following FDR's death in April 1945, Congress became a little anxious that future presidents would stay in office even longer than he had, thereby upsetting the delicate balance of power among the three branches of government. Roosevelt already had the wealth (millions), the real estate (a fat Hyde Park mansion), the nepotism, the luck (well, except for the polio), the portraits, the prominent relatives named George (a cousin) and John (his sixth child), both bankers . . . how much more powerful could or should a president get?

The answer: not much. On March 21, 1947, Congress proposed the Twenty-second Amendment, which set a two-term limit for the presidency of the United States. It was ratified on February 27, 1951, and unless the amendment is repealed,[18] the United States is no longer in danger of a Fidel Castro coming along and being president for nearly fifty years, as Castro did in Cuba. (*He* was a guy who understood dynasty.)

WHAT'S THE DIFFERENCE BETWEEN A DEPRESSION AND A RECESSION?

A "depression" is an economic situation so dismal that even people who have no understanding of economics get it, as the word also means "pathological sadness" (see page 78). It is typically marked by disease, high unemployment, heavy consumption of blues music, and saccharine movies aimed at boosting public morale, such as the Shirley Temple films. A "recession" is simply a decline in the gross domestic product for two consecutive quarters.

17. Another way of spelling "material." Perhaps they gave it this fancy spelling since it was going to Europe.
18. Thirty-fourth president Dwight D. Eisenhower wasn't a fan of the amendment and wanted it repealed. Fortieth president Ronald Reagan expressed a desire to repeal it, too, but Congress wouldn't listen to either of them. Ha!

Dynasty, Cuban style—Fidel Castro (left) and his brother Raúl

WHAT IS A CONSTITUTIONAL AMENDMENT, AND HOW DOES ONE GET PASSED OR REPEALED?

Generally speaking, it's tough to change or "amend" the Constitution. But if something is very, very wrong (for instance, slave ownership), a law can be written to address the problem. Any member of Congress can propose an amendment, but it takes a two-thirds majority in both the Senate and the House of Representatives to pass it. An amendment doesn't become law until a three-fourths majority of all states ratify it—either by convention or by popular vote, whatever Congress decides. It takes a new amendment to repeal a previous amendment. Another reason it's tough to change the Constitution: members of Congress generally don't like to spend any more time voting on bills than they absolutely have to.

The 1787 draft of the U.S. Constitution, on display in Washington DC. To test the conventional wisdom about how hard it is to amend the Constitution, we visited the National Archives in DC with a Sharpie. How'd we fare? In spite of the temptation, the authors did not attempt a National Treasure*–style heist and overhaul of our country's founding document.*

DYNASTY #4
The Kennedy Family
(It's Pronounced "Chow-dah.")

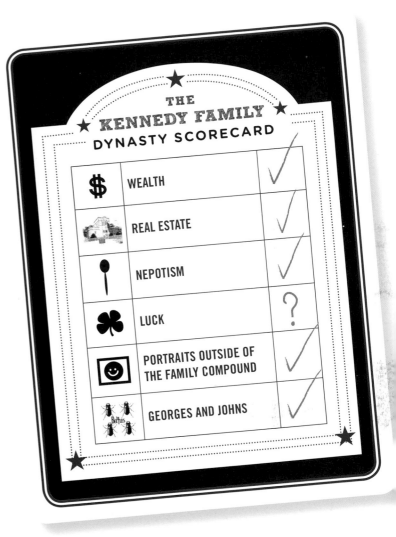

$	WEALTH	✓
🏛	REAL ESTATE	✓
	NEPOTISM	✓
☘	LUCK	?
☺	PORTRAITS OUTSIDE OF THE FAMILY COMPOUND	✓
🐞	GEORGES AND JOHNS	✓

The Kennedys were the quintessential twentieth-century American dynasty in that they earned (and still earn) millions, invested (and still invest) in swank real estate, cashed in on luck (as bootleggers during Prohibition), named several family members George or John to stack the deck in their favor (including the dynasty's sole president), and graced numerous painted portraits hung outside their Hyannis Port compound, all during . . . well, the twentieth century.

Joe Kennedy

LET'S ALL RAISE A GLASS TO PROHIBITION

Prohibition is the name of America's "dry" period, otherwise known as the Roaring Twenties—because even though the Eighteenth Amendment outlawed the sale of liquor, a lot of people got drunk anyway. It's also ironic, and logical, that this period was followed immediately by the Great Depression, as both depression and bafflement over loss of money are common symptoms of hangovers. The Eighteenth Amendment is the only amendment to the U.S. Constitution ever to be repealed—by the Twenty-first Amendment.

Joseph P. Kennedy was the dynasty's Abraham, a patriarch of biblical proportions. His sons include John, aka Jack, the thirty-fifth president of the United States; Robert, aka Bobby, the U.S. attorney general under John and later a U.S. senator from New York; and Edward, aka Ted, arguably the Democratic Party's most powerful senator until 2008, when brain surgery sidelined him from making his trademark anti-Republican outbursts.[19]

Joe Kennedy made his fortune by investing in films, banks, and liquor distribution. During Prohibition he allegedly doubled his money by smuggling booze from Canada into the United States, but like all competent alleged crooks, he was never convicted of or even charged with any crime.

In an effort to improve his shady reputation, Joe Kennedy dove into politics during the 1932 presidential election, becoming one of Franklin Roosevelt's most ardent and generous supporters. Roosevelt rewarded Kennedy by appointing him the first chairman of the federal Securities and Exchange Commission (SEC).[20] The close relationship between Joe Kennedy and FDR bears mentioning only because it's no coincidence—just another fun example of the incestuous nature of American dynasties. It also explains quaint phrases such as "a patriarch of biblical proportions" and "the old boy network." Look hard enough, and you'll find that most powerful American dynasties, presidential or not, are somehow connected.

19. Ted Kennedy was indeed the most vocal of what conservative pundits called the "Bush Bashers."
20. The SEC, in its own words, exists "to protect investors, maintain fair, orderly, and efficient markets, and facilitate capital formation." One possible interpretation: it exists to protect "the old boy network."

HARD-KNOCK LIVES: THE "KENNEDY CURSE"

In spite of their unimaginable wealth and success, the Kennedy clan has suffered more than its share of misfortune—so much so, in fact, that some people believe the family is cursed. (Tecumseh was not entirely responsible, at least as far as we know, though Jack was the final victim of his curse.) Take a look and judge for yourself.

CHRONOLOGY OF THE KENNEDYS' SERIES OF UNFORTUNATE EVENTS

KENNEDY FAMILY MEMBER	TRAGIC DEATH, ACCIDENT, OR PERSONAL STRUGGLE
JOSEPH P. KENNEDY JR.	Dies when the plane he is flying mysteriously explodes over the English Channel, August 12, 1944
KATHLEEN KENNEDY	Dies in a plane crash in France, May 13, 1948
JOHN F. KENNEDY	Assassinated by Lee Harvey Oswald (according to the Warren Commission) on November 22, 1963
EDWARD (TED) M. KENNEDY	Back broken and lung punctured in a plane crash on June 19, 1964 (several of his aides were killed)
ROBERT F. KENNEDY	Assassinated by Sirhan Sirhan the night of June 5, 1968
EDWARD (TED) M. KENNEDY	Chappaquiddick (See "How Come Ted Kennedy Gave Up on Becoming President After One Lousy Try?" on page 56)
JOSEPH P. KENNEDY II	Boards a plane on February 23, 1972, that is hijacked by terrorists and flown to South Yemen; freed two days later
EDWARD M. KENNEDY JR.	Loses right leg to bone cancer on November 17, 1973
ROBERT F. KENNEDY JR.	Arrested for possession of heroin on September 11, 1983
DAVID A. KENNEDY	Dies of an overdose of cocaine, Mellaril, and Demerol on April 25, 1984
PATRICK J. KENNEDY	In treatment for alcoholism and cocaine addiction for most of 1986; re-enters treatment, for addiction to painkillers, in 2006
MICHAEL L. KENNEDY	Dies in a skiing accident on December 31, 1997
JOHN F. KENNEDY JR.	Dies when the plane he is flying crashes off Martha's Vineyard on July 16, 1999; his wife and her sister also killed
EDWARD (TED) M. KENNEDY	Diagnosed with a brain tumor on May 20, 2008; dies on August 26, 2009

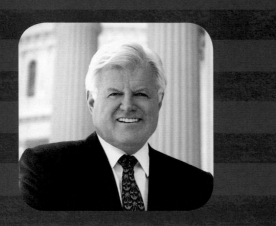

HOW COME TED KENNEDY
GAVE UP ON BECOMING PRESIDENT
AFTER ONE LOUSY TRY?

You'd think Ted—the Kennedy clan's former *Godfather*-style head of the family—would have been a shoo-in given his decades of service in Congress, his pedigree, and his exalted status in the Democratic Party. But the truth is, he could never quite live down Chappaquiddick. This is the name of a scandal that took place near the exclusive resort town in Martha's Vineyard where he drove his car off a bridge on July 18, 1969. Kennedy managed to escape and swim to safety after the car plunged into the water, but his passenger, a campaign worker named Mary Jo Kopechne, drowned. Rumor had it Kennedy was drunk at the time (he was scion to a booze mogul, after all) and Miss Kopechne was his mistress, but these rumors were never proven. Still, thanks to some powerful family lawyers, he pled guilty and got off with only a suspended two-month sentence for leaving the scene of an accident—a verdict some see as a miscarriage of justice on par with the O. J. Simpson acquittal.

Following World War II, Joe Kennedy used his considerable clout to kick-start his son John's fledgling political career. John, a witty and likeable war hero, appreciated his father's help, as he knew little of politics and had pretty much coasted through life on his charm and good looks. His father knew a valuable commodity when he saw one. "We're going to sell Jack like soap flakes," he famously declared—probably because soap flakes, whatever they are, were a valuable commodity at the time.

Joe Kennedy's relentless marketing paid off. John was young, yes, but that meant he brought the possibility of hope and change, unlike his cynical Washington-insider adversary, Richard Nixon. Sure, he was a minority many loathed—a Catholic—but freedom of religion is a cornerstone of the nation's founding.[21] He was an intellectual, too: the Pulitzer Prize–winning author of *Profiles in Courage*, which chronicled the brave politics of John Quincy Adams and other U.S. senators. Finally, unlike his political rival Richard Nixon, he never appeared sweaty or unshaven on television. A lot of historians credit his masterful use of this exciting new mass medium—the grainy black-and-white news broadcast—to catapult his career. Imagine what he could have done with YouTube.

---

21. As the first Catholic presidential candidate ever, John F. Kennedy's choice of running mate, Lyndon B. Johnson, was shrewd. Johnson was able to attract many Southern Democratic voters who otherwise wouldn't have voted for a Catholic or an urbane New Englander—largely because he was neither of those, and because he wore big Texan hats.

Sound familiar? Yup: the branding of Barack Obama owes more than a little to the branding of JFK. John Quincy Adams wouldn't have stood a chance against either of them.

Richard Nixon attempts to conceal his sweaty, unshaven jowls while debating John F. Kennedy on TV in 1960.

As far as the dynastic qualities of the Kennedys go, it could be argued that JFK's tragic assassination had the perverse effect of making the Kennedys even *more* powerful, at least in terms of how history will remember them. JFK accomplished a great deal during his two years and ten months in office. Notably, he averted nuclear war with the Soviet Union during the 1962 Cuban Missile Crisis; he laid the foundation for the landmark Civil Rights Act of 1964; and he poured billions of dollars into NASA, which made good on his promise to put a man on the moon by the end of the decade.[22]

OBAMA-KENNEDY FACE-OFF	BARACK OBAMA	JOHN F. KENNEDY
Preached Hope and/or Change	✓	✓
Bestselling Author	✓	✓
Minority	✓	✓
Clean-Shaven	✓	✓
Stylish, Pearl-Wearing Spouse	✓	✓

22. During the following decade, the 1970s, a man even played golf on the moon. Neat! It's possible that NASA's billions could have been better spent on, say, educating the underprivileged, feeding the poor, or curing disease. But that's a matter of opinion.

On the other hand, he cheated on his wife in the White House swimming pool, the Lincoln Bedroom, and a side room next to the Oval Office—with a different woman in each place. History has not been as kind to, say, Bill Clinton, regarding infidelity. Would JFK's trysts have blossomed into multiple Monicagates had he not been shot? (Granted, the truth about his infidelity didn't come out until long after his death.) What about his addiction to painkillers? Or the lies he told about his health: namely, that it was good? (He suffered from chronic back pain and Addison's disease most of his adult life.)

Marilyn Monroe was linked to JFK—particularly after a PG-13 rendition of "Happy Birthday"!

Maybe these questions are better left unasked, as they can never be answered. (But they are fun to debate over soda and chips. You could even use this book as a handy tray or placemat.) It's much more pleasant to remember the Kennedy White House as "Camelot,"[23] that shining castle on the hill. Then again, there was cheating in the Camelot of myth, too: Guinevere cheated on King Arthur with Lancelot.

---

23. Camelot was a mythical place where for a brief period hope, justice, courage, and honesty were exalted. A Broadway musical production called *Camelot*, based on the King Arthur legend, was a huge hit during Kennedy's presidency. Rumor has it JFK often spun the soundtrack on the White House turntable. Because the musical's theme so closely matched the longing for hope felt by many of Kennedy's mourners, the association was cemented. True or not, it's fun to imagine JFK kicking it like a DJ.

THE BUSH FAMILY
DYNASTY SCORECARD

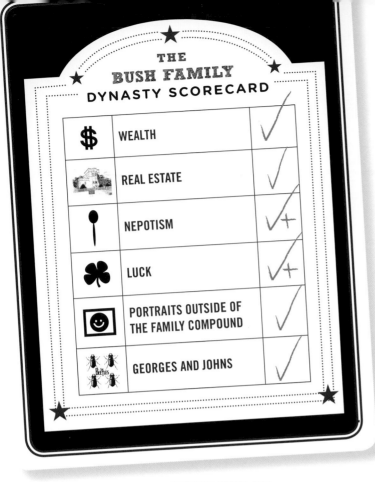

$	WEALTH	✓
🏠	REAL ESTATE	✓
❗	NEPOTISM	✓+
☘	LUCK	✓+
☺	PORTRAITS OUTSIDE OF THE FAMILY COMPOUND	✓
🪲 BEETLES	GEORGES AND JOHNS	✓

A dynasty in the making: George H. W. Bush and his wife, Barbara, holding baby George W.

DYNASTY #5
The Bush Family
(Don't Misunderestimate Them.)

Talk about a dynasty worthy of myth or epic. Yes, the Bushes—George H. W., forty-first president of the United States, and George W., forty-third president of the United States—bring drama, intrigue, vengeance, family honor, and wacky malapropisms[24] to the rich banquet of American history. Given that there are so many lenses through which to view the Bush dynasty and its complexities, perhaps it's best to pick just one: oil.

Oil made the family its vast fortune, dating back to 1924—when George W. Bush's grandfather Prescott Bush became vice president of Harriman & Co., an oil-drilling company based in Texas. His son, George H. W., went to work for the family business and later founded his own oil company, Zapata Petroleum Corporation, in 1953.

During this time, George H. W. made lots of friends in politics. At the end of the 1960s these political connections led him to embark on a new career: that of a civil servant who held even more high offices than John Adams.[25] As both politician and oilman, he cultivated many relationships and business partnerships with oil-rich nations. Some relationships were trickier to navigate than others.

Take Iraq, for instance. As director of the CIA from 1976 to 1980, George H. W. (right) spied on Saddam Hussein. But as long as Iraq's oil kept flowing to the U.S., he didn't consider Hussein an enemy, per se—just someone to keep an eye on.

As vice president under fortieth president Ronald Reagan, George H. W. actually considered Iraq an ally.[26] The Reagan administration began supplying Hussein with billions of dollars in military aid to fight the Iranians in the Iran–Iraq War, even going so far as to send Donald Rumsfeld (then U.S. Special Envoy to the Middle East) on a goodwill mission to Baghdad.

---

24. The act of misusing words ridiculously, such as George W. Bush's: "They misunderestimate me." True story: the first book in which coauthor Andisheh Nouraee's work ever appeared was a compilation of Bush malapropisms by Jacob Weisberg. Search for "george w. bush andy nouraee npr" and you'll find it.

25. These include congressman (Republican, Texas), U.S. ambassador to the United Nations, chairman of the Republican National Committee, chief of the U.S. Liaison Office in the People's Republic of China, director of the CIA, vice president, and president.

26. In the "the enemy of my enemy is my friend" sense.

IRAN AND THE U.S.: A NOT-SO-SECRET HISTORY

During the 1960s and 1970s, oil-rich Iran was ruled by the Shah Reza Pahlavi ("shah" means king), a U.S.-backed secular dictator much like Saddam Hussein, though not *quite* as psychopathic. In 1979, a coalition of Muslim fundamentalists drove the shah from power. Led by Ayatollah Khomeini, these rabble-rousers turned Iran into a Muslim theocracy. Not only that, they seized the American embassy and held fifty-three U.S. diplomats captive for 444 days. Perhaps cruelest of all (at least in terms of how they've affected American dynasties), they denied the U.S. access to Iran's oil. Since then, the U.S. and Iranian governments have been bitter enemies, which explains why John McCain sang "Bomb Iran" to the tune of the surf-rock classic "Barbara Ann" during his unsuccessful 2007–2008 campaign for presidency. Either that or he was shamelessly pandering to hawkish Republicans. Or both.

Donald Rumsfeld and Saddam Hussein exchanging smiles and a hearty handshake, circa 1983

At the time, Iran's brand-new anti-U.S. theocracy was believed to be a far bigger threat to U.S. interests than Iraq. The Iran–Iraq War ended in a stalemate in 1988, with both sides declaring victory. (Nearly a million soldiers and civilians died.) The oil supply from Iraq to the U.S. reached an all-time low.

Two years later, as forty-first president, George H. W. changed his tune about Hussein completely. Following the 1990 Iraqi invasion of Kuwait—another huge supplier of U.S. oil—he deemed Hussein an "enemy of freedom"[27] in adherence to FDR's "good neighbor" policy.

In early 1991, George H. W. put together an international coalition to drive the Iraqi Army out of Kuwait with minimal casualties. He did not, however, attempt to drive Hussein from power. He just made sure that the U.S. once again had safe access to Kuwaiti oil. Besides, as he explained in his 1998 memoir, occupying Iraq would not only cost billions of dollars and countless American lives, it would infuriate Arabs worldwide and violate one of our nation's core post–Cold War principles: the United States does not declare war unilaterally. We declare war only with the support of other nations, and preferably through the UN. To do otherwise would be both stupid and unethical.

Flash forward to March 2003.

George W. is the forty-third president of the United States. With his War on Terror, he has further updated FDR's "good

---

27. Actually, Kuwait was and is a dictatorship, too—ruled by the al-Sabah family. So in this case, Hussein was technically an enemy of other dictatorships. But "enemy of freedom" has a better ring to it.

neighbor" mandate. U.S. policy regarding foreign aggression becomes two-pronged: (1) Any terrorist act against an ally can be considered a terrorist attack against the United States; (2) Any sovereign nation that sponsors or harbors terrorists can be attacked preemptively. George W. insists that the U.S. must deal with Saddam Hussein, who he says poses a grave and imminent threat because Hussein is reconstituting his nuclear weapons program and has links with Al-Qaeda.

On March 19, 2003, it's bombs away over Baghdad.

We cover the Iraq War in chapter four. The central question about the Bush dynasty is this: why did George W. invade Iraq if his father knew it was such a bad, bad idea? George W. has offered various explanations over the years: Saddam *was* a threat, though not a nuclear one. He *did* sponsor and harbor

terrorists, though not Al-Qaeda. Most of all, it is in the United States' best interest to spread democracy.

But many former W. and H. W. Bush administration officials offer a simpler explanation: George W. wanted access to Iraq's oil, and Saddam Hussein prevented him from getting it.

One cynical way to argue this view is to pose a disturbing hypothetical question: if twenty-first-century U.S. foreign policy consists in large part of spreading democracy and preemptively attacking nations that harbor or sponsor terrorists, why haven't we invaded Saudi Arabia? That country is a dictatorship, ruled by the al-Saud family. Women's rights are suppressed; dissidents are beheaded; all religions except an especially draconian sect of Sunni Islam, Wahhabism, are suppressed. The Saudi government has provided millions of dollars to organizations that the U.S. has deemed "terrorist." Fifteen of the nineteen September 11 hijackers were from Saudi Arabia—as is Osama bin Laden himself. But the United States continues to consider Saudi Arabia a close ally.

Could it be that the answer there, too, is oil? Specifically, that we have easy access to Saudi oil, and that the Bush family and its political allies in the U.S. oil industry profit handsomely from their close business relationship with the House of Saud? Prince Bandar bin Sultan, former Saudi Arabian ambassador to the United States, was once so close to the Bush family that George W. affectionately nicknamed him "Bandar Bush."

George and "Bandar Bush" kick it in Crawford, Texas, less than one year after 9/11.

Or perhaps—if you examine recent history through the lens of the Bush dynasty itself—you could argue that George W. was motivated to invade Iraq, at least in part, to avenge his father's honor. A lot of powerful people viewed George H. W.'s conclusion to the Gulf War as an inept failure, seeing as the U.S. didn't get any Iraqi oil in its aftermath. From this perspective, by toppling Hussein, George W. took care of unfinished Bush family business. To add a little spice to this argument, one could even speculate that George W. was motivated to *outdo* his father. Until September 11, 2001, George W. stood in his father's shadow, never quite measuring up to the statesman, oilman, intellectual—or president—that George H. W. was.

But alas, this is a debate best left to a large chunk of time and a surplus of snack food. As of this writing, both George W. and George H. W. insist that they are on the exact same page regarding Iraq, U.S. foreign policy, and, of course, oil. George W. says that he has no regrets. He made his decision about Iraq, and he sticks by it. He is, in his own words, "The Decider." Perhaps this is his most dynastic legacy: the power bequeathed to him by wealth, land, luck, name, and nepotism ensures that his decisions will affect the entire planet for decades to come.

George W. Bush on the verge of deciding something

OUR TOP FIVE AMERICAN NONPRESIDENTIAL DYNASTIES
More Oil, Guns, and Money

In the Soviet Union, capitalism triumphed over communism. In this country, capitalism triumphed over democracy.
—*Fran Lebowitz*

Just because you aren't president of the United States doesn't mean you can't manipulate the fates of millions of people, all while sipping brandy from the comfort of your library, laughing: *"Mu-hu-hu-ha-HA!"* (Kidding.) But in this day and age, being president might even constitute a liability. A February 2008 Gallup Poll put George W. Bush's approval rating at 19 percent, setting a new record for the lowest in United States history.[28] His approval rating when he left office was the lowest of any president since approval ratings started being measured.

In any case, as we've just seen from studying the presidents, big business plays an important role in the establishment of dynasties. The power to win friends and influence people, to establish universities and foundations, to improve the world through philanthropy, to affect the policies of governments both global and local . . . all of it comes down to the simple desire to create or sell something many people will consume, thereby controlling as much of their lives as possible.

---

28. The previous record holder was thirty-third president Harry S. Truman, whose approval rating dropped to 22 percent in a Gallup Poll taken in February 1952. But by the time he left office he had a much higher approval rating than George W. Bush.

THE CARNEGIE FAMILY
DYNASTY SCORECARD

$	WEALTH	✓
	REAL ESTATE	✓
	NEPOTISM	✓
♣	LUCK	✓
☺	PORTRAITS OUTSIDE OF THE FAMILY COMPOUND	✓
	GEORGES AND JOHNS	

The house that steel built

Andrew Carnegie

DYNASTY #6
The Carnegie Family
(How to Win Rich Friends and Influence Rich People)

Before oil (the twentieth century's fast track to wealth), there was steel (the nineteenth century's fast track to wealth). The Industrial Age relied on steel for building railroads, constructing the machines that produce beer cans, and creating bigger and better vaults to secure the riches of the dynasties that produced the steel. By far the biggest U.S. steel company was . . . well, the aptly named U.S. Steel. Founded by a Scotsman, Andrew Carnegie, it was known as "Carnegie Steel" before his family became so absurdly rich that a surname wouldn't suffice. The Carnegies are also known for their hand in promoting education and railroads. And move over, Oprah! The true father of self-help was millionaire industrialist Dale Carnegie.

THE VANDERBILT FAMILY
DYNASTY SCORECARD

$	WEALTH	✓
🏢	REAL ESTATE	✓
👤	NEPOTISM	✓
☘	LUCK	✓
☺	PORTRAITS OUTSIDE OF THE FAMILY COMPOUND	✓
🐞	GEORGES AND JOHNS	✓

CNN's Anderson Cooper—yep, he's a Vanderbilt!

Cornelius Vanderbilt

DYNASTY #7
The Vanderbilt Family
(The Wu-Tang Clan of Dynasties. Seriously.)

This New York City family gave us CNN's Anderson Cooper[29] and dabbled in shipping and railroads, much like the Carnegies. And education! Nashville, Tennessee's Vanderbilt University wouldn't exist were it not for a $1 million gift from "Commodore" Cornelius himself in 1873. Plus, they boast more George Washingtons than the first president's own family.[30]

The first Vanderbilts (then spelled "van der Bilt") arrived from Holland in America in 1650 and set up shop as farmers on Staten Island.[31] The family lived rather modestly until the mid-nineteenth century, when "Commodore" Cornelius Vanderbilt started a business building luxury residences (including one for himself) and made vast millions. Upon his death in 1877, he was the richest man in America. You can thank the Vanderbilts for helping to found the Metropolitan Opera and the Columbia University Medical Center, among other institutions. So say you suffered some terrible affliction during a presentation of *Il Trovatore* at the Met and you had to be rushed to the Columbia University Medical Center, where you were saved. You could say that the ghost of Cornelius Vanderbilt had a hand in your entire unforgettable evening. Spooky!

Gloria Vanderbilt surrounded by her company's greatest assets

---

29. Anderson's mom is Gloria Vanderbilt, the heiress turned fashion designer who helped turn the American public on to the concept of "designer jeans." Prior to Vanderbilt, the words "designer" and "jeans" were what "bacon cheeseburger" is to "kosher." Calvin Klein owes the family a debt of gratitude.

30. George Washington Vanderbilt III (1914–1961) was a famous yachtsman. This is a common profession or hobby only for members of dynasties, as few people outside dynasties can afford yachts.

31. Home of the Wu-Tang Clan, but not so much farmland anymore.

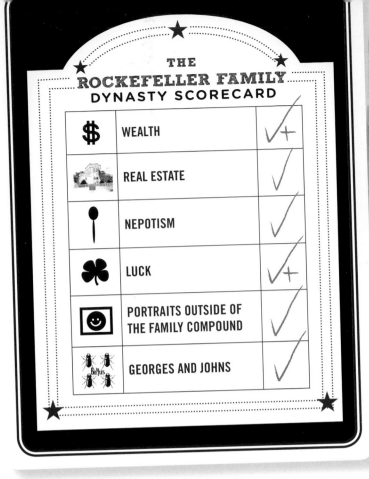

THE
ROCKEFELLER FAMILY
DYNASTY SCORECARD

$	WEALTH	✓+
	REAL ESTATE	✓
	NEPOTISM	✓
☘	LUCK	✓+
☺	PORTRAITS OUTSIDE OF THE FAMILY COMPOUND	✓
	GEORGES AND JOHNS	✓

John D. Rockefeller and John D. Rockefeller, Jr. Nothing says dynasty like matching names and matching top hats.

DYNASTY #8
The Rockefeller Family
(*Without Whom* 30 Rock *Might Be* 30 Vand)

You have to give this family credit: they were the first to see that steel wasn't the future. In 1970s Pittsburgh, the pollution from steel mills was so bad that a white shirt would turn brownish gray by midday, simply from being exposed to the air downtown. But it wasn't only pollution. Steel began to be produced more cheaply abroad than in the U.S. (namely in China), plus automated steel-producing factories put people out of work—for the simple reason that they require fewer people to operate than the old-fashioned factories that required . . . um, people (see *The Terminator* films).

Like the Bush family, the Rockefellers bet on oil and it paid off. The Rockefellers also built a huge complex of buildings in midtown Manhattan, Rockefeller Center (right), where many TV shows, such as *Saturday Night Live*, are conceived and filmed.[32] (Now the complex is proudly owned by the real estate company Tishman Speyer.) Nelson Rockefeller, the family's most famous and accomplished member since founder John D., was the forty-first vice president of the United States—nominated by thirty-eighth president Gerald Ford, after Richard Nixon resigned from the presidency in 1974. But the family's most dynastic legacy by far is that their name has become synonymous with wealth itself.

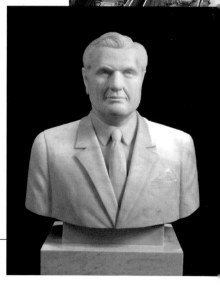

A bust of Nelson Rockefeller. It could be argued that busts are even more dynastic than portraits.

32. The hit comedy 30 Rock gets its name from the address of this very place.

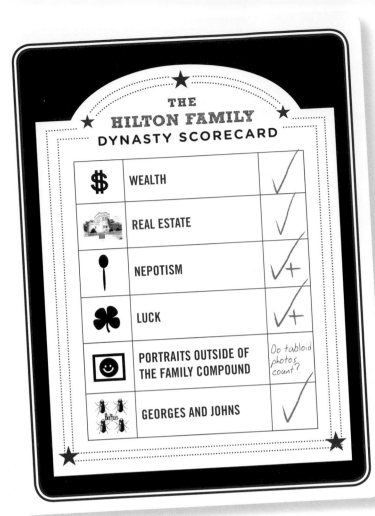

THE HILTON FAMILY
DYNASTY SCORECARD

$	WEALTH	✓
🏨	REAL ESTATE	✓
	NEPOTISM	✓+
☘	LUCK	✓+
☺	PORTRAITS OUTSIDE OF THE FAMILY COMPOUND	Do tabloid photos count?
🪲🪲🪲 BEETLES	GEORGES AND JOHNS	✓

The paparazzi jostling for a photo of Paris Hilton

DYNASTY #9
The Hilton Family
(Perez Not Included)

Okay, we know what you're thinking: "But this is a civics book!" We won't be discussing Paris here. (But a quick aside—did you see what she was wearing the night Britney got caught flashing the camera? OMG! That girl has got to get a new stylist . . .) Anyway, the Hiltons made more money by establishing a hotel chain—which ironically relies on transport, oil, and steel—than most industrialists (even the Vanderbilts) made by establishing their own dynasties. They are the richest American hoteliers ever, period.

Oh, and don't forget about poor Nicky. Why does Paris get all the attention?

The hotels that provide Paris and Nicky with some handy pocket change

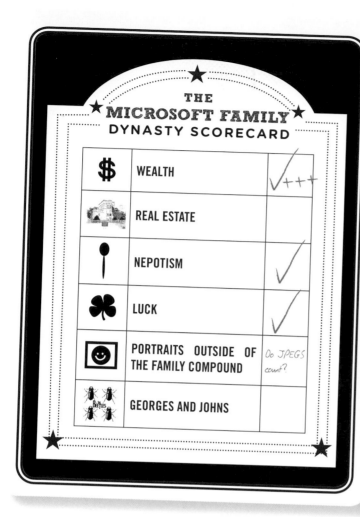

THE
MICROSOFT FAMILY
DYNASTY SCORECARD

$	WEALTH	✓+++
🏠	REAL ESTATE	
	NEPOTISM	✓
☘	LUCK	✓
😊	PORTRAITS OUTSIDE OF THE FAMILY COMPOUND	Do JPEGS count?
🐞 BEETLES	GEORGES AND JOHNS	

DYNASTY #10
The Microsoft Family
(Ka-ching!)

Well, Microsoft isn't a family exactly, but how do we even define "family" in the twenty-first century? The point is, Bill Gates is the world's second-richest man—valued, even in financially dismal 2010, at $53 billion—and his company consistently earns more money per annum than most third-world nations. Interesting fact: at age nineteen, before he became a billionaire inventor and entrepreneur, Gates was arrested for a traffic violation in Albuquerque, New Mexico (see page 21). So in police files, his past is even seedier than Joe Kennedy's, who was never arrested. He's since shaped up, however. The Bill & Melinda Gates Foundation—dedicated to improving health care and reducing poverty worldwide—is the largest charitable organization in the world, with an endowment of nearly $30 billion.

THE THREE STAGES OF BILL GATES
Student inventor, age 13, with Paul Allen in 1968 (top); young mogul, age 30, in 1985 (middle); and philanthropist, age 53, with wife Melinda, in June 2009 (bottom)

OUR FAVORITE EPISODE OF *DYNASTY*

This seminal Reagan-era prime-time drama lasted even longer than the Reagan presidency itself. The first episode aired on January 12, 1981; the series finale (disregarding the 2006 reunion) aired on May 10, 1989. In full color, heavy makeup, and lots of hair product, *Dynasty* chronicles the secrets, loves, passions, and betrayals of a family headed by—you guessed it—the owner of a huge oil company.

The cast of Dynasty . . . *in dry clothes.*

Meet Blake Carrington, the patriarch of biblical proportions, as played by John Forsythe . . . Alexis, the scheming ex-wife, as played by Joan Collins . . . Krystle, the new wife with a pure heart but many demons, as played by Linda Evans . . . and, of course, the young and troubled Sammy Jo, as played by Heather Locklear.[33]

Given that there were 217 episodes of the program all told, you might think it would be difficult to choose a favorite. But Andy, Jodi, and Dan decided unanimously on the very last one—#217, "Catch 22"—in which Krystle and Alexis wrestle each other into a swimming pool. To this day, it remains the highest-rated episode of a "nighttime soap" in TV history.

"MERITOCRACY"
It's More Than Just an SAT Word; It's the Touchstone for an Argument!

For as long as there has been an America, there has been the "American Dream." Your own version of the American Dream may differ from the next person's, of course, depending on what your goals are, how much sleep you get, how much loot you've got stashed in offshore bank accounts, etc.—but we're willing to wager that your dream includes a whole lot more than forty acres and a mule, and probably even more than just owning your own home. (Unless your home has been featured on MTV's *Cribs*.) Traditionally in America, the proverbial sky has been the limit. Any dream goes!

---

33. At the time, Heather Locklear was married to Mötley Crüe drummer and infamous bad boy Tommy Lee.

If becoming president of the United States is the ultimate measure of success, then we needn't look any further than the post-2008-presidential-election bestseller lists for proof that the American Dream *can* come true.[34] (Well, so long as you have fierce ambition and a verging-on-compulsive work ethic, and no small amount of that pesky luck, either.) Even the Obama family dog, Bo, is a superstar. Of course, Barack Obama isn't the only person—living or otherwise—who provides proof of the American Dream come true. So does his wife, Michelle. So do Horatio Alger[35] and Thomas Paine and Jay-Z and Susan B. Anthony and Martin Luther King Jr. . . . really, anyone in America (and there are too many to list here) who rose from humble beginnings to dizzying heights of self-made success.

The American Dream, realized

FORTY ACRES AND A MULE? REALLY—THAT'S IT?

If you're wondering where the phrase "forty acres and a mule" comes from—aside from Spike Lee's film production company—it was the compensation promised to former slaves directly following the Civil War. The idea was that these newly freed people would have a better shot of achieving the American Dream if they could own property themselves. The result? In early 1865, every eligible African American adult male received forty acres of land to farm and a mule to pull a plow. (Plows, like batteries, were not included.) By June 1865, roughly 10,000 former slaves were settled on plantation land in areas of Georgia and North Carolina. In perhaps the cruelest historical example of a "psych!" however, President Andrew Johnson decided to reverse the order and return the land to its original white owners. To this day, the phrase "forty acres and a mule" remains symbolic of the broken promises made to African Americans during Reconstruction and beyond. It's also probably why a majority of historians lump Andrew Johnson in with George W. Bush as one of history's worst presidents.

34. Among Obama-related titles: Barack; Barack Obama: Son of Promise, Child of Hope; Yes We Can—and those are just on the children's bestseller list. His own books, Dreams from My Father and The Audacity of Hope, also dominated the bestseller lists.

35. The nineteenth-century equivalent of Stephen King (at least in terms of book sales), Horatio Alger was the author of over 270 bestselling mass-market novels about down-on-their-luck boys who achieve fabulous wealth and success through grit, determination, and the steadfast belief that by serving others you also serve yourself. You can thank Horatio Alger for the cliché "rags to riches." Seriously, you can. You can also thank him for the cliché "a Horatio Alger story," which means the same thing.

But as we've read in this chapter and seen with our own eyes—or at least on TV—many people have certain advantages when it comes to achieving success because they were born into dynasties.

One might argue that George W. Bush isn't as intellectually curious as some because he didn't give much thought to his education. His years at the finest private schools, colleges, and universities were taken care of by nepotism and his family's wealth. Long story short: he didn't have to work for his education, so he felt entitled to it. No doubt John Quincy Adams, Franklin D. Roosevelt, and John F. Kennedy believed that *they* were entitled to a few things, too. The same goes for Barack Obama.

But, hey, who can truly know what someone else believes or thinks—or even feels entitled to? After all, we can only imagine what Benjamin Harrison felt entitled to as he stumbled around the White House in the darkness, refusing to use his newfangled electricity.

DISCUSSION QUESTIONS
(OPTIONAL)

1 Is oil the real key to dynastic wealth and power in the twenty-first century?

2 What happens when oil runs out? Will wind, solar energy, biofuels, or coal take its place?

3 Speaking of which, will oil, a finite resource, run out anytime *soon*?

4 Is it in a dynasty leader's best interest to conceal certain parts of his innermost psyche while appearing to be "accessible" to the public he serves?

5 Does owning a gun help to establish a dynasty? And does this explain why gun sales skyrocketed by an astounding 70 percent in the weeks following Barack Obama's election, in spite of the fact that the rest of the economy was in the toilet?

CHAPTER 3

ECONOMICS MADE FUN

(Or, Check Out These Photographs of Adorable Animals!)

INTRODUCTION
A Citizen's Guide to Money

When we think of the word "economics," we think of pulling out our fingernails slowly. It sounds incredibly boring. But it's really important, because money is one of the—maybe even *the*—major force driving politics, government, and the world. So how do we give you a little info about this vital topic without boring you? The obvious choice was to include irresistible photos of adorable animals to give your eyes and brain a break—after all, millions of you click onto the Web for your daily cute fix. The other obvious choice was to keep it brief. That's why you'll find this to be the shortest and sweetest chapter in the book.

Don't be scared. This won't be too painful.

Our country's economy—and its approach to economic principles—affects everything from how much we pay for a soda to the houses we live in to our relationship with the rest of the world. It helps to know the key players and the rules of the game, so here's a quick rundown.

PAPER MONEY
How Does It Work?

Why does paper money hold value while, say, rocks you pick up behind your house don't? Because money—whether it's coins, paper, or gold doubloons—is a contract: a medium of exchange that everybody's agreed to, without ever saying so. That's why a dollar bill, printed on pretty much worthless paper, can be worth a hundred pennies while a penny, which costs more to make than a $100 bill does, only represents one cent. Our society as a whole has agreed to honor each piece of currency as having a certain value.

Most of the Western world used to trade gold instead of paper money. In that case, there *was* a more straightforward connection between a piece of gold and its worth—whatever it weighed was its value. But society still had to agree on that value. Plus, transporting gold around was kind of pesky for anyone without a hefty schooner or pirate ship. So eventually, *most* of the world switched to paper and coins.

THE GODFATHER OF ECONOMICS: JOHN MAYNARD KEYNES

Keynes was a British economist who had a major impact on modern economic theory and U.S. economic policies. He's important because his theories still influence the way our government handles our money (and also the way we wear our mustaches). He's largely responsible for the conviction that the government needs to be deeply involved in running an economy. Bailouts, for instance—when the government steps in and lends money to companies in order to avoid economic crises for the country as a whole—are pretty Keynesian. Many people disagree with Keynes's assertions, and with the U.S.'s frequent adherence to his ideas. He is not to be confused with James Brown, the Godfather of Soul.

James Brown is largely responsible for people feeling nice, like sugar and spice.

THE AWARD FOR MOST PHYSICALLY PAINFUL MONEY GOES TO . . .

Kissi money was once the agreed-upon currency in parts of West Africa. Its value was determined by how long the particular piece of money was. If a piece of your Kissi money broke, a witch doctor had to put it back together. Though from the looks of Kissi money, we presume he spent most of his witch-doctoring days handing out Band-Aids.

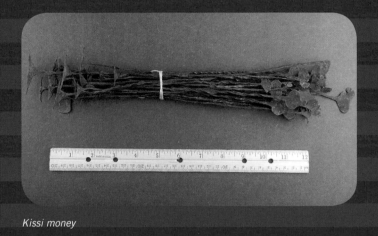

Kissi money

Once we made the switch, we (and lots of other countries) still used something called the "gold standard" to back up our currency—as in, if you had paper money issued by the government, that piece of paper was a promise that the government had enough gold to back it up. (Theoretically, you could trade the government your paper money for gold bricks, if you were into that kind of thing.) We kept the gold standard until 1971. These days, paper money is "agreed" to hold value on its own without gold standing behind it (though our government does have a reserve of gold in Fort Knox as a kind of backup— about one-fifth of the value of all the dollars in circulation).

THE U.S. ECONOMY
What's in Uncle Sam's Wallet?

Why was the Great Depression so sad? Why do people in government argue about balancing the budget? Who's steering our economy? And how does a mortgage crisis happen? Here's a rundown on the inner workings of our country's cash flow.

WHAT'S A GDP?

GDP, or gross domestic product, measures two things: how much money everyone in the country makes, and how much everyone in the country spends. Economists use all sorts of factors to calculate the total, and even then it's still inexact. But most agree that the GDP, which is expressed in a dollar amount, is the best indicator we have for how "healthy" our economy is. At the printing of this book our country's GDP was estimated by the IMF, the International Monetary Fund, to be $14.9 trillion.

"Healthy" is based on the assumption that most people would like to make more money and spend more money. For instance, in 1930 our GDP was much less than it is now. Your great-grandmother may have had to save her pennies to buy, say, a box of those newfangled tea bags people kept talking about. You, on the other hand, can probably afford to drink tea all day long. In other words, our GDP has grown and, generally speaking, we make more and spend more than our parents and grandparents did, even factoring in the recent economic downturn.

You can find the most up-to-date info about the GDP at www.bea.gov. But keep in mind that the GDP can't measure factors like safety, health, clean air, or intangible things linked to overall happiness. Our GDP may grow at the expense of other things not counted in currency, so the GDP is only part of the story.

WHAT'S A BUDGET DEFICIT AND WHY DOES EVERYONE TALK ABOUT A BALANCED BUDGET?

The government finances itself by collecting the taxes we pay. When the government spends more money than it makes, it has a "budget deficit." If the government spends less than it makes, it has a "budget surplus." And if what the government spends equals what it makes, it has a "balanced budget."

To pay its bills during a deficit, the government has to borrow

money from banks. How? At least partly by offering bonds that people like us buy through those banks. The government basically takes a loan from the American people and pays us interest on it. Your grandpa Joe then buys said bonds and gives them to you for your graduation.

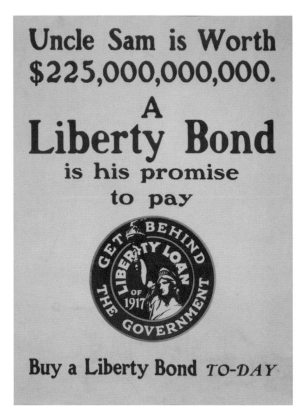

Bonds are the government's way of saying, "I'll pay you back. I swear."

The more the government borrows from banks, the less money is available for other, nongovernmental borrowers (like people who want to start a business or invest in one). The less money there is to borrow, the more it costs to borrow it. And since it costs more to borrow, people borrow less. That means people end up spending less and investing less.

So *theoretically* (an important word in economics), a budget deficit reduces the economy's growth rate. A budget surplus, on the other hand, *theoretically* works in reverse: it lowers interest rates and stimulates new businesses, homes, and growth. For complex reasons, people often debate these outcomes, and their pros and cons.

RIGHT SAID FED
What's the Federal Reserve and What Does It Do?

Congress created the Federal Reserve ("the Fed") in 1914, after a bunch of bank failures left a lot of people suddenly broke. It was decided that we needed a central bank to safeguard the nation's economy (banks included) and keep it healthy.

The Fed is sort of like an economic puppet master. It's supposed to supervise our banking system and help keep prices and our currency stable, employment high, and interest rates reasonable. It does this by passing regulations and, in large part, by deciding how much paper money to print and when to put that money into circulation (more on that on page 79). The Fed also sometimes makes loans to other countries in rare times of economic crisis (crises that could "trickle down" and hurt the U.S.).

Not everyone agrees that having a Federal Reserve is a good idea. And it has sometimes been criticized for being too secretive about what it does with the public's money.

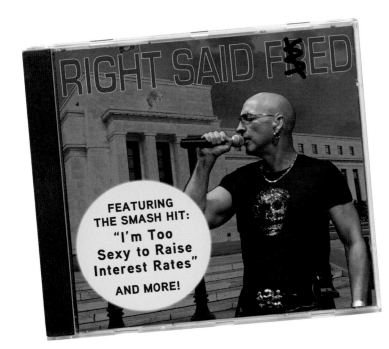

WHAT'S THE FDIC?

The Federal Deposit Insurance Corporation is the federal government's way of guaranteeing the safety of the money you deposit at your bank. If the bank ran out of money and couldn't pay you what they owed, the Fed would step in and foot the bill.

WHO'S ALAN GREENSPAN?

Greenspan was chairman of the Fed from 1987 to 2006. He's controversial for his support of more competitive markets with fewer regulations—the kind of economic philosophy that many blame for the 2008 subprime mortgage crisis (see page 76). On the other hand, his term spanned nearly two decades, so someone must have thought he was doing something right.

INTERESTED IN INTEREST RATES?

Interest rates are the fees banks charge you to borrow money. If you borrow $100 (to buy a nice gift for Dan, Jodi, and Andy, c/o Walker & Company, 175 Fifth Avenue, New York, NY 10010), at an 8 percent annual interest rate, and you pay back the loan in exactly one year, you owe $108.

Which isn't all that much when you think about the joy the gift will bring to our faces.

The Fed doesn't set interest rates, but it does regulate them. How? By being a lender and a borrower. The more the Fed loans banks, the more money banks have available to loan to borrowers. The more money the banks can loan, the lower the interest rates are. On the flip side, the more money the Fed borrows (for government projects, to pay off debts, to finance a deficit . . .), the less the banks have available to lend, and the higher the interest rates become.

So the Fed can manipulate the economy by manipulating interest rates. If it thinks the economy is growing too rapidly, or if it wants to encourage more people to save instead of spend, it can borrow more money and raise interest rates, thereby slowing growth by lowering the amount of loans given. And it can do the opposite if it wants to encourage spending or speed up economic growth. Whether the Fed is right about when to interfere, and the effects of its interference, is another story, and one that is often debated.

OOPS! THE SUBPRIME MORTGAGE CRISIS AND ECONOMIC COLLAPSE
Why'd It Happen? Who's to Blame? Why Did It Affect the Whole World?

It started with home loans. Thanks to a strong housing market in which everyone selling a home was making a lot of money, banks went for a bigger piece of the profit pie by making home loans to borrowers who had once been considered risky—like people with bad credit or low income. These were called subprime loans, because the borrowers were "sub-prime." These borrowers believed (or were led to believe) that they could later sell their homes for a profit, or refinance (renegotiate) their loans if their payments got too high (which depended on interest rates). But when interest rates rose, home sales slowed down while payments leaped up. Suddenly, buyers were left with homes they could no longer pay for.

When the buyers couldn't pay their mortgages, the banks took the homes back, which is called foreclosing. Banks (and the investment firms that backed their loans) were now losing money. They got cautious about lending—making it harder for people to get loans at all, even ones they could afford. In the meantime, many financial institutions were losing money from all the unpaid mortgages and had to declare bankruptcy.

Banks worldwide began to lose money from all those bad housing debts. (Additionally, the interconnectedness of the world economy means that a failure in any big economy—especially one as large as ours—has a domino effect). The U.S. government developed a $700 billion "bailout" plan to rescue many of the companies involved, afraid of what their collapse could do to the U.S. economy.

People like Old Man Potter (pictured below) rubbed their hands together excitedly, their mouths curling into bitter smiles at others' misfortune.

Who was to blame? The banks that made risky loans in the hopes of making more money? Home buyers who bought houses they couldn't afford in the first place? The U.S. government and the Fed, for not having better laws in place for this kind of stuff? Old Man Potter? Maybe all of the above.

Old Man Potter, the greedy tycoon of It's a Wonderful Life, *likes to see people lose their money because he is just plain mean.*

WHAT'S A RECESSION?
Does It Involve Red Rover?

Technically speaking, a recession is when the GDP starts to roll backward (get lower) for two or more quarters of the year, causing falling incomes and unemployment. Recessions involve lots of factors and aren't always easy to predict, but they are believed to result largely from attitudes. Not "attitudes" like the one your dog gives you when he has to go for a walk and it's raining. We're talking about people's feelings about the economy. Let's say there's a natural disaster, and people begin to feel worried about the economy and their future financial stability. They cut back on spending to be safe, and stores and factories respond to the lower sales by reducing employees or wages. Their employees (or ex-employees) then spend less, and . . . you see what we mean: a cycle has started.

If the government thinks a recession is a-brewing, it can choose to act by either increasing the money supply (à la the Fed) or increasing government spending—the rationale being that by spending on goods, the government is creating jobs. Some believe this helps lessen the length and strength of a recession. Others believe it contributes to the problem and that the market would be better off left to recover on its own. Many economists believe that recessions eventually correct themselves, that reductions in demand (spending) cause price levels to fall. Lower prices then encourage more spending, and things bounce back.

Hang in there; we'll get through this together.

WHY DO SOME PRESIDENTS GIVE US FREE MONEY?

After 9/11, Congress worried about fearful American attitudes leading to a slowing of spending that would lead to a recession. They passed a tax cut in 2001, including an immediate tax rebate check, to get people buying again. Whether it was really helpful or not is up for debate.

WHAT WAS THE GREAT DEPRESSION?
And Why'd It Happen?

A depression is like a recession on steroids. The experts disagree on what caused the Great Depression of the early 1930s, but many believe it was that people were spending less due to a lack of access to money (even the money they had), thanks to problems with the banking system and crashing stock prices. Many people blame the severity of the Great Depression on the Fed's failure to act; they say the Fed should have released more money into circulation and that its failure to do so deepened the crisis.

Jose Canseco and Mark McGuire; their oversized bats foreshadowed their oversized muscles—courtesy of steroids.

WHAT'S INFLATION AND WHY DOES IT HAPPEN?
Is There Such a Thing as Deflation?

The value of a dollar (or of any currency, for that matter) is never really fixed. Why? Because prices are constantly changing—in our country and relative to the other currencies of the world. Paper money may look permanent, but what it *means* to the people using it is not. (Remember: what money is worth is not a fixed value but a contract agreed to by society.)

Inflation is when the value of a currency drops. Suddenly, you need more dollars to buy the same old stuff.

Don't run for the hills. We're halfway done already.

WHY ARE THERE SO MANY MILLIONAIRES IN ZIMBABWE?

The highest rate of inflation in the world right now is in Zimbabwe, where the rate is estimated to be at 150,000 percent of the Zimbabwe dollar's real value. A loaf of bread, the last time we checked, cost 1.7 million Zimbabwe dollars. People carry their money around in sacks.

It's believed that inflation happens when a government decides to print too much money, usually in order to pay off debts. This means there is more paper money in circulation, while the resources that that money represents (the true value) have stayed the same, which makes each bill worth less.

"The Great Sag of 1873–96" was followed a century later by the scandalous denim droop of 1996.

Wages are often tied to inflation. For instance, a company might give its employees inflation-based raises, to keep their pay equal to rising prices. The U.S. dollar is currently considered to be a very stable currency, with low inflation.

Deflation is rare in the U.S., but it has happened in the past. "The Great Sag of 1873–96," for instance, was marked by a huge demand for cash that wasn't available. Prices fell, and it cost fewer dollars to buy stuff.

TRADESIES
International Trade

Trade agreements, currency (and how it works), and the trade organizations that rule the world's money—here's a look at how we play with others.

WHAT DOES IT MEAN WHEN PEOPLE SAY THE DOLLAR IS STRONG OR WEAK?

A strong dollar means that, compared to other currencies, the dollar has a high value. That means we are able to buy more foreign currency or goods more cheaply than another country may be able to buy goods or currency from us. The strength of our dollar is due to many things, including how much debt we have and how other countries perceive the stability of our economy.

Having a strong currency isn't always a good thing. It discourages other countries from buying our goods because the prices become too high. So, exports benefit from a weaker currency (which makes it cheaper for other countries to buy our stuff), and imports benefit from a stronger currency (because it's cheaper for us to buy other countries' stuff).

THE EURO

In 2002 many European nations adopted one currency—the euro. They did this for a few reasons: to make trade among themselves easier, to help with currency stability, and to give Europeans a warm fuzzy feeling about one another.

WHAT'S A TRADE DEFICIT?

When we are importing more than we're exporting, we have a trade deficit. It basically means we're spending more on trade than we're earning from it.

WHY DOES THE GUY FROM COLDPLAY WRITE "MTF" ON HIS HAND AND PIANO?

Well, first you have to know that "MTF" stands for Make Trade Fair, and second, you have to understand tariffs. A tariff is a tax on goods crossing the border of a country (pick a country, any country)—usually on goods coming *in*. The point of tariffs is to make the home country's products more appealing by making products from other countries more expensive. So if you're Dutch and you want to sell Heineken beer to the U.S., for instance, you often have to pay to play—in the form of a tariff, making a bottle of Heinie more expensive than a Bud Light.

Now, back to that guy from Coldplay. There are two kinds of trade that people are alluding to when they write "Make trade fair" on their hands: fair vs. free. "Free trade" supports lower tariffs everywhere, higher import quotas (upping the number of imports the U.S. is allowed to take in), and the reduction of other trade barriers. Supporters of free trade argue that fewer

tariffs = greater openness = greater competitiveness, which means everybody gets what they want easier and cheaper.

"Fair trade" is a movement, started in the 1960s, that demands that farmers and other laborers get a "fair" price for their goods and for their labor, rather than just a competitive one—or an outright exploitative one. Early supporters of fair trade included religious organizations and radical student and political groups, but these days it's more mainstream. Supporters of fair trade argue that *free* trade benefits only the wealthy, devastating farmers and others by forcing them to lower their prices in order to compete with bigger players in a tariff-free world market. Often, these prices are so low that they keep the producers in poverty. A certified fair trade label lets shoppers know they're paying "fair prices," i.e., enough for farmers and laborers to live on.

WHAT'S NAFTA AND DO WE HAFTA HAVE IT?

NAFTA stands for North American Free Trade Agreement and it's between Canada, Mexico, and the U.S. It was signed into law in 1992 with the purpose of eliminating the majority of tariffs on trade among the three countries. The upside is supposed to be increased trade, making everyone better off because they are able to buy and sell more, and more cheaply. Critics say that it only benefits the business owners doing the importing and exporting, leaving the working classes worse off.

For instance, it's argued that Mexican farmers can't keep up with our farmers—who are subsidized (financially cushioned) by our government—and therefore are plunged deeper into poverty.

What's afta NAFTA? Some people feel that NAFTA needs to be scrapped altogether, while others argue it needs to be revised to be more beneficial to the people it's failed so far and to take more responsibility for regulating the environmental and labor standards involved in all that trading.

ECONOMIC REVOLUTIONARIES

The Zapatistas of Mexico are a group of armed revolutionaries who oppose NAFTA and the type of global trade it represents. They claim that such trade agreements oppress the poor around the world.

IMF, WTO, WB. HUH?

In 1944, on the heels of World War II, forty-four nations (led by the U.S. and the UK) met at Bretton Woods, New Hampshire, to discuss how to create a system of international economic cooperation that would contribute to global stability. Thanks to their big roles in winning the war, the U.S. and the UK were the most popular kids in school and led the pack.

Here's what came out of the meetings: the International Monetary Fund (IMF), the International Bank for Reconstruction and Development (which later became the World Bank), and an organization—soon called GATT (General Agreement on Tariffs and Trade)—which eventually became the World Trade Organization (WTO).

Critics argue that Bretton Woods and the organizations it created were flawed from the start, as they came from a small number of "leader" states making decisions for the world system.

"All of these acronyms make my head hurt."

THE IMF VS. THE WWF

The IMF is an organization of 186 countries that gives short-term loans (raised from the money countries pay when they join the IMF) to member countries in financial trouble. These loans come with conditions, requiring the borrowing country to adopt a set of economic policies and financial measures based on what the IMF thinks will make the country more capable of paying back its loan. These policies often include things like reducing tariffs on imports, increasing interest rates, and cutting back on government programs and subsidies to save money.

Critics argue that IMF policies create rather than alleviate poverty. By forcing countries to cut tariffs and social programs, these policies, critics say, take money, jobs, and support away from the people who need it most—the countries' poor. These critics also argue that it's unethical for the IMF to impose its own economic theories on countries that might wish to run themselves differently.

Countries are encouraged to join the IMF because it promises increased investment and trade opportunities. But there's also a lot of controversy about whose interests the IMF serves, as the influence of its members is based on the size of their economies. Thus developed countries like the U.S.,

Bretton Woods

Japan, and the UK have the lion's share of "say" in decisions that affect everyone.

For these reasons, thousands of workers and students passionately protest the IMF every year.

According to an informal survey, the WWF (World Wildlife Fund) could easily kick the butt of the IMF, because its clients include the Siberian tiger and the brown bear.

The Siberian tiger could easily eat any human member of the IMF

THE WORLD BANK, OR "THE OTHER WB"

The World Bank makes loans (with money it makes on the bond market) to countries for improvements in agriculture, infrastructure, farming, health issues (such as AIDS), education, the environment, and gender fairness. Its stated mission is to help developing countries eliminate poverty and create sustainable economic growth.

World Bank

Critics say that the World Bank's true purpose is not to reduce poverty but to support U.S. business interests. Like the IMF, it supports policies based on economic theories favored in wealthy Western countries. And many argue that the World Bank's policies have actually increased poverty, contributed to environmental problems, and been detrimental to public health and cultural diversity. The president of the bank is always an American, nominated by our president (though subject to the approval of the other member countries), and decisions can be passed only with votes from countries whose shares total more than 85 percent of the bank's shares (i.e., the wealthiest countries).

World Bank—bloodsuckers or blood donators? One Boston-based protest group made their feelings clear.

STICKING IT TO EL HOMBRE: THE BANK OF THE SOUTH

The Bank of the South (Banco del Sur) is a monetary fund and lending organization first championed by Venezuelan president Hugo Chavez (more on Hugo Chavez on page 104). It makes loans to nations in South America for government programs and economic development—essentially telling the World Bank and the IMF *hasta luego*.

THE WORLD TRADE ORGANIZATION

The WTO regulates trade around the world. It's responsible for negotiating new trade agreements and policing member countries' adherence to the agreements. Since 97 percent of world trade is governed by the WTO, it is pretty much the only game in town. If you want to trade with other countries, you have to follow the WTO's rules.

Countries vote on the WTO's policies. Voting rights are weighed by a country's share of world trade. Seeing a pattern here? Right again—the wealthiest countries get the weightiest votes. Like the IMF and the World Bank, the WTO supports economic policies that open up trade as much as possible, a system that critics argue favors wealthier nations while disenfranchising poorer ones that have a hard time competing.

IMF:
www.imf.org
THE WB:
www.thewb.com
WORLD BANK:
www.worldbank.org
WORLD TRADE ORGANIZATION:
www.wto.org

We made it! We deserve a nice, long nap now.

DISCUSSION QUESTIONS
(OPTIONAL)

 How balanced is your own budget? Do you think it's important for the U.S. to have a balanced budget? Or are overspending and borrowing okay? Why or why not? Who do you borrow money from? Do you ever pay them back?

2 What would you buy if the dollar was, say, a hundred times stronger than the euro?

3 Do you think the IMF, World Bank, and WTO are slightly villainous? Or do you think that's just hype?

CHAPTER 4
DIPLO-MESSY
Foreign Affairs (But Not in the "People I've Kissed on Vacation" Sense)

INTRODUCTION

"Hey, America, This Is the World.
World, This Is America."

"你好"

"Relax. She's just saying 'hello.'"

Diplo-Messy is our way of helping you do that. Don't thank us. It's not a favor. You paid us. You did pay for this book, right?

The globalization of the U.S. economy, the development of China into an economic superpower, cross-border migration, international health scares like SARS and swine flu, and, of course, the ongoing war on terror, mean that what happens in Karachi can have as much effect on Americans as what happens in Kansas City. Not that much happens in Kansas City, anyway.[1]

THE WAR ON TERROR™

Whatever you think of ex-prez George W. Bush and his presidency, don't let it be said he didn't care about your feelings.

On September 20, 2001, with the ruins of the World Trade Center in New York still smoldering and Americans fearful and angry, President Bush stood in the well[2] of the Capitol and did something unprecedented.

He declared war on the American public's negative emotions.

"Freedom and fear are at war," he said. America was about to wage what Bush famously called a War on Terror.™

The closest the U.S. had ever come to waging war on an emotion was in 1933, when Franklin Delano Roosevelt famously told the American people,

Foreigners can be quite difficult to understand.

They typically live outside the United States and frequently communicate using exclusionary code words known as "foreign languages."

Despite their unwillingness to make it easy on us, we Americans have no choice but to pay attention to foreigners.

"The only thing we have to fear is fear itself . . . and spiders."

He stopped short, however, of actually ordering the U.S. Army to lob artillery at fear.

As The Decider, Bush displayed no such hesitation.

---

1. There are two large cities in the U.S. called Kansas City—one in Missouri and another just across the state line in Kansas. If you are a resident of Kansas City and are offended by our suggestion that not much happens in Kansas City, rest assured that we are referring to the other Kansas City.

2. "But I thought the Capitol had running water." It does. The "well of the Capitol" is a fancy name for that spot in the House of Representatives where presidents give speeches. Water is available there, but it's usually served in glasses, not buckets.

The U.S. military had a clear mandate: to target and destroy terror. The logistics of how this worked are still unclear. (We're guessing that if our armed forces spotted terror, they were ordered to shoot it. Perhaps guilt, shame, and loathing were simply to be detained and subjected to "coercive interrogation.") But based on the events that followed Bush's declaration, we think he may have dubbed America's response to 9/11 a War on Terror™ because the phrase was catchy and vague.

Think about it. If Bush had simply called his initiative a "war against the Al-Qaeda terrorists who attacked us on 9/11," he would have had a harder time rallying public support for other initiatives that didn't directly relate to 9/11: namely, the Iraq war.

Calling it a War on Terror™ was clever branding, but was it clever policy?

Let's look at some other wars against vague concepts to see how it stacks up.

In the 1960s, President Lyndon B. Johnson declared a War on Poverty. Important social programs such as Medicare[3] arose from the initiative, but last time we checked, there's still plenty of poverty around. Poverty–1, U.S.–0.

Johnson's successor, Richard Nixon, declared a War on Drugs. It's been going on for nearly four decades, has cost the United States approximately eight bajillion dollars, and has landed millions of Americans in the slammer.[4] (Not to mention the shooting war this has triggered south of the border in Mexico.) Plus, drugs are even more easily available to Americans now than they were when the war started. Drugs–1, U.S.–0.

Like the Taliban, marijuana is a tougher war opponent than we thought.

And, by the way, the U.S. isn't the only country to have declared war on inanimate objects. The Indian government recently dispatched its military to fight a War on Garbage.

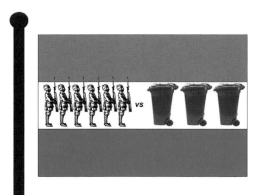

China has repeatedly declared War on Internet Smut. It seems clear that the War on Terror™ has one main thing in common with these other wars: it can't be won. It's reasonably safe to assume that terror will be around for as long as human beings are able to experience emotions.

WHAT IS TERRORISM AND WHY DO WE THINK OF BEARDS 'N' FUNNY HATS WHEN WE HEAR THE WORD?

As you might have guessed, it's not actually terror we need to fight—it's anti-American terrorists.

Thanks to 9/11, when Americans think of terrorists, they think of bin Laden and his cronies: fanatical militant Muslims who attack civilian and government targets.

But terrorism is by no means exclusive to fanatical Islam. Terrorism is violence against civilians committed by people who aren't uniformed members of a country's military. It has been, and continues to be, committed by Christians, Jews, Hindus, Muslims, atheists, criminals, guerrilla armies, soldiers, spies, religious extremists, radical environmentalists, antigovernment rebels, and jerks.

---

3. Medicare, in a nutshell, is the closest the U.S. comes to nationalized health care. As part of the Social Security Act, it guarantees citizens sixty-five and older health insurance. No, this doesn't have anything to do with terrorism, but we thought you might be curious.
4. "Slammer" is a popular slang term meaning "pokey," "hoosegow," or "mandatory municipal motel."

Prior to 9/11, in fact, the deadliest terrorist attack on U.S. soil was the 1995 bombing of the Alfred P. Murrah Federal Building in Oklahoma City. It was carried out by two U.S. Army veterans, Timothy McVeigh and Terry Nichols, who believed the U.S. government had become tyrannical. They decided to attack a government building, killing 168 innocent people.

"WHITE POWER!"
THE UGLY RALLYING CRY OF AMERICA'S UGLY HOMEGROWN TERRORISTS
(That's Why a Lot of Them Wear Masks, Right? Because They're Ugly)

Not to scare you or anything, but—as the Oklahoma City bombing showed—there's a pretty big terrorist threat in our own backyard. The Ku Klux Klan was founded in 1866 by six Confederate veterans who terrorized newly freed slaves by playing dangerous and even deadly pranks on them. Throughout the next hundred-plus years, both its level of violence and membership spiked. The pranking quickly evolved into lynchings—lynchings that went largely unprosecuted. At its peak in the mid-1920s, the Ku Klux Klan boasted over four million members, roughly 15 percent of the entire voting population, including future Supreme Court justice Hugo Black.[5] Its power greatly diminished, however, when several of its leaders were discovered to be corrupt, alcoholic sex-offenders. Still, with America's first African American president in office, hate groups like the Klan have "kicked it up a notch." And they are dangerous. But it's also important to remember that they are not very powerful and, in most instances, not terribly attractive, either.

For more information about America's homegrown terrorists and how you can help stop them, visit the Southern Poverty Law Center, a nonprofit organization dedicated to educating Americans about hate crimes: www.splcenter.org.

5. At the same time that there was a former Klansman Supreme Court justice named Black, there was a non-Klansman justice named Byron White. Wonder if they ever giggled together about that? And, adding one more color to the palette, both Black and White voted in favor of public-school desegregation in the 1954 landmark _Brown v. Board of Education_ decision.

Former Supreme Court Justice Byron White. Despite having the words "white" and "supreme" on his business card, he supported civil rights.

THE PEAS-IN-A-POD HATE CHART

....

AL-QAEDA VERSUS THE KU KLUX KLAN—MORE IN COMMON THAN EITHER GROUP WOULD PROBABLY LIKE TO ADMIT

	AL-QAEDA	KU KLUX KLAN
Big fan of the Internet	✓	✓
Distributes cheap literature and writes nasty blogs filled with typos and grammatical errors	✓	✓
Boasts lots of splinter groups or "franchises" that adopt the famous Al-Qaeda or Ku Klux Klan name	✓	✓
Has its own brand of unlistenable heavy metal music		✓
Encourages "lone wolf" attacks—homespun DIY terrorist operations inspired by fanatical ideology but with no ties to a bigger, formal organization	✓	✓
Members often dress in white robes	✓	✓
Constantly begging for money	✓	✓
No kegs allowed at meetings	✓	
Largely inspired by the long-winded writings of lonely, hate-filled goofballs	✓	✓
Prefers photos of its members in outdoorsy situations, with faces concealed and machine guns brandished	✓	✓

And the only deadly foreign terrorist attack on our nation's capital? It was not the 9/11 attack on the Pentagon. The Pentagon is actually located in Virginia. It was the 1976 car bombing of Chilean dissident Orlando Letelier in Washington DC by agents of Chile's military dictatorship.

Clearly, no religion, ethnicity, or political persuasion has a monopoly on terrorism. Terrorism is an example of something military types call "asymmetrical warfare."

Al-Qaeda, like the Ku Klux Klan, wants to wage war against the United States government. Because we have the most advanced military in the world, they can't defeat us on a regular battlefield. Instead, they attack us in indirect ways, trying to hit us where we're most vulnerable.

SALMAN RUSHDIE, THE TARGET OF HISTORY'S ARGUABLY MOST FAMOUS FATWA

Like other fundamentalist Islamic groups, Al-Qaeda also issues "fatwas," calls for murder and destruction in the guise of religious edicts. On February 14, 1989, Iranian Supreme Leader Ayatollah Khomeini issued a fatwa condemning British writer Salman Rushdie to death for blasphemy against Islam in his novel *The Satanic Verses*.

For most of the 1990s, Rushdie lived in fear and refused to appear in public. In 1998, the Iranian government formally distanced itself from the Ayatollah's decree, though the fatwa was never lifted. In 2005, Khomeini's successor, Ayatollah Ali Khamenei, reaffirmed the "sacred duty" of fundamentalists to rub Rushdie out. Rushdie had long since become bored with being afraid, however, as evidenced in his cameo in the 2001 hit romantic comedy *Bridget Jones's Diary*.

Living in a free society makes us especially vulnerable to this type of warfare. We can all largely come and go as we please, and a terrorist often takes advantage of that, by dressing like a student and exploding a suicide bomb on a train or, as happened on 9/11, by dressing business casual and hijacking a jet.

To sum up: terrorists resort to terrorism not only because they're ruthless and desperate, but also because they lack alternative means for violence. We're guessing that if Al-Qaeda—or for that matter, the Ku Klux Klan—had regiments, tanks, and aircraft carriers, they'd use them.

MOMMY, WHERE DOES TERROR COME FROM?

Like a lot of things Americans seem to dislike, terrorism is French.

Or more precisely, the word is French. The government violence that followed the French Revolution in 1789 was known as *la terreur*.

How terrifying was *la terreur*?

You've no doubt heard the metaphor "heads are gonna roll."

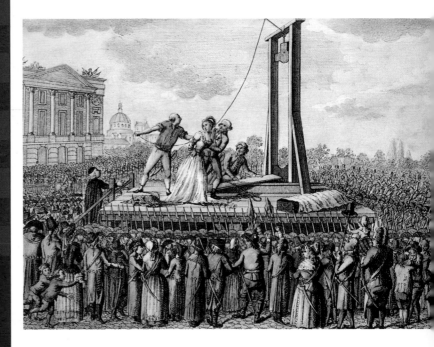

French queen Marie Antoinette's meeting with the guillotine: "Don't worry, Your Majesty. Your severed head gets its own special, royal basket."

Well, heads rolling was not a metaphor during *la terreur*. Some historians estimate forty thousand Frenchies were separated from their heads during the year and a half that followed the French Revolution. *Mon Dieu!*

TERRORIST GROUPS WE LOVE TO HATE

Funny: while government-sponsored terrorism is often the deadliest kind (for example, the genocide against civilians in Darfur, the so-called "Dirty War" against leftists in Argentina in the 1970s, and the Nazi Holocaust), Americans don't typically associate terrorism with men in uniform.[6]

Instead, when we consider terrorism, we often envision pesky "non-state actors"—angry radicals with beards, bomb belts, and balaclavas.

America's official list of terrorist organizations resides in the Office of the Coordinator for Counterterrorism in the U.S. Department of State headquarters in Washington DC.

The list is in the fourth drawer of the file cabinet by the water cooler, filed between "Terriers (Boston and Jack Russell)" and "Tex-Mex, Menus from Restaurants That Deliver to the Department of State." (Kidding!)

It's a hefty document and is divided into two lists: terrorist groups that concern us a lot, and terrorist groups that concern us slightly less.

The main list has names you've probably heard on the news: Al-Qaeda, Hamas, Hezbollah, etc. These are the ones whose worrisome activities presumably changed the colors on our nation's nifty color-coded terror-alert system.

The second list boasts one genuinely famous name (Irish Republican Army) and several names that sound too made-up to be scary. Are you afraid of the Revolutionary Proletarian Initiative Nuclei?[7] We neither.

The big kahuna of terrorist groups these days is, of course, Al-Qaeda. Al-Qaeda's modus operandi or MO (yes, that's Latin, meaning "how they do") is different from that of your typical terrorist groups. Most terrorists have a country-specific beef.

For almost ten years, a handy government color-coded chart let Americans know how scared they should be.

Por ejemplo: FARC, the Colombian rebel and terrorist group, is at war with the Colombian government. They tend to limit their mischief making to Colombia itself. Hezbollah largely confines itself to the southern half of Lebanon.

Al-Qaeda has no national agenda because they have no nation. Them suckas is global. The organization's members, let's call them "Al-Qaedudes," want to rid all Muslim countries of Western influence. They want the U.S. and Israel gone from the Middle East. They want to oust U.S.-allied leaders of Muslim countries like Saudi Arabia and turn back the clock to what they consider the good old days of Islam: a period between the seventh and tenth centuries, when Muslim lands from the Atlantic to the Indian oceans were ruled by one Muslim leader and Islamic law was the policy of the land.

---

6. Upon rereading, maybe "funny" wasn't the best first word for that sentence.
7. Founded in Rome in 2000, this radical leftist group opposes most of the Italian government's policies but has yet to actually kill anybody over them.

Basically, Al-Qaeda wants to party like it's 999.

Al-Qaeda, which means "the base" in Arabic, was founded around 1988 in Pakistan by Osama bin Laden and a few close pals—mostly as a means to provide safe havens or "bases" for Muslim Arabs who had traveled from the Middle East to Afghanistan in the 1980s to fight the Soviet Union's occupation of the country, and who viewed themselves as "holy warriors" (in Arabic, *mujahideen*).

WHY IS OSAMA BIN LADEN THE SMUG, SMILING FACE OF TERRORISM, ANYWAY?

Short answer: it's all about the Benjamins. Osama bin Laden's family is filthy rich. To give you an idea of *how* rich, Osama's father, Sheikh Mohammed bin Laden, had twenty-two wives and fifty-two children, including Osama—and all of those still living are multimillionaires. Osama's inheritance enabled him to fund and arm Al-Qaeda. Without bin Laden's millions, Al-Qaeda would be dirt-poor.

Incidentally, forty-first prez George H. W. Bush spent many of his years in the private sector in business with members of the Saudi Binladin Group (see the Bush Dynasty, pages 59–62). But don't worry: Osama bin Laden is not part of this "family business." How embarrassing would *that* be for the Bush family?

The United States had no beef (halal or otherwise) with early Al-Qaeda. In the 1980s, their enemy was *our* enemy: the Communist Soviet Union. The U.S. funneled billions in cash and weapons to arm the *mujahideen* and other anti-Soviet rebels in Afghanistan. We didn't care if these rebels were tall, sexy, homely, overweight . . . or, yes, Islamic militants who might eventually turn their weapons on innocent U.S. civilians. All we cared about was sticking it to the Commies. And we did. And Al-Qaeda was happy.

Al-Qaeda didn't start focusing its bad juju on the U.S. until after the first Gulf War (1991). Granted, they were already a little pissed off at the U.S. See, once the Commies were defeated, the U.S. stopped supplying the *mujahideen* with money and arms. We didn't really thank them or gently punch them in the arm and say, "Way to go, team!" The U.S. just wanted to forget all about its nasty little proxy war against the Soviet Union in Afghanistan.

With the Iraqi invasion of Kuwait in August 1990, the U.S. had much bigger concerns in the region. To keep Saddam Hussein's grubby hands off our—we mean, off *Kuwaiti* and *Saudi*—oil, the U.S. moved a huge military force into the Saudi desert. This force stayed even after Saddam Hussein was defeated and Iraqi troops withdrew from Kuwait.

Al-Qaedudes were displeased. Saudi Arabia is home to Islam's two holiest sites, Mecca and Medina. Islam's founder, the prophet Mohammad, was born in Mecca and died in Medina (see page 160). Islamic fundamentalists believe American troops are infidels, as welcome in Islam's holy land as a Pussycat Dolls video is on the pope's iPod. They weren't too happy about Saddam Hussein's army being so close to Saudi Arabia, either.

In the buildup to the March 2003 invasion of Iraq, the Bush Administration repeatedly cited Saddam Hussein's "links" to Al-Qaeda as evidence of the imminent terrorist threat Iraq posed to the U.S. But in fact, no such links *existed*.

On the contrary, Al-Qaeda hated Saddam Hussein as much as we did.[8] In the fall of 1990, with Kuwait occupied by the Iraqi army, bin Laden himself even went before the Saudi royal family and volunteered to kick Saddam Hussein out of Kuwait with his battle-hardened *mujahideen*—provided that Saudi Arabia kicked the U.S. off its soil. But the Saudis believed that the U.S. military would do a better job of protecting Saudi Arabia from

The extent of Saddam Hussein's links to Osama bin Laden

Saddam Hussein than a ragtag army of scruffy fundamentalists, so they refused bin Laden's offer.

In outrage and protest of the continued infidel presence on holy land, Al-Qaeda started attacking U.S. troops overseas when opportunities presented themselves: first in Yemen in 1992, then in Somalia in 1993.

But even newshoundy Americans had very little clue about Al-Qaeda until August 7, 1998, when two nearly simultaneous Al-Qaeda attacks on the U.S. embassies in Kenya and Tanzania killed or wounded more than five thousand people.

Suddenly, Osama bin Laden had secured the number-two spot on America's foreign bogeyman list, after Saddam Hussein.

The U.S. retaliated against the embassy hits with missile strikes in Afghanistan and Sudan. The Afghanistan strike hit some Al-Qaeda training camps. The Sudan strike actually hit a pharmaceutical factory the U.S. seems to have mistaken for a weapons factory. Aspirin, anthrax—they both start with *a*. Easy mistake, we suppose.

SAYYID QUTB, THE GUY MOST RESPONSIBLE FOR FILLING OSAMA BIN LADEN'S HEAD WITH ALL SORTS OF COCKAMAMIE IDEAS

Sayyid Qutb (1906–1966) was a self-proclaimed intellectual, a geek, and founder of the Egyptian Muslim Brotherhood—as well as the author of *Milestone*, a book demanding modern-day Muslim societies be governed by the laws of Islam instead of by secular laws. Qutb's ~~ramblings~~ writings inspired Osama bin Laden and his right-hand man, Ayman Al-Zawahiri, to become terrorists. Many "credit" Qutb with being the "father" of the fundamentalist Islamic terrorist movement. Make that "blame."

---

8. It's true. On principle, Al-Qaeda despises all secular Islamic dictators—largely because they want to downplay the role of fundamentalist Islam in their governments.

After 9/11, of course, the fight against Al-Qaeda was stepped up considerably. In 2001 and 2002, the U.S. destroyed Al-Qaeda's safe haven in Afghanistan. But it's not clear that pounding on Al-Qaeda has weakened it. In fact, there's strong evidence to the contrary.

In 2009, according to the Department of State's annual Country Reports on Terrorism, 14,971 people were killed in terrorist attacks around the world. That's up from 3,547 people in 2001. Using our nuclear fusion–powered (aka solar) calculator, we determined that's a fourfold increase in terrorism deaths since the 9/11 attacks, and since the War on Terror™ was declared.

Terrorism is also a boom industry in Afghanistan. The first country to experience the joys of the American War on Terror™ has seen terrorist attacks and fatalities rise every year since the United States began shifting its attention to Iraq in 2002. In 2008, 4,673 people were killed, injured, or kidnapped by terrorists in Afghanistan—up from 1,540 in 2005.

Another boom industry in Afghanistan is drugs. After the fall of the Taliban in 2002, opium production skyrocketed. Say what you will about the Taliban, they *were* good at scaring Afghanistan's warlords and drug kingpins into keeping their opium production on the DL. With the Taliban out of the picture? *Fuggedaboutit.* Anyone with a poppy seed and a dream could make a fortune there. As of 2009, 90 percent of the world's heroin comes from Afghanistan, and the heroin is cheaper and purer than it has been in a generation. And while Al-Qaeda and Taliban sympathizers publicly deplore drug use, they aren't averse to profiting from it. In fact, the Taliban arms its ongoing war against the U.S. with drug money. It's the old "desperate times call for desperate measures" rationale.

Afghans are known for their distrust of outsiders and lustrous coats.

Opium poppies—don't worry, they use a different kind for poppy-seed buns.

COME, MR. TALIBAN, TALLY ME BANANA

The Taliban is the Muslim fundamentalist group that ruled Afghanistan from 1996 until 2001. Infamous for banning girls' education, suppressing all forms of popular culture, and forcing Afghan men to grow beards, they earned our ire by hosting Osama bin Laden's Al-Qaeda while it planned and executed the 9/11 terror attacks. The U.S. overthrew the Taliban in 2001 but never really killed the movement or its top leaders. The primary U.S. military mission in Afghanistan today: to weaken the Taliban movement enough to hand off the anti-Taliban fight to Afghanistan's central government. The Obama Administration believes pulling out of Afghanistan with the Taliban as strong as it is now would inevitably result in the Taliban taking over the whole country again.

One of only two known photos of Taliban leader Mullah Omar. Handsome, eh?

So, the U.S. invasion of Afghanistan didn't so much damage Al-Qaeda as cause it to evolve. Now its members aren't simply committing senseless acts of violence and preaching a fundamentalist world takeover; the more hypocritical among them are selling drugs to fund their operations. What a world!

Another example of Al-Qaeda's evolution: with the Taliban no longer able to play host to them in Afghanistan, many Al-Qaeda leaders simply moved, walking across the border to the loosely governed tribal areas of Pakistan.

Since 2002, the menace of Al-Qaeda in Pakistan has grown considerably. This is particularly terrifying (note that "terrifying" and "terror" come from the same root), as Pakistan is one of the few countries in the world with a functioning nuclear arsenal. It's no secret that many members of the ISI, the Pakistani intelligence service, are Al-Qaeda and Taliban sympathizers. Pakistan's government, historically as stable as sand castles, doesn't do much to instill confidence in our own intelligence community. A January 2009 article in *The New York Times Magazine* suggested Pakistan's nukes pose the greatest terrorist threat to the United States ever, period. Terrified yet? We'll stop typing here, as our fingers are shaking too much.

Now, what else can we do to scare you?

Well, after the U.S. invasion of Iraq and the chaos that ensued, an Al-Qaeda branch sprang up there as well.

Only, it wasn't really the same Al-Qaeda. It was a separate movement mimicking the tactics and rhetoric of the original Al-Qaeda. And it wasn't a single group anymore.[9] Al-Qaeda became a brand, like a fast-food franchise—different owners, same lousy taste. Except fast food probably kills more people.

Al-Qaeda and Al-Qaeda-like attacks also started happening around Europe. On March 11, 2004, coordinated backpack bombings in Madrid's rail system killed 191 people in an attack that came to be known as "3/11." On July 7, 2005, suicide bombers detonated three explosions within fifty seconds of each other in London's transit system, killing fifty-six people, including four of the attackers.

You da bomb in Al-Qaeda Jeans.

Again, these attacks weren't carried out by people with written orders from bin Laden. Rather, they were carried out by "lone wolves" who adopted an Al-Qaeda-ish, anti-Western ethos (see the Hate Chart, page 89).

One of the saddest ironies in all of this? Al-Qaeda in Iraq wouldn't have existed were it not for the U.S. invasion. Some would say that the War on Terror™ has been responsible for giving birth to the very terrorist groups it seeks to destroy.

The Lone Wolf terrorist in action

9. Abu Mus'ab Al-Zarqawi, the deceased Al-Qaeda leader in Iraq, did pledge an oath of allegiance to Osama bin Laden in October 2004, but this was largely symbolic—like a promise ring.

TERRORIST GROUP/BOY BAND	MOST FAMOUS MEMBER	RELIGION	GOAL	HAM?	BEARDS?	FUN FACTS
AL-QAEDA	Osama bin Laden	Sunni Islam	Turn the world into a single Muslim fundamentalist state	No	Yes	In 2007, bin Laden released a video telling Americans their taxes would be lower if they succumbed to Muslim rule
FARC	Víctor Julio Suárez Rojas (Nickname: Mono Jojoy)	They're Marxist-Leninists, so officially none	Topple Colombia's U.S.-allied government and replace it with Communism	Of course; it's a staple of the Latin-American diet	Mustaches, actually	FARC arms its savage war by making and selling cocaine; cocaine users in the U.S. are bankrolling a bloody war
HAMAS	Sheikh Ahmed Yassin (deceased)	Sunni Islam	Conquer Israel, unite it into a big Palestinian state	In their name, yes; in their bellies, no	Yes	Won control of Palestinian parliament in 2006 after the U.S. forced Palestinian elections
HEZBOLLAH	Hassan Nasrallah	Shia Islam	Fight Israel, protect Lebanese Shiites from rival Lebanese factions, provide health care for poor	No	Yes	Unequivocally condemned 9/11 attack of Twin Towers as massacre of innocents
LASHKAR-E-TAIBA	Dawood Ibrahim	Sunni Islam	Take mostly Muslim Kashmir state from India and join it to Pakistan	No	Yes, except when they're trying to infiltrate Indian targets disguised as Hindus	Ibrahim is a former Bollywood movie producer, drug dealer, and pimp; not sure how he squares any of that with his vehement religious views
*NSYNC	Justin Timberlake	Christian	Sell music, concert tickets, and an assortment of plastic crap with their pictures on it	Yes, and Lance Bass started a production company called Bacon & Eggs	Joey Fatone had one	The name of then-heaviest member of *NSYNC is Joey Fat One! (Okay, Fatone)

OTHER ALS OF NOTE

AL PACINO: Oscar-winning Italian American actor, star of two of the best movies ever made (*The Godfather, The Godfather: Part II*) and one of the worst (*Gigli*). His rendition of gangster Tony Montana in 1983's *Scarface* is referenced in two other chapters of this book.

AL CAPONE: A notorious Chicago gangster who amassed a small fortune selling booze while booze was illegal in the U.S. Eventually went to jail, not for booze or murder but for tax evasion. Prior to Al-Qaeda, Capone was America's least-loved Al.

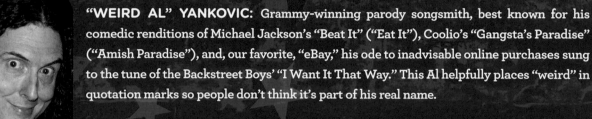

"WEIRD AL" YANKOVIC: Grammy-winning parody songsmith, best known for his comedic renditions of Michael Jackson's "Beat It" ("Eat It"), Coolio's "Gangsta's Paradise" ("Amish Paradise"), and, our favorite, "eBay," his ode to inadvisable online purchases sung to the tune of the Backstreet Boys' "I Want It That Way." This Al helpfully places "weird" in quotation marks so people don't think it's part of his real name.

DOES AL-QAEDA HATE US BECAUSE OF OUR FREEDOM?

In the months and years following 9/11, many politicians and conservative commentators suggested Al-Qaeda was at war with us because they disdain American freedoms such as unfettered political speech and gender equality.

If you think about it, the notion is absurd.

Don't give Al-Qaeda a lot of credit—they are seriously backward people who oppose all of our basic values. But that's not why they attack us.

If Al-Qaeda chose their targets with the goal of destroying personal freedom, they'd attack Sweden, Norway, or Canada. They'd sure be easier targets than the U.S. What's Sweden gonna do if it's attacked? Drop used Volvos on bin Laden?

They attack us because we're a political and military giant. We have soldiers stationed throughout the Middle East and Asia. We support Israel. We prop up dictators throughout the Muslim world. Practically and symbolically, we do a lot of stuff they oppose.

Yes, they hate our freedom. But they attack us because our foreign policy interests clash with theirs.

~~NOOKYULAR~~ NUCLEAR PROLIFERATION
This Section of the Book Is da Bomb

With the pile of dough we expect to make in royalties from this book (sorry to sound like show-offs, but we're talking potentially *hundreds* of dollars), we three have decided to buy a nuclear weapon.[10]

We're not trying to start any trouble. Honest, we're not.

You see, we've noticed that when you have a nuke, people treat you differently—with more respect and deference.

People once eager to tussle with you suddenly want to talk out their problems with you. Having a nuke is a bit like having a giant, mean dog in your front yard. Minus the giant poop.

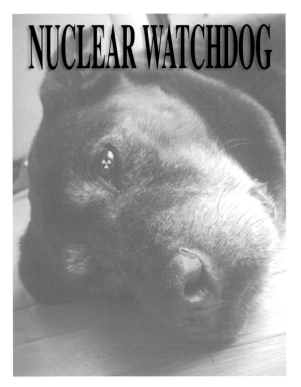

Who's a good little nuclear watchdog?

If you think we exaggerate the magical, attitude-adjusting power of a nuclear weapon, consider the U.S.'s relationship with Pakistan.

Frenemies!

From 1999 until 2007, Pakistan was a military dictatorship. It supported the wicked Taliban regime in neighboring Afghanistan by creating a sanctuary for the Al-Qaeda terrorists who plotted 9/11. Pakistan even hosted Al-Qaeda on its own soil and, as of this writing, is probably home to Osama bin Laden.

But wait, there's more.

Pakistan launched terror attacks against neighboring democratic India. It even sold weapons of mass destruction to some of America's biggest enemies.

By several measures, Pakistan has been a force of violence and extremism in ways that threaten U.S. security far worse than Iraq ever did.

But while the U.S. was diving headfirst into Iraq, Pakistan's dictator, General Pervez Musharraf, was being hailed by the White House as a friend and vital ally in the so-called War on Terror.™

---

10. Andisheh just put up a new shelf in his garage and thinks he has just the spot for it.

Why? The answer is simple.

Nukes.

Pakistan had 'em. Iraq didn't. You can't jerk around a country with nukes. And you sure can't invade them like we did Iraq.

The formula's pretty clear. When you don't have a nuke, but you're accused of trying to get one, you're World Public Enemy #1. Once you have one, however, world leaders treat you like you're all of a sudden way sexy and they're on a third date with you. You can say all kinds of stupid stuff, but the world is gonna think it was interesting, smart, and funny and say it would love to continue this conversation over dessert.

WHAT ARE NUKES AND WHERE DID THEY ALL COME FROM?

You'll have to wait until next year for our science textbook, *Dork Now, Rich Later*, for the technical explanation, but here's the short answer for the what and how of nukes.

Even the teeny-tiniest nuclear weapon is more powerful and destructive than the most powerful conventional weapon. An American missile with a regular explosive can find and

Contrary to myth, nuclear weapons do not come from the stork.

destroy a large building. By harnessing the same energy source that the sun has been using for the past 4.57 billion years[11]— nuclear fusion—the same missile with a nuclear explosive will destroy a city and the millions of people who live there.

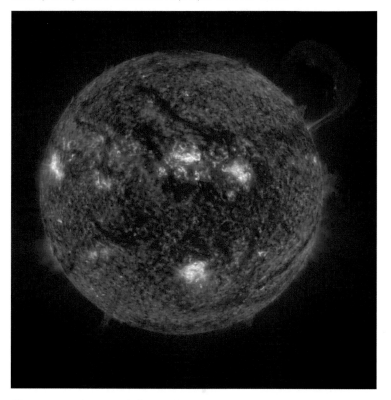

The sun, our solar system's first nuclear weapon

WHO HAS NUKES?

Membership in the nuclear club is exclusive. The U.S. and Russia are the oldest and biggest nuclear powers. Each has more nukes than the rest of the world combined.

The UK tested its first nuke off the coast of Australia in 1952. France exploded its *le Nuke* in the Sahara desert in 1960. China exploded its first nuke in 1964. It was made from a copy of a Russian bomb design. Both nations were Communist at the time and, like good Commies, they shared.

---

11. The sun is a mass of incandescent gas. It doesn't look a day older than 4.5 billion years, if you ask us.

India exploded its first nuke in 1974. We kid you not: India's government dubbed its bomb "Smiling Buddha" and insisted its testing was a "peaceful" explosion. To keep the peace, Pakistan exploded *its* first nuke in 1998.

Although North Korea has tested nuclear bombs, it is not yet thought to have the ability to fire a nuclear weapon at anyone. Israel is thought to have nukes, but that's never been proven.

With the exception of the occasional James Bond villain, no individual has now or has ever had a nuke.

"India named a nuclear weapon after me? Okay, that's funny."

NUCLEAR NON-PROLIFERATION TREATY (NPT)

~~Nashville Public Television is a community-funded broadcaster founded in 1962 to bring quality, non-commercial television programming to north-central Tennessee.~~

The Nuclear Non-Proliferation Treaty (formally known as the Treaty on the Non-Proliferation of Nuclear Weapons) is an international agreement designed to halt the spread of nuclear weapons.

Ratified in 1970, the agreement allows the five nations who already had nukes (the U.S., what was then the USSR, the UK, France, and China) to keep them. The other nations that signed had to promise never to develop nukes.

In exchange, the already nuclear states promised to never use nukes on them. Furthermore, the treaty allows nations to develop peaceful nuclear-power programs. Because the technology used to make fuel for nuclear-power plants is so similar to the technology used to make fuel for nuclear weapons, the signatory nations are obligated to allow the International Atomic Energy Agency (the IAEA, an arm of the United Nations) access to their nuclear facilities.

India, Pakistan, and Israel never signed the NPT and therefore aren't violating it by having nukes. North Korea did sign the treaty, but it withdrew as a result of its escalating quarrel with the Bush Administration earlier this decade. Shortly after North Korea canceled its NPT subscription, it tested a nuke.

Even though compliance is voluntary, the NPT has been a successful treaty. In nearly forty years, countries have cheated here and there, but only one signatory (North Korea) actually dropped out and built a nuke.

The NPT's three biggest challenges at the moment involve the U.S. and three countries whose names start with the letter *I*.[12]

In 2006, the U.S. reached a landmark trade deal with India. We agreed to sell them nuclear-power-plant technology to help provide energy for their growing population and economy.

You might be thinking, what's the big deal? The U.S. and India are grown-ups. They should be able to decide whether they want to send each other nuclear love notes.

"This baby will power millions of customer-service calls!"

---

12. *Ay-yay-yay.*

Perhaps. But the U.S. signed the NPT. Selling nuclear technology to India—despite its near four-decade refusal to sign the NPT, and despite its already building and testing nuclear weapons—is like the U.S. flipping the bird at all the nations that signed the NPT all those years ago and continue to follow it. It's another example of the phenomenon we mentioned at the beginning of this section—when you get a nuke, people bend over backward to be nice to you.

Among the nations that are annoyed about the U.S. agreement with India is Iran. As this is being written, the U.S. and Europe are getting their briefs and boxers in a wad over Iran's nuclear program.

You don't trust me with nuclear technology? That hurts.

Iranian president Mahmoud Ahmadinejad

Iran's nuclear program is for nuclear power—so says the IAEA and the U.S. intelligence establishment. Iran has apparently violated provisions of the NPT by not revealing every detail about its nuclear program, but by and large it is in compliance.

The U.S. and Europe say that Iran should not be allowed to develop its own nuclear fuel to power its fledgling nuclear-power program. Iran cannot be trusted, they say, because nuclear-power-plant fuel and nuclear-weapon fuel are made by the same process. If you can make nuclear-power-plant fuel, you can make nuclear-weapon fuel.

Iran points out, correctly, that it has signed the NPT, which gives Iran the right, by international treaty, to develop its own nuclear-fuel program. Iran insists it wants nuclear power for electricity only, but loudly notes that the U.S. has no business lecturing anyone about the NPT when the U.S. is selling nuclear technology to India and giving gazillions in military aid to the Middle East's only likely nuclear-weapons power, Israel.

The U.S.-India deal, plus the Iran-U.S.-Europe-Israel nuclear standoff, points to the need for a revised, twenty-first-century NPT that, at the very least, acknowledges that the world's balance of power has shifted away from North America and Europe.

THE COLLAPSE OF THE SOVIET UNION AND NUCLEAR PROLIFERATION

The end of the Soviet Union was a mostly, but not entirely, good thing.

Yes, democracy has flourished in eastern and central Europe, but the threat of nuclear annihilation, the Cold War's ever-looming doomsday, hasn't actually gone away. In fact, the likelihood of a Soviet nuke being used to attack the U.S. or Europe may actually be higher now than it was when there was an actual Soviet Union.[13]

It turns out the Soviet Union's nuclear arsenal was quite a bit sturdier than the Soviet Union itself. The collapse of the USSR left thirty-five thousand working nuclear warheads and enough radioactive material for forty thousand more warheads scattered across a country that once took up one-sixth of the earth's land.

---

13. The world could end at any minute and here you are, wasting your life reading this book. Go out. Hug a kitten. Climb a mountain. Take the kitten to the mountain with you. Be sure to take some tuna and water to share.

BELOYARSK
NUCLEAR REACTOR
Yard Sale
~~KEEP OUT~~

worst things that could ever happen in the world, ever,[14] neither party has made securing loose nukes a policy priority.

However, the new START (Strategic Arms Reduction Treaty), ratified at the end of 2010, shows that most members of the two parties are at least willing to work with Russia to reduce the number of nukes we have to, say, a number that will destroy every major city only once. For want of a better word, it's a start.

Instead of being protected by a military superpower, many of these weapons now sit in rickety warehouses guarded by lonely, underpaid guards and scientists. Old Navy has better inventory control on its $15 cargo shorts than many of these Russian facilities have on their nukes.

According to a 2007 story in *The New York Times*, eighteen attempts to smuggle nuclear weapons and materials—many from the former Soviet Union—have been thwarted since 1998. That number hints at an even more disturbing number: how many attempts were *not* thwarted?

Many terrorist groups, including Al-Qaeda, want nuclear weapons. Despite the recognition by both Republicans and Democrats that a terrorist with a nuke is high on the list of the

Try to hide these.

SAM NUNN HAS A FUNN HOBBY

The world's top loose-nuke-gatherer-upper is actually a private citizen—the former U.S. senator from Georgia Sam Nunn. His Nuclear Threat Initiative (NTI) uses donations from rich people like Warren Buffett and Ted Turner to secure as much loose nuclear material around the world as it can. We're not sure what Nunn does with the nukes, although we've been warned repeatedly to stay out of his garden shed.

We're kidding, of course; he doesn't have nukes. Securing nukes means beefing up the security around nuclear facilities. Sometimes it's as simple as fences and locked doors. In Russia, where NTI has done a lot of work, securing nukes often means moving nuclear materials from shabby, remote facilities to well-maintained, better-guarded facilities.

14. The official list of Worst Things That Could Ever Happen, Ever, places "nuclear terrorist attack" at number eight on its list, sandwiched between "space-alien attack on Earth" and "another _Matrix_ sequel."

ROGUE STATES AND BOGEYMEN

If this book accomplishes one thing, we'd like for it to be that we get so rich we can warm ourselves each winter by burning piles of $100 bills.

If this book accomplishes two things, we'd like one to be the money-fire thing and the other to be that readers can watch the news or listen to government officials without getting swept away by misleading spin or petty nonsense.

One of our least favorite forms of public misinformation is foreign-policy demagogy. Demagogy is the practice of misleading people by appealing to their fears, biases, and prejudices.

"Illegal immigration threatens U.S. national security," is an example of classic demagogy. Illegal immigration has a long list of actual ill effects, none of which include terrorists disguised as Mexican roofers swimming to America to blow up the Golden Gate Bridge.

Winston Churchill, FDR, and Stalin made strange bedfellows. Relax, that's a figure of speech.

Representative Tom Tancredo (R-CO) has built a career on playing up the threat posed by illegal immigration and antagonizing legal immigrants by complaining about Spanish-language books in Denver's libraries. Incidentally, all four of Tancredo's grandparents were born in Italy.

One of the most popular forms of foreign-policy demagogy is something we call the bogeyman technique. Foreign policy can be pretty messy and complicated. Good and evil aren't always easy to figure out. There are enemies and there are frenemies.

For example, to defeat Adolf Hitler, the twentieth century's most infamous mass murderer, the U.S. and England had to team up with Joseph Stalin, the twentieth century's *second*-most infamous mass murderer.

Were Roosevelt and Churchill evildoers for teaming up with such an unambiguously evil man as Stalin? Of course not. To save the world from Hitler, they had to hand over Eastern Europe to Stalin. There was no way around it.

Not surprisingly, Roosevelt and Churchill did not tout their policy as a bargain with the devil.

On the contrary, the war propaganda arms of both governments presented Stalin as a right-thinking proponent of goodness. Public criticism of Commie Russia was actually censored in the West during the war. Consider this: a certain awesomely awesome British author named George Orwell could not publish his awesomely awesome novel *Animal Farm* during World War II. No British publisher wanted to touch it because of its allegorical criticism of Stalin's Soviet Union.

That sort of outright censorship is virtually impossible in the age of electronic communication. Instead of trying to hide information from us, our leaders try to manipulate us by constructing compelling narratives of good versus evil.

We ordered the Animal Farm *cover and got this instead. Stupid photo agencies.*

That's where the bogeyman technique comes in.

It's a lot easier to sell Americans on a foreign-policy initiative when there's an icky bogeyman on whom to focus our righteous anger. You can't have cops without robbers. You can't have Itchy without Scratchy, Superman without Lex Luthor, or James Bond without a foreign-accented criminal mastermind.

And you can't have U.S. foreign policy without a bogeyman.

You must have only one of two requirements to be a bogeyman: you must either have facial hair or wear a military uniform.

BOGEYMAN	FACIAL HAIR OR MILITARY UNIFORM	EVIL DEEDS	BOGEYMAN COVER-UP
MAHMOUD AHMADINEJAD *(1956–present)* Iranian bogeyman	Mustache, and usually a raggedy, Members Only–ish jacket that really needs to be dry-cleaned	Engaged in a war of words with the U.S. and Israel that has turned international institutions against Iran; insinuated Iran actively seeks the destruction of Israel; hosted a Holocaust-denial conference	He's not Iran's supreme leader; Iran's major political decisions are made by Ayatollah Ali Khamenei, whose title really is Supreme Leader
HUGO CHÁVEZ *(1954–present)* Venezuelan bogeyman	Frequently wears a uniform, with a beret	Has repeatedly made crude comments about Bush and former Secretary of State Condoleezza Rice; has restricted free media in Venezuela; has largely failed at his attempt to alleviate poverty in Venezuela	He was freely elected in 1998, 2000, 2004, and 2006; though he has never threatened the U.S. with military action, we've threatened him—in fact, we backed a nearly successful coup d'état against him in 2002
SADDAM HUSSEIN *(1937–2006)* Iraqi bogeyman	Both	Murdered opponents of his regime; used poison gas on his own citizens; invaded Iran and Kuwait	Saddam was an ally of the United States throughout the 1980s; even though there was no evidence linking him to 9/11, he was so plainly evil that as many as 60 percent of Americans blamed him for it at one point
KIM JONG IL *(1941–present)* North Korean bogeyman	Always appears in photos wearing black or olive-green fatigues	Maintains the world's last Stalinist state; threatens nuclear war on his neighbors; lets millions of North Koreans starve while he and his inner circle live lavishly	Kim didn't drop out of the NPT or test a nuke until after Bush and Company repeatedly threatened him with attacks
ROBERT MUGABE *(1924–present)* Zimbabwean bogeyman	Mustache—in a style we call the Vertical Hitler	Confiscated productive farmland from white farmers and doled it out to cronies who didn't know how to farm! In just a couple of years, Zimbabwe went from food exporter to famine state; one-quarter of the country's thirteen million people now subsist on international food aid	The interracial strife Mugabe exploits to stay in power is a result of Zimbabwe's near-century-long colonization by Britain

GETTING NEIGHBORLY WITH CUBA

What we give to Mexico

"Say hello to my little country."

With all the ill will directed at the U.S. these days,[15] it's easy to forget that the U.S. gets along fantastically well with most of its closest neighbors.

The U.S.–Canada border, for example, is the longest unfortified border in the world. Canada's our bestest friend and our biggest trading partner. Each year, Canada sends us billions in oil, gas,[16] comedians, hockey players, funny accents, and migratory birds.

In return, we send Canada *Law & Order, Law & Order: SVU, Law & Order: Criminal Intent*, prescription drugs, and busloads of old people shopping for those prescription drugs because they're cheaper in Canada than they are here.[17] When the weather's warm, we also send back most of the birds.

And despite the hubbub surrounding illegal immigration, the U.S. gets on quite well with Mexico, too. Each year, we send Mexico tens of thousands of vacationers. In return, Mexico sends us hardworking laborers, petroleum, endless free refills of the chip basket, and the irresistible two taco/one enchilada combo plate. Be careful, the plate is very hot.

What Mexico gives us

There's really only one close neighbor with whom we have a bad relationship.

---

15. Multiple studies of world public opinion since 2001 have found that the U.S. is less popular than getting kicked in the head, and only marginally more popular than getting stabbed in the eye while fire ants attack your groin. Check out www.pewglobal.org for slightly more precise wording.

16. Contrary to myth, we get more oil and gas from Canada than we do from Saudi Arabia.

17. Even though most of them are actually made here.

"Bad" really isn't the word. Awful, terrible, horrendous—a relationship so atrocious that American passports are actually preprinted with the fact that we're not allowed to travel there.

That country, as you might have gathered from the title of this section, is Cuba.

Cuba is a Spanish-speaking island nation about ninety miles south of Key West,[18] Florida (home of singer Jimmy Buffett, but don't hold that against it—it's actually a nice place to visit). Cuba sits at the intersection of the Atlantic Ocean, the Gulf of Mexico, and the Caribbean Sea. It's about the size of Pennsylvania, but with better weather.

Jimmy Buffett—Key West's most popular son, after Ernest Hemingway

WHY IS CUBA AN ENEMY OF THE U.S.?

The U.S. government will tell you it's because Cuba is a communist dictatorship—ruled from 1959 to 2008 by Fidel Castro and then, as of February 2008, by his brother Raul.

Pretty much all of the bad things you might hear about the Castro dictatorship are true. The dictators have, in fact, squashed political dissent, jailed critics of their government, and suppressed free enterprise.

Fidel Castro, being all Communisty and stuff

But is that the real reason Cuba is an enemy of the U.S.?

Not really. Being a cruel dictatorship has never, by itself, made the U.S. completely shun another nation. In reality, Cuba's government is no more repressive and undemocratic than many nations the U.S. actually counts as friends—Saudi Arabia[19] and Turkmenistan[20] spring to mind.

What makes Cuba an enemy of the United States is that the Castro regime has, over the decades, gotten under the skin of several politically powerful constituencies in the U.S.

See, for more than 450 years prior to Castro's ascent, Cuba was a political and economic plaything of two very powerful nations.

---

18. Key West's Ernest Hemingway Home and Museum, where the esteemed author supposedly wrote _A Farewell to Arms_, is now home to sixty polydactyl cats—meaning they have six or seven toes on their paws.

19. Since 1932, Saudi Arabia has been ruled by Ibn Saud and five of his sons. The current king, Abdullah, was born in 1924.

20. Turkmenistan's freaky dictator Saparmurat Niyazov was so crazy, he changed the name of the month of April to "Mother." Not for mothers in general, but for his own mother, whose image he put on countless statues and plaques around the country.

From 1511[21] to 1898, Cuba was a colony of Spain. Spain gave Cuba a language (Spanish), a religion (Catholicism), and two diseases (smallpox and measles) that killed off most of the native population.

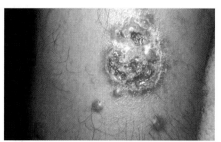

Smallpox: not the nicest gift to bring when you arrive on someone's island

Then, in 1898 the U.S. whooped Spain in the Spanish-American War and took Cuba under its wing. Though Cuba was never formally a U.S. possession (like Guam or Puerto Rico), the U.S. meddled incessantly in Cuba's national affairs up until the Cuban revolution.

In 1959, Castro took power from a dictator named Fulgencio Batista. Batista was a crook and an incompetent. But he was our crook and incompetent, so we got along with him swimmingly.

He protected American corporate plantations in Cuba (fruit and sugar, mainly) and turned Cuba's capital, Havana, into a gambling and nightlife mecca for the U.S.'s superrich. The Havana of Batista's day was often referred to as the Latin Las Vegas.[22]

Cuban dictator Fulgencio Batista—a bad guy, but our guy

The Batista regime concentrated the nation's assets in the hands of a small number of wealthy Cubans and foreigners. The U.S. didn't mind, but Fidel did. When Castro toppled Batista's regime in 1959, he tried to make a clean break with Cuba's battered childhood.

The sting from Castro slamming the door on our Yankee behinds might not have lasted so long if not for the Cold War. With the U.S. hostile to his government, Castro courted protection from the one country that could provide it: in the late 1950s and early 1960s, that meant the Soviet Union.

HOW DID THE COLD WAR PLAY OUT IN SUCH A HOT COUNTRY?

The U.S. and the Soviets were deep into the Cold War—a tense standoff that played itself out in proxy battles all over the world. In the USSR, Cuba saw a protector. In Cuba, the Soviets saw a palm-treed aircraft carrier and missile base just ninety miles off the coast of Florida. Cuba was a giant middle finger for the Soviets to wave at the U.S.

With Cuba and the Soviets paired up, Castro's opponents (many of whom fled to the U.S.) argued to the U.S. government that toppling Castro wasn't just a way to restore the old system—it was a way to thwart Soviet expansion into the Americas.

So attempt to thwart we did—with the U.S.-funded disastrous Bay of Pigs Invasion of Cuba in 1961 by anti-Castro exiles. And in the years that followed, we funded various efforts to assassinate Castro and his top lieutenants.

Cuba's Bay of Pigs, or at least what we imagine it to look like

---

21. When Columbus sailed across the ocean blue in 1492, he saw Cuba but didn't stop there.
22. Never mind that the actual Las Vegas is pretty freakin' Latin. It's 25 percent Hispanic and its name means "the meadows" in Spanish.

Okay, so that kinda explains why the hatin' started. But why has it continued nearly two decades since the end of the Cold War?

The answer is American presidential politics. You know how people call Florida a "swing state"? That doesn't mean spouse swapping (although we're not saying that doesn't happen in Florida—warm weather and sunshine can cloud your judgment). "Swing state" means it's pretty evenly divided between Republicans and Democrats (see Swing States, page 35).

Like all but a handful of states, Florida gives all of its presidential electoral college votes to the candidate who gets the most popular votes. If one candidate gets 50.1 percent of the vote and another candidate gets 49.9 percent of the vote, the candidate with 50.1 percent gets *all* of Florida's electoral college votes. In 2004 and 2008, that meant twenty-seven[23] electoral votes, the fourth-highest electoral vote total after California, Texas, and New York—and nearly 10 percent of the 271 you need to become president (see The Electoral College, pages 34–36).

Because Florida is a swing state, small losses in Florida's large and politically powerful Cuban community can lose you the state. As long as presidential candidates feel like they need to court anti-Castro Cuban American votes or risk losing Florida, candidates from both parties will be tempted to embrace hard-line anti-Castro policies.

CIGARS

Cuba is known for its exceptional tobacco plants and cigar makers. Though legend has it that Communism has hurt the quality of Cuban cigars, they're still prized among U.S. cigar smokers—in part because their importation to the U.S. is banned. Cuban cigars are readily available in most other Latin American countries.

Andisheh has traveled to Latin America a few times on vacation. Each time he went, at least one of his friends asked him to bring back Cuban cigars. Andisheh's attorney advises him not to reveal whether he complied with his friends' requests.

A Cuban cigar factory in 1912, before Castro ruined it with Communism, repression, and, um, quality health care for all workers

---

23. In chapter one, we discussed Florida's decisive twenty-five electoral votes in the 2000 election. Florida's population growth, as measured in the 2000 census, gave it an additional two representatives. So in 2004 and 2008, Florida had twenty-seven electoral college votes.

GUANTÁNAMO BAY

Even though Cuba is an enemy nation, the U.S. has a military base there. Since the Spanish-American War, the U.S. has maintained a military facility on Cuba's west coast at a harbor called Guantánamo Bay.

The U.S. says Cuba gave the base to us for as long as we want. Cuba says the deal wasn't really an agreement at all. Rather, it was forced down Cubans' throats at a time when the U.S. was Cuba's colonial overlord in all but name.

Recently, instead of using Gitmo (as it's often called) to thwart Communism, we used it to warehouse accused terrorists without trial. President Obama ordered the Gitmo prison shut down, but the naval base remains.

Gitmo prison: "C'mon in, the weather's great. No, seriously. The weather is great."

RISING JADE, ENIGMATIC DRAGON TIGER, AND OTHER HELPFUL CLICHÉS ABOUT CHINA

By the time you're done with school, you'll have taken several American history classes and read or skimmed dozens of books on the topic. But you still won't know it all.

We mention that only to help you understand what a pain in the pupu platter it is to cram everything about China into a few short pages. China is a four-thousand-year-old civilization with 1.3 billion people. No wonder it's a lot easier to use weird, condescending clichés (insert sound of gong here) than it is to actually dig into China's history and politics.

Let's be honest, though. It's partly China's fault.

It's all the way over in Asia. It takes at least twenty hours to fly there—longer than a fully charged iPod battery can last. iPods? Yup, made in China. Call us conspiracy theorists, but we wonder: did they make the battery life specifically less than an America–China journey to deter us from coming over, nosing around, and demanding hamburgers?

How long is the flight to China from the U.S.? This man was clean shaven when the plane took off.

FROM REPRESSIVE, BACKWARD, AGRICULTURAL WASTELAND TO REPRESSIVE, BACKWARD, INDUSTRIAL AND FINANCIAL SUPERPOWER IN A GENERATION!

For most of its four-thousand-year history, China was an A-list cultural, political, and technological achiever.

Paper? Invented in China circa 100 CE. Opera? Invented in China circa 200 CE. Ridiculously long stone walls that you can see from outer space? Invented in China circa 500 CE. Gunpowder? Invented in China circa 800 CE. Food that simultaneously tastes sweet and sour? Invented in China circa 1700 CE. Fine china? Invented in Lansing, Michigan.

Just checking to see if you're paying attention. Fine china (porcelain) was indeed invented in China, around two thousand years ago.

Communist Chinese dictator Mao Zedong

What goes up must come down, and come down China did. The fourth quarter of the last millennium was not good to the Chinese.

By the turn of the twentieth century, China was obscenely poor and weak—trampled constantly by foreign invaders. Its political and economic landscape had more in common with medieval Europe than with anything we'd consider modern.

When China finally got the foreigners out in 1949, the decline hastened. Communist dictator Mao Zedong's record of mass murder makes Hitler seem like an underachiever.[24] The "Cultural Revolution" he instigated in 1966 was a tidy euphemism for the ten-year period of strife, bloodshed, and repression.

Two of China's most amazing inventions—the Great Wall and Sweet-and-Sour Chicken!

---

24. Because China is ruled by Communists, the world has never had a full accounting of how many people Mao killed. His early agricultural and industrial policy diktats, dubbed the "Great Leap Forward," triggered a famine that left at least 16.5 million, possibly 30 million, dead. Estimates of the number who died in political violence also reach the millions.

China's rapid turnaround began in the 1980s. After Mao kicked the bucket in 1976, a predictable power struggle ensued. When the dust settled, a guy named Deng Xiaoping was running the show.

Deng's bright idea: unleash China's entrepreneurial culture without giving up the Communist Party's control of the country. He turned China into a commie-capitalist hybrid. Commitalism. Capunism. Something like that.

He let the Chinese people start their own businesses, as well as allowing them to do business with foreigners.

They make good stuff in China now.

Contrary to myth, Chinese factories don't just make things cheaply. They make things very well and very quickly. TVs, computers, smartphones, dumbphones, medicines, and those indoor-outdoor thermometers people keep buying for their dads—they all come from China now.

Deng Xiaoping (clapping for Jimmy Carter) added capitalism to Communism, creating the sweet-and-sour sauce of economic systems.

Buoyed by cheap labor, protectionist government policies, and a centuries-old entrepreneurial tradition that survived Communism intact, China's manufacturing economy blossomed like a lotus in eternal springtime. (Sorry, we're addicted to funny Chinese clichés now.)

By the 1990s, China had become the world's leading producer of cheap plastic crap.

In and of itself, that was a huge transformation. But it didn't stop there. China quickly progressed from cheap plastic crap to expensive plastic crap and then, well, pretty much every manufactured product you can think of—plastic or otherwise.

VOULEZ-VOUS APPRENDRE UNE MEILLEURE LANGUE QUE FRANÇAIS?[25]

No offense to France, but why, oh, why do so many public schools in the United States offer French language lessons but not Chinese? French is great. As we've learned in this chapter, it was once the "language of diplomacy." It's beautiful and widely spoken—not just in France but in Canada and in a large chunk of Africa and Southeast Asia.

But France's hold on the world is waning while China's is waxing. English is the default international language now, and it's not inconceivable that Chinese will be number two during our lifetime.

Merci beaucoup pour les bons temps,[26] but if a school has to choose, it might be wise to choose Chinese. Just throwing that out there.

25. Would you like to learn a better language than French?
26. Thank you very much for the good times.

Au revoir, *middle-school French class.*

China is the undisputed champion of mass-produced consumer goods. If you think we're exaggerating, go to Target or Walmart and start looking at the bottom of every object you can find. If security hassles you, show them this book.

AN AMERICAN COMPANY

Package and Product Designed in the U.S.A.
MADE IN CHINA

Even the computer that this chapter was written on was made in you-know-where.

More important than merely making stuff, China's economic machine has lifted an estimated four hundred million people out of poverty in only a few decades. Never in human history has so much poverty been eradicated so quickly. By any objective measure, that deserves a big WOW.

But it's still a one-party, big-brother state where criticizing the government will land you in jail, and simply Googling information critical of the government can land you on a police watch list.

THE U.S. AND CHINA
It's Complicated

Could you please pass the 10W-30?

If the U.S. and China were a couple, their Facebook status would be "It's complicated."

The U.S. and China are totally up in each other's biz-ness.

The only country with which the U.S. does more trading than China is Canada—but that's only because Canada sells America huge quantities of a gooey natural resource we can't live without: ~~maple syrup~~ petroleum.

China takes a lot of the money it collects from selling us stuff and invests it back into the American economy. As of November 2008, China had purchased $680 billion in U.S. government bonds. And it still had nearly $2 trillion in cash reserves.

By many measures, the U.S. and China are pals. But when you turn on cable news or eyeball the China section of your local bookstore, you might get an entirely different impression.

Many American politicians and political prognosticators view China not as a business partner but as a growing threat. Some prophesy an inevitable war with the U.S. as the two global giants compete for finite natural resources and political influence.

In fact, the U.S. and China have actually already fought a war.

During the Korean War (1950–1953), U.S. troops advanced so close to North Korea's border with China that China joined the North Koreans in fighting the U.S. The border between North and South Korea today closely matches the front line separating Chinese and U.S. troops at the end of the war.

China and the U.S. no longer have any real quarrel over Korea, but they do have one big sore spot: Taiwan.

When the Communists took over China in 1949, the overthrown former government set up shop in Taiwan, a large island off China's southern coast.

CHINA

Not so fast, Taiwan.

TAIWAN

Land of Confucian

From 1949 until 1972, the U.S. acted like the government in Taiwan was actually the official government of all of China. We even made sure Taiwan controlled China's vote in the UN.

In 1979, the U.S. formally recognized Communist China as the official government of China. Additionally, we agreed with Communist China that Taiwan should eventually be reunified with the mainland.

Nevertheless, we still sell billions of dollars' worth of weapons to Taiwan to defend itself from a mainland Chinese attack. We also broadly hint (but never promise) that our navy will intervene if China invades Taiwan.

China is, as you might expect, annoyed by this. They believe we have as much right to tell them what to do with Taiwan as they have a right to tell us what to do with New Jersey.

Speaking of which, what the heck are we gonna do with New Jersey?

Where were we? Oh, yeah.

Short of a shooting war, many Americans who want a less-friendly relationship with China would be happy if we at least toughened up our trade policy.

One of the reasons China is able to export goods cheaply is because its government manipulates the country's currency and limits imports. Also, Chinese businesses don't have to comply with Western-style labor laws preventing exploitation of workers. And as we've all learned from the pet-food/baby-food/lead-paint-in-toys scares of recent years, Chinese manufacturers aren't subject to the same environmental or safety standards as their American or European counterparts. The "get tough with China" crowd suggests slapping Chinese-made goods with taxes and quotas as a way of leveling the playing field.

Someone got into the Chinese kibble again.

IT'S RAINING MEN IN CHINA

In 1982, a one-hit-wonder disco act known as the Weather Girls had a smash hit with "It's Raining Men." The song imagined a fantastical world where single, attractive men were so plentiful, they fell from the sky like rain—uninjured!

Believe it or not, such a world exists. To control its population, China does not allow married couples to have more than one child. Forced to choose, many Chinese families prefer to have boys. It's not uncommon for a couple to abort female babies so that their only child is male. There are 120 boys born in China for every 100 girls, the largest male-to-female disparity in the world.

If you've ever glimpsed a fraternity party, you know how obnoxiously young men, even the nice ones, can behave when there aren't young women around. Marriage, or even just a stable relationship, tends to have a pacifying effect on men.

The millions of Chinese men who want a mate but cannot find one pose a serious threat to society. In their seminal work on demography, *Bare Branches*, Valerie M. Hudson and Andrea M. den Boer say theft, rioting, and militarization are all side effects of having too many men and not enough women.

What's good for the Weather Girls isn't necessarily good for the rest of us.

WILL CHINA STUMBLE?

Even if you don't prophesy war with China or worry that China's economic rise might threaten U.S. prosperity, there's still reason to worry about China. Its success challenges the American and European view of the world.

Americans and Europeans believe political freedom and economic prosperity go together like chocolate and peanut butter, like high school and musical, like General Tso's Chicken and free fortune cookies. China's economic juggernaut suggests a one-party, autocratic, dissent-intolerant, big-brother state is just as capable of producing happy citizens as multiparty democracies.

General Tso's Chicken: finally, rampant militarism we can support.

Fans of freedom and democracy can't help but be weirded out by that. If China becomes a globe-straddling superpower like the U.S., will China begin exporting Chinese non-democracy as aggressively as the U.S. and Europe like to push their forms of democracy? Will the world's dictators and autocrats point to China's economic miracle as justification for suppressing political dissent in their own countries?

It's a reasonable concern. After all, the U.S. goes out of its way to support its like-minded friends; there's no reason to think China won't do the same.

WHY DOES SUDAN ♥ CHINA?

In exchange for Sudanese oil, China uses its UN veto to protect the murderous Sudan government from sanctions related to its genocidal policies in Darfur. China's position is that Western democracies have no business telling other governments how to handle their internal affairs.

On the other hand, many China watchers think that China's growing middle class will inevitably lead to greater political freedom and democratization. For example: water and air pollution in China is astonishingly awful. Chinese people are increasingly upset at their wretched environmental regulations. At what point does the upset become a mass protest or a full-fledged political movement? At some point, will the Chinese people be so fed up with their government's control of political speech and behavior in general that they rebel? If they do, keep an eye on the millions of unattached Chinese men we mentioned on the previous page!

So far, there hasn't been much sign of agitation. And that's kinda scary.

Mmm, just another beautiful, smoggy day in Beijing! Cough, cough . . .

WHY IS GENERAL TSO'S CHICKEN SO TASTY?

General Tso's Chicken is probably the most popular Hunan-style Chinese dish served in American Chinese restaurants today.

Why is it so tasty? Because it skillfully combines several elements that American palates traditionally savor: it's a nice chunk of meat; it's breaded; it's fried; it's sweet; it's tangy from ginger; and it's spicy from chili peppers.

If you go to China, though, don't expect to find it on a restaurant menu. An actual Hunanese general, General Tso lived from 1812 to 1885. But his association with the chicken is totally fabricated. General Tso's Chicken appears to have been invented in New York in the 1970s.

Sticking a dead general's name on the chicken dish was simply clever marketing. Tso has as much to do with fried chicken dishes as affable tigers have to do with sugary cornflakes.

A MUSLIM AND A JEW WALK INTO A COUNTRY
A Short Guide to the Israel-Palestine Conflict

Concerned this book wouldn't otherwise generate enough hate mail, we've decided to write a section about the Palestinian-Israeli conflict.

Okay, that's not actually true.

We mean, it is true—this is the section. But it's not true that we're fishing for hate. With the exception of popular conservative TV hosts like Bill O'Reilly, whose on-air rage would help our book sales, we're not interested in making anyone angry.

Bill O'Reilly, a man we'd like to anger

It's an unfortunate fact of life that public discussions about Israel and Palestine tend to get mean and personal. Every syllable is parsed for real or imaginary bias.

To some people, the fact that the first sentence of this section says "Palestinian-Israeli conflict" instead of "Israeli-Palestinian conflict" is a sign that we three authors are card-carrying members of the militant Palestinian group Hamas.

We assure you it's not true. Hamas doesn't even issue membership cards.

To others, the fact that we used the phrase "Palestinian-Israeli conflict" instead of "Israeli occupation of Palestine" is a sign that we're paid Israeli propagandists.

We're not . . . although now that Dan and Andisheh think about it, Jodi did recently buy a new car. Where did this money come from? *Hmm.* We'll have to check the wiretaps of Jodi's phone usage. (Thank you, USA PATRIOT Act!)

Jodi's car, or the illicit earnings of a secret Israeli agent?

IF HAMAS DOESN'T ISSUE MEMBERSHIP CARDS, WHAT *DOES* IT DO?

HAMAS
Membership Card

NAME: Andisheh Nouraee
AGE: 23
HEIGHT: 6'4"
VIEWS: 2 da x-treme
TEMPER: ill

Totally not real. For starters, I'm only 5' 9".

Well, to begin with, Hamas holds 76 of 132 seats in the parliament of the Palestinian National Authority—which means it gets to decide what's best for Israeli-occupied Palestine. As of this writing, that means war with Israel. Owing to Hamas's use of suicide bombings and rockets, and its dogged refusal to recognize Israel's right to exist, the United States and most of its allies consider it a terrorist organization. It doesn't help that money from Iran keeps Hamas well-armed and well-funded,[27] and that Iran's bogeyman prez Mahmoud Ahmadinejad makes provocative anti-Israeli gestures like saying they'll be wiped off the map and denying the Holocaust. But Hamas also builds hospitals, schools, libraries, and day-care centers, and it has been effective in rooting out high-level government corruption. (Scare tactics *do* work, for better or worse.) Its cable channel, al-Aqsa TV, features news as well as anti-Semitic children's programming.

Hamas's slogan, which, depending on your point of view, can be interpreted in about as many ways as the Koran or the Bible, concludes with the phrase: "Death for the sake of God is the loftiest of wishes." Um, yikes (see the War on Terror™, page 86).

The point is that nothing we say or do is going to change one simple fact: Israelis, Palestinians, and their various supporters have irreconcilable, opposing narratives.

The pro-Israeli side believes Israel has strived to live in peace in the Middle East but has constantly been thwarted— first by neighboring Arab armies, then by Palestinian terrorists.

The pro-Palestinian side believes Israel is essentially a latter-day European colony that denies Palestinians the right of self-determination.

---

27. Ironically, most of Hamas's funding—well over 50 percent—comes from Saudi Arabia, which the U.S. calls one of its biggest allies in the War on Terror™. So how can a country be an ally in the War on Terror™ on one hand and a giant ATM for terrorists on the other? If we could answer that question, we would be much less sad and confused than we are now. A little help, anyone? (See Dynasty, pages 59-62.)

One side is never going to convince the other. Never.

Our intention is not to tell you which side to pick but to help you figure out what the sides are saying.

So, shalom and salaam. Or, if you prefer, salaam and shalom.

"Shalom" is the Hebrew word for salaam. "Salaam" is the Arabic word for peace. "Peace" is the English word for shalom. Rinse. Repeat.

HAVE THEY REALLY BEEN KILLING EACH OTHER FOR CENTURIES?

Nearly every day, some smarty-panted commentator acts all wise and pants-wearing by saying Israelis and Arabs have been killing each other for centuries.

The implication of the "for centuries" meme[28] is that the Israeli-Palestinian conflict is an intractable ancient blood feud: a Middle East Hatfields versus McCoys based in ancient scripture; the Mecca-oys versus Hatbergs, and therefore it's a waste of time for mere mortals to try to solve it.

'Tis not true. The Israeli-Palestinian dispute is not, at its core, a religious feud. No one is arguing over the nature of God, or whether Mohammad could beat Moses in paintball.[29]

The Israeli-Palestinian conflict is about land. Two groups of people claim the same land as their homeland.

And, no, it hasn't been going on for centuries, either. It's been going on for decades.

Don't get us wrong. Religion fuels the conflict. If the Torah told Jews that their promised land was Terre Haute, Indiana, instead of Palestine, this chapter about war in the Mideast would probably be about the Midwest. Territorial compromise is much harder when the territory you're compromising about is sacred to you (see Jerusalem: It's Mine, Mine, Mine!, page 161).

Okay, maybe Mohammad is better at paintball.

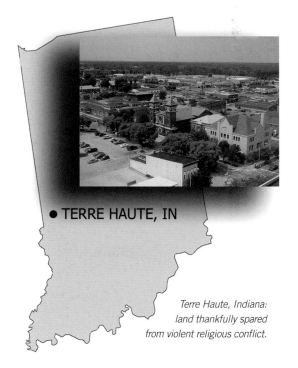

● TERRE HAUTE, IN

Terre Haute, Indiana: land thankfully spared from violent religious conflict.

---

28. A "meme," in case you are wondering, is a cultural idea that is passed along from generation to generation, much like a genetic trait. To put it another way, a meme is the verbal equivalent of, say, male-pattern baldness.

29. Moses' ability to move vast oceans would probably make him the favorite in any such match.

Israel, East Jerusalem, the West Bank, and Gaza combined are the size of Massachusetts. With twelve million people jammed in, however, it's got nearly twice as many people as New England's hardest-to-spell state.

At its core, Israel-Palestine is a war about a lot of people wanting not a lot of land.

HOW ISRAEL CAME TO BE

Israel was founded in 1948, but its roots go way, way, way, *way* back. To Genesis, in fact. Not the band that brought you the 1986 number-one hit single "Invisible Touch"—although they go pretty far back, too. We're talking "first book of the Torah" Genesis.

Genesis the band and Genesis the book: both begat many timeless hits.

In the Book of Genesis, you can find the likes of Abraham, Jacob, and Isaac wandering the land[30] that comprises modern-day Israel.

Though the Bible explains how the land of Israel is holy and precious to Jews, it explains nothing about why Jews and Muslims fight. Islam wasn't founded until 600 or so years after the New Testament was written (see Living with Mono(theism), page 144).

A better starting point for explaining today's fighting is 1881 in, of all places, Saint Petersburg, Russia. If you're looking for a scapegoat to pin the Israeli-Palestinian conflict on, you could do worse than Ignacy Hryniewiecki.

In addition to having probably the most made-up-sounding last name you'll find in this book, Hryniewiecki[31] was a cold-blooded assassin.[32] On March 1, 1881, he killed Czar Alexander II of Russia with a grenade. Hryniewiecki and his coconspirators were hoping to topple the Russian monarchy.

Our chosen scapegoat for this chapter, Ignacy Hryniewiecki

They failed. But in the process, they succeeded in setting off a chain of events that led to the enduring Israeli-Palestinian conflict.

Russian aristocrats spread the myth that a Jewish conspiracy was responsible for the killing. Anti-Jewish riots, known as pogroms, began. The pogroms continued for years and spread throughout Europe, inspiring a mass exodus of European Jews to the U.S.

His target, Czar Alexander II

Many of their children and their children's children eventually gave birth to famous Jewish Americans like Bob Dylan and Joan Rivers. If you enjoy enigmatic acoustic singer-songwriters and/or mean-spirited red carpet coverage on E!, you sorta have Ignacy Hryniewiecki to thank.

Joan Rivers, the child of Russian Jewish immigrants, ended up making a living mocking celebrities' outfits outside award ceremonies.

30. With the exception of begetting, there is no more popular activity in the Old Testament than wandering.
31. No small achievement for a book with "Andisheh Nouraee" on the cover.
32. Don't let the bow tie fool you.

Slightly more germane to our current topic, the pogroms also galvanized many Jewish intellectuals around the idea that Jews needed a home country of their own: a place where their lives and livelihoods were not subject to the whims of bigoted aristocrats and the ignorant rioters who followed their cues. Among those intellectuals was an Austro-Hungarian lawyer and journalist named Theodor Herzl.

In 1896, Herzl wrote an influential book called *Der Judenstaat. En inglés, por favor,* that means *"The Jewish State"* in German.

Theodor Herzl, founder of Zionism

Herzl was freaked out by the pogroms in Russia and *le freaked* even more that they had spread to places like France, where *liberté, égalité, fraternité,* and kissing with tongue supposedly reigned supreme.

Herzl and his fellow Zionists became convinced Jews needed Jewish leaders, a Jewish army, and a Jewish country. After some debating, Zionists decided their state needed to be in Palestine[33] because it was promised to Jews in the Torah.

Inspired by Zionism, European Jews began moving to Palestine by the boatload.

HOW PALESTINE STILL HASN'T COME TO BE

As it turned out, there was a tiny complication in the Zionist plan to pack up the JU-Haul and move the family to Palestine.

A turn-of-the-twentieth-century Palestinian man, blissfully unaware of the crap awaiting his unborn family and neighbors

There were already people living in Palestine.

Today, we call them Palestinians.

Back then, though, they weren't called that. They were the Arab residents of the Ottoman Empire's province of Palestine. Palestine was a Turkish possession, ruled from the empire's capital, Istanbul.

At their peak, Ottoman Turks ruled a vast territory covering the Middle East, north Africa, and part of southeast Europe. They also popularized a style of cushioned footstool known as an ottoman.

In the late nineteenth century, however, the Ottomans (the empire, not the footstools) were in terminal decline. Their empire was so flimsy, they were actually called "The Sick Man of

Ottoman emperor

---

33. *Other locations considered by early Zionists for a Jewish homeland include East Africa and Argentina. Just imagine how much more exciting bar mitzvahs would be if you danced the hora and the tango.*

Europe." They were so sickly that when the first wave of Zionists showed up in Palestine, they were too weak to respond.

The Ottoman Empire croaked during WWI and its Middle East possessions were nabbed by the Brits and the French. If you look at a map of the Middle East, you'll notice that many of the borders are long, straight lines. The borders are that way because the Brits and the French literally sat down with maps and pencils and drew the modern Middle East.

The lucky Brits got Palestine. And they, too, permitted European Jews to migrate to Palestine en masse.

From the time the Brits grabbed Palestine until the

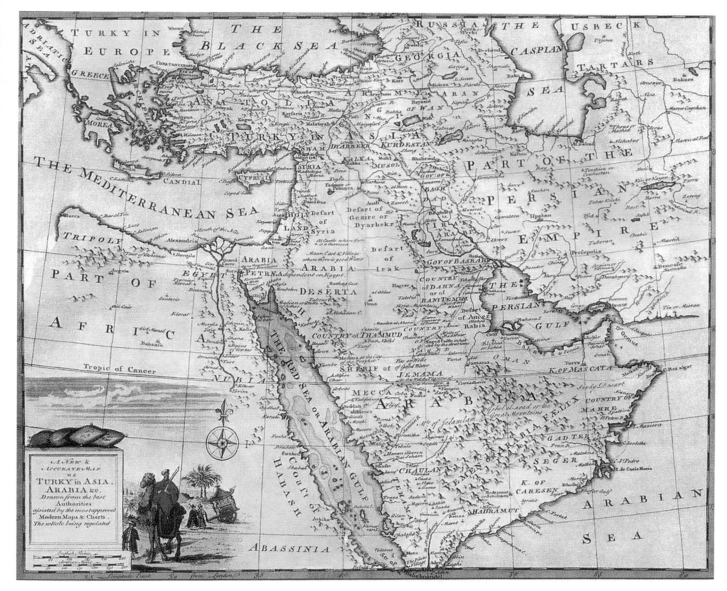

The Ottoman Empire, circa 1750

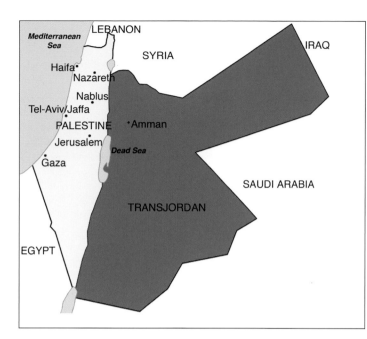

British Mandate of Palestine; note the straight lines.

Anti-Zionist uprising in Palestine in 1920

THE BIRTH OF ISRAEL
One Person's Independence Is Another Person's Catastrophe

beginning of WWII (from the late 1910s to the late 1930s), around 300,000 Jews arrived in Palestine from Europe. The Brits even promised Jews they would eventually have their own state there.

The Arabs who already lived in Palestine were mighty annoyed at the newcomers and the Brits. Many Palestinians believed their land was being swiped from them.

The annoyance was expressed verbally, but also with occasional rioting. From 1936 to 1939, Arab Palestinians actually fought a guerrilla war against the Brits and the Jews to stop the Jewish migration—one of the earliest iterations of the Jewish-versus-Palestinian fighting still going on today.

Zionist European Jews considered a move to the Holy Land the fulfillment of Biblical promise and nationalist ambitions. Palestinian Arabs considered the same actions colonization by yet another foreign overlord. Palestinians wanted and still want Palestine for themselves. They don't think they should be paying the price for European anti-Semitism.

Two people. One land. The Palestinian-Israeli conflict in a nutshell.

At the same time Palestinians were ticked at the Brits, so were the Zionists. In their opinion, the Brits simply weren't allowing in Jews fast enough.

Remember, by the mid-1930s, Germany was under the complete control of Adolf Hitler. Hitler didn't hide his desire to kill Europe's Jews. The urgency of Jewish worry during this period can't be understated. Before Zionists began their migration to Palestine from Europe, there were thousands of Jews living in Palestine and throughout the Middle East. Before the 1930s, they actually got on relatively well with their Muslim and Christian neighbors. It wasn't all macaroons and kick ball, but Jews in the Middle East were definitely a lot better off than Jews in Europe. They certainly were not subject to any nasty pogroms.

Metal gates reading "Arbeit Macht Frei" or "Work Will Make You Free" appeared at the entrance of several Nazi death camps.

As we will learn in chapter five, Islamic scripture officially recognizes and tolerates Judaism and Christianity. Muslims believe they share the same God as Christians and Jews. It's one of the sadder ironies of the Palestine-Israel dispute: throughout the Middle East, anger at Zionism has morphed over time into flat-out hatred of Jews.

During WWII, the doomsday scenario feared by Zionists became reality: multiplied by six million. The Nazi Holocaust killed approximately two-thirds of Europe's nine million Jews.

Recognizing the urgent need for a safe Jewish homeland, the UN (essentially the U.S. and Europe) divided Palestine into two countries: a Jewish one called Israel and an Arab one called Palestine.

Jerusalem, which is holy to Jews and Muslims as well as to Christians, was designated an international city[34] (see A Fightin' Mad Timeline, pages 162–163).

The Arabs in Palestine as well as in neighboring countries were angry about Israel's creation.

Adolf Hitler's genocidal war against European Jews accelerated emigration to Palestine.

Among the survivors, memories of the Holocaust broadened and deepened support for Zionism's goals. Being the target of a state-sponsored mass-murder spree focused Europe's Jews on their collective survival.

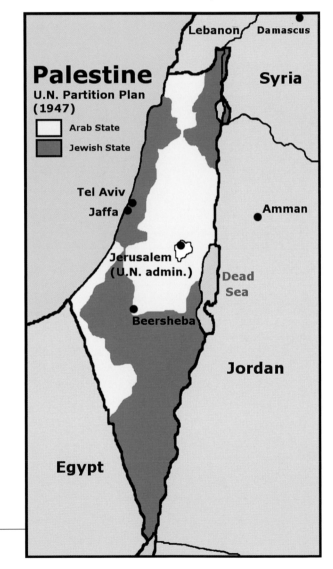

In response to the Holocaust, the British divided Palestine into a Jewish state and an Arab state. Compare this to the map on p. 121.

34. *Poor atheists. How come they don't get a city? No, wait: Vegas!*

King Abdullah, who was Muslim, chillin' with some of his Christian homies in Jerusalem

They believed the UN was imposing a European colony for Jews on Palestine. Palestinians believed, and still believe, they were displaced as penance for European anti-Semitism. On May 15, 1948, the day after Israel (with the UN's blessing) declared its existence, neighboring Arab states invaded.

How'd the war turn out?

Well, Israel commemorates the fighting as their war of independence. Arabs refer to the war in Arabic as *al Nakba,* which means "the catastrophe" in English.

It also means catastrophe in French. *Catastrophe* is a French word, ya know.

Palestinian Arabs and their neighboring Arab allies were beaten badly by Israel. When the fighting stopped in 1949, Israel grew beyond its original UN borders to roughly the shape it is today. Not only did it maintain the land allotted to it by the UN, but it also captured nearly all of the land the UN had granted for an Arab Palestine.

Approximately 700,000 Palestinian civilians left their homeland. Many fled to avoid the violence around them. Many were driven from their homes by Israeli forces intent on removing as many non-Jews as possible from Israel. When you hear about Palestinian refugees in the West Bank, Gaza Strip, and the countries that surround Israel, they are these now-elderly refugees and their descendants.

The official line in Israel used to be that Palestinians up and left voluntarily. But people don't abandon their homes voluntarily. In recent years, several Israeli historians have debunked the "they left voluntarily" story as pernicious myth. Palestinians

Palestinian refugees flee to Jordan in 1949, after the 1948 war.

were forced out. The war left Palestinians a stateless people. Palestinians are perfectly correct to call it their catastrophe.

It's important to note that Arab leaders played a crucial role in the Palestinian catastrophe. Arab states dove face-first into a war they couldn't—and didn't—win. To fight Israel's existence was a strategic error of monumental proportions. Without that first Arab-Israeli war, it's possible a Palestinian state might have developed right alongside Israel.

WAR AND PEACE AND WAR AND PEACE AND WAR AND PEACE, ETC.

Even though their forces were beaten back, it took a while for Arab nations to accept Israel as a part of the Middle East's dusty landscape. The end of the war in 1949 wasn't peace. It was pause.

In 1967 Israel walloped the militaries of Egypt, Syria, and Jordan in a six-day-long war known, coincidentally enough, as the Six Day War. Israel captured East Jerusalem, the West Bank, Gaza, and (from Syria) the Golan Heights. The Arab alliance against Israel had blockaded Israel's Red Sea port and was preparing to invade, but Israel acted quickly and flattened enemy forces while their engines were still warming up.

In 1973, the Arab states tried and failed to retake the land Israel won in 1967.

It wasn't until 1979 that Arab nations effectively resigned themselves to Israel's existence.

That was the year Egypt and Israel made peace by signing the Camp David peace treaty on the White House lawn.

In exchange for returning the Sinai peninsula to Egypt (along with the U.S. promising to send billions in annual ~~bribes~~ aid payments to Egypt), Israel received a promise of peace and full diplomatic recognition.

Egypt is the Arab world's most populous and militarily hefty country. Once Egypt shook hands with Israel, the likelihood of an Arab military conquest of Israel dropped from slim to none.

Anwar Sadat, the Egyptian president who signed the treaty with Israel, was assassinated by Muslim radicals in Egypt who were opposed to the deal. Arab governments publicly pooh-poohed Camp David, but no Arab army tried to invade Israel again. Arab nations largely abandoned the Palestinian cause.

The conflict in the Middle East today is a fight between the Israeli military and Palestinian guerrillas (aka terrorists). Each side accuses the other of fighting dirty. At the risk of irritating, well, everyone, we have to admit that they're both right.

Israel removed hundreds of thousands of Palestinians from their homes in 1948 to shore up their security after they were attacked by their Arab neighbors, and won't allow them back.

The Israeli occupation of Gaza and the West Bank after the 1967 war has inflicted untold misery. Millions of innocent Palestinians live in a sort of purgatory. They have no state or effective government.

Egyptian president Anwar Sadat, U.S. president Jimmy Carter, and the Israeli prime minister Menachem Begin celebrate the Camp David peace treaty with an awkward three-way handshake.

They are unable to travel freely from town to town within their own territory. Countless Palestinians in the territories have had their homes bulldozed by Israel. Illegal Israeli settlements occupy much of the most desirable land (and, to this day, continue to sprout). Though Israel ditched its settlements in Gaza in 2005, it still controls all traffic in and out, for security reasons. Gazans aren't just denied access to Israel but also to Egypt, the sea, and air travel. Gaza is an open-air prison of 1.5 million people.

Palestinians in the West Bank can't go more than a few miles without passing through Israeli military checkpoints. Palestinians can't visit friends or relatives in the next town, can't go shopping, and can't even get to a hospital without going through an Israeli military checkpoint. The checkpoint system so strangles Palestinian movement, the UN says sixty-nine Palestinian women gave birth at Israeli checkpoints between 2000 and 2006.

Cut off from the world by the Israeli military, the Palestinian economy is in shambles. The unemployment rate hovers near 30 percent. In Gaza, 80 percent of the residents rely on international aid to eat.

What Israel has done to Palestinian civilians is awful. So is what Palestinian militants have done to Israeli civilians.

Since the late 1960s, Palestinians have inflicted an organized guerilla war against Israel that has left thousands of innocent Israeli civilians dead. Remember—this is in addition to the wars and general ill-temperedness directed at Israel from surrounding Arab states. Is it any wonder Israelis feel under siege?

The single most infamous terror attack against Israel actually took place in Munich, Germany, during the 1972 summer Olympics. Terrorists disguised as athletes murdered ten Israeli Olympic athletes and one coach. Israel's clandestine response—a calculated series of assassinations of Palestinian militants—was later chronicled in the 2005 film *Munich*.

The deadliest attacks by Palestinians against Israelis came during the so-called al-Aqsa intifada, an uprising that began

More than half of the people trapped in war-destroyed Gaza are children.

Palestinian terrorist at the 1972 Israeli Olympic team's suite in Munich

in September 2000 and still isn't officially over (see A Fightin' Mad Timeline, pages 162–163). It included a horrifying wave of suicide attacks on Israeli civilian targets like restaurants, buses, and discos, killing hundreds of Israelis and prompting Israel to construct a security fence and wall across the West Bank.

Today, Israelis are safer from Palestinian terror atttacks than they've ever been. In 2009, not a single suicide bomb was detonated in Israel. It's not for lack of trying on the Palestinian side, but Israel's military actions of the past decade have sharply reduced the terror threat to Israeli civilians.

Militants in Gaza still lob as many rockets as they can at Israel, but they seldom injure or kill Israelis. The rockets are small and about as accurate as bottle rockets. Fifteen Iraelis were killed by Palestinians during 2009.

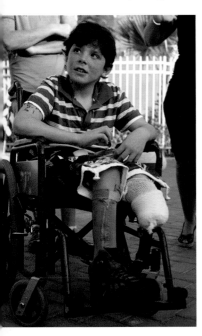

Israeli Osher Twito lost his leg in 2008 when a Palestinian rocket slammed into him. He was only eight years old.

It's gonna end. Right? After all, even history's most sickening, seemingly interminable interludes (slavery, Communism, the heyday of rap-metal) eventually come to an end.

Here are two possible outcomes, in order of likelihood.

1. THE TWO-STATE SOLUTION

In 1967, the UN Security Council passed Resolution 242, nudging Israel to give up the land it had just won in the Six Day War in exchange for a peace settlement with its Arab neighbors. Of course, the Arab states say they'd back such a deal, since it would mean recovering the land they lost in the war they started. Not surprisingly, Israel doesn't seem interested at the moment.

It's not that Israel isn't willing, under certain circumstances, to trade land for a peace deal with Palestinians. They've already done that—they gave back the Sinai Peninsula, which they won in the 1967 war, leading to peace with Egypt. But the Arab-backed land-for-peace goal wants to return Israel's borders to what they were before the 1967 Six Day War. Israel doesn't feel that is in its best interest.

Israel annexed East Jerusalem during the 1967 war and vows never to surrender it. Successive Israeli governments have worked to fill East Jerusalem with Jews (approximately 185,000 live there today), while trying to squeeze out Arabs. Have you ever squeezed an Arab? They don't like it.

Israel may give up some of East Jerusalem's Arab 'hoods so that Palestinians can put a capital in Jerusalem, but Israel is not going to give up the whole thing.

Then there's the West Bank. Parts of it are so densely packed with Israeli settlers, it would be a political and logistical nightmare to uproot them. A phrase often uttered by politicians and analysts is "the facts on the ground." This means, instead of making a peace deal based on the lines of a 1967 map, a peace deal should be crafted to reflect Israel's settlement patterns of the West Bank since 1967.

A land-for-peace deal would likely require Israel keeping parts of the West Bank, in exchange for giving Palestinians parts of what is currently Israel-proper. There are 295,000 Israelis and 2.5 million Palestinians living in the West Bank.

Third, there's the right of return. International law says war refugees have a right to return to their homes after the war is over.

There are millions of Palestinian refugees in the countries and occupied territories surrounding Israel. If all or even a substantial portion of them return, Israel would probably cease to be a majority Jewish state, which was kinda the point of Israel in the first place. Israel's population is already 20 percent Palestinian (or Israeli Arab, as they're usually called).

When you hear American or Israeli politicians talking about the importance of maintaining a "Jewish homeland," it typically means they're saying they don't support the Palestinian full right of return in the event of a peace settlement.

2. THE ONE-STATE SOLUTION

A growing number of Arab commentators suggest that, instead of two countries, Israel-Palestine should be one country.

Israel doesn't want this to happen, for reasons we've already gone over.

But Israel has never really reconciled itself with the two-state solution, either. Israelis rightly complain that Palestinian leaders are irresponsible and lousy. At the same time, though, the tactics of Israel's occupation make the occupied territories impossible to govern. All the stuff governments are supposed to control—land use, water, policing, travel, etc.—is controlled by Israel.

Forging and brokering a peace agreement between Israel and Palestine will require a large-scale foreign intervention. International troops will have to patrol Palestine for militants before Israel lets Palestine be an independent nation.

In the meantime, mountains of development money will have to start pouring into Palestine. Palestine's desperate poverty must be relieved if militant movements are to be weakened. Honestly, it may be impossible. Look at Palestine on the map: it's not even clear that Palestine can survive as a nation in a two-state solution. The West Bank is landlocked and disconnected from Gaza.

At the time of this writing, with a precarious UN cease-fire in place to prevent Israel and Hamas from reducing Gaza to rubble, it's difficult to imagine cooler heads prevailing any time soon to create a lasting peace.

On that distinctly unfunny note, we wrap up our brief history of the Israeli-Palestinian conflict.

A two-state solution would look something like this.

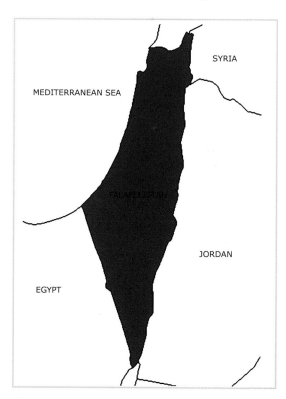

A one-state solution would combine Arabs and Jews into one nation. We propose calling it "Falafelistan" since both sides agree on falafel's divine deliciousness.

ALL TOGETHER NOW
The United Nations

The United Nations is like Miracle Whip or Heidi Montag. It persists, despite the facts that no one admits to liking it nor understands quite how it got into a position of such prominence.

The United Nations' headquarters in New York City

Heidi Montag, version 1.0

But unlike lab-created sandwich spreads and surgically enhanced TV starlets, the UN is quite useful. Here are some things you may not know about the UN:

★ The United Nations feeds 110 million people each year, half of them children. (We're guessing the other half are adults.)

★ The United Nations has helped nearly fifty million refugees start new lives. Refugees are people driven from their countries because of violence or disasters.

★ As of 2008, the United Nations had roughly 88,000 peacekeepers in seventeen countries trying to halt wars, or at least slow them down.

★ The words "United Nations" are an anagram for "detain in snout," "anus dentition," and, rather aptly, "a disunion tent."

See? You like the UN more already and you're, what, only 170 words into this section.

HOW THE UN CAME TO BE
(Looking Back to BCE)

Conflict is part of human nature. For as long as there have been two people on earth, there has been fighting.[35] The United Nations exists to counter human impulse. It exists to promote the peaceful resolution of the world's conflicts.

The need for a world forum to help peacefully settle international disputes has been evident since the beginning of history. We mean that literally. The first history book[36] ever written was Thucydides' *The History of the Peloponnesian War,* about the idiotic war fought in the fifth century BCE between Athens and Sparta.

Ancient Greece was violent. Even the pencil sketches fought.

---

35. For a deep, thoughtful explanation of why humans can't seem to resolve conflicts peacefully, you'll have to wait for the publication of our upcoming book on conflict resolution, tentatively titled _Sit Down and Shut Up_.

36. Actually, it wasn't a book; it was a scroll of papyrus. But why nitpick?

Diddy: a bust of Thucydides, author of The History of the Peloponnesian War. *We assume he had eyes in real life.*

THE LEAGUE OF NATIONS

Only after the industrial-scale carnage of WWI (1914–1918)[37] did world leaders finally see the wisdom of building a permanent venue for world diplomacy.

Yep, it's the same Woodrow Wilson (see p. 43).

In 1918, with the war nearing its end, U.S. president Woodrow Wilson[38] gave a speech calling for the formation of a league of nations where conflicts could be talked out.

Europe's leaders thought Wilson's idea was swell. They loved it so much, in fact, that when the treaty officially ending the war was signed in 1919, they went ahead and formed a league of nations. Coincidentally, or perhaps because they weren't terribly imaginative, they called it the League of Nations.

In his history, Thucydides (or, as we like to call him, Diddy) tells how the Greek powers Athens and Sparta pounded the kappa kappa krappa out of each other for nearly a decade, only to turn around and sign a peace deal that saw the return of all the territory each had just captured.

What the—? The two sides destroyed one another for a *tie*! Pointless, huh?

Sadly, it took humankind more than two millennia for the Diddy's words to sink in. We know it's a slow read, but come on!

World War I was the first large war to include aircraft, machine guns, tanks, and poison gas.

---

37. In 1916, for example, French and German troops spent nearly the entire year fighting for a single small town called Verdun, in northeastern France. When the battle was over, 300,000 French and German soldiers were dead—the population of Pittsburgh or Anaheim—and the battle lines were pretty much where they were on the day the battle began.
38. America's first alliterative president; he was followed by Calvin Coolidge, Herbert Hoover, and Ronald Reagan.

Bearded, bundled up, and looking at you sideways, Henry Cabot Lodge even looks like an isolationist.

A conference hall was built. A Nobel Peace Prize was awarded (to Wilson). And forty-four countries joined the League on the first day.

Sadly, the U.S. wasn't one of them. Huh?

Despite Wilson's enthusiasm, the U.S. Senate voted nay on joining the League. Led by isolationist Senator Henry Cabot Lodge,[39] the Senate thought staying out of the League would decrease the likelihood of U.S. involvement in a second world war. Good one, Henry.

Reluctance to get involved in Europe's diplomatic biz-ness is actually an old American trait. It makes sense if you think about it. Remember, the U.S. was founded by people who were so sick of Europe that they sailed a large ocean to get away from it (see America's First Witch Hunt, page 139). Our first president, George Washington, once called treaties with foreign governments one of the "most baneful foes of republican government." Them's fightin' words!

Historians today almost all agree that the U.S.'s failure to join spelled doom[40] for the League of Nations. The League may have gained a parking space, but it lost the world's biggest, most prosperous, most dynamic democracy from its negotiating table.

But in fairness to American isolationists, it's not clear that even an active U.S. membership would have changed the League's fate.

The League of Nations was, by design, pretty toothless.[41] It could make declarations, but it had no way of enforcing them. When Nazi Germany, imperial Japan, and fascist Italy began pounding their war drums in the mid-1930s, the League of Nations could only whine and whimper. Without any military at its disposal, the League could get about as forceful as using ALL CAPS and underlining.

In 1939, a mere two decades after the League of Nations was formed to prevent another world war, World War II began. D'oh! This was especially frustrating because Germany basically wanted to save the face it lost by being crushed in World War I. To do so, it set about trying to conquer Europe. The League of Nations was supposed to stop the pesky Germans at the first sign of trouble. Oh, well.

World War II was the deadliest conflict in human history by far. We haven't topped it yet, knock on wood. It's the only conflict ever where human beings actually used nuclear weapons against each other. (Or, more specifically, the United States used nuclear weapons against Japan.)

The atomic bomb explodes over Nagasaki, Japan.

---

39. Voted "Senator whose name most sounds like a musty old hotel" in the 1919 Senate yearbook.
40. O-O-O-M.
41. So toothless, it couldn't even make the "th" sound.

World War II's unprecedented destruction awoke the United States to the idea that the world wouldn't ignore us just because we ignored *it*. Try as we did to avoid the fighting, the Japanese dragged us in with their attack on Pearl Harbor—followed immediately by Hitler's declaration of war against the U.S.

President Franklin D. Roosevelt's administration believed that cooperation between governments was no longer a pie-in-the-sky fantasy but a necessity. So, in the middle of WWII, the Roosevelt Administration began to push its allies to formally create a new-and-improved League of Nations—a tougher, less dithering, more American organization.

To that end, the United Nations boasts two key features the League of Nations lacked.

See, it really is like the grown-ups' table. No sporks allowed!

1. THE SECURITY COUNCIL

The fifteen-member Security Council[42] of the UN decides issues of war and peace. If the UN is a dinner party, the Security Council is like the grown-ups' table.

The Security Council itself is comprised of five permanent members: the U.S., Russia (formerly the Soviet Union), the UK, France, and China.[43] The Security Council requires only a majority vote before approving action, but permanent members have veto power over any UN vote.

By contrast, the old League of Nations couldn't even order lunch without unanimous consent.

2. ITS OWN FIGHTING FORCE

The other tool the UN has that the League did not: the use of force. Though the UN does not have a military per se, its member nations make troops available for UN-sanctioned military missions.

Since its inception, the UN has deployed its blue-helmeted peacekeepers on sixty-three missions.

A typical UN peacekeeping mission involves monitoring cease-fires between opposing military forces and trying to protect civilian populations caught between warring parties. UN peacekeepers even helped found a country, aiding East Timor's transition to independence after it freed itself from Indonesian control.

UN peacekeepers in Ivory Coast. There's more muscle in this picture alone than the League of Nations had during its entire existence.

---

42. The original council had eleven members. It was expanded to fifteen in 1965, after the UN ambassador from Luxembourg found four extra chairs in the UN headquarters basement. Okay, not really the chairs part.

43. When China's government was toppled in 1949 in a Communist revolution, the UN did not recognize the Communists as the legitimate government of China. Instead, control of China's UN seat was retained by the deposed government, based in Taiwan. The Chinese government in Beijing wasn't seated at the UN until 1971.

UNIMOSITY

The UN is more American than apple pie. Apple pie is actually from northern Europe. Surprise!

The UN was conceived at the Dumbarton Oaks mansion in Washington DC. It was named by FDR. Representatives from fifty nations signed the UN charter in San Francisco. Its headquarters is in Manhattan.

Take that, apple pie!

So then why do a majority[44] of Americans dislike the UN?

Simply put: for most of its history, the UN hasn't done what the U.S. has wanted it to do.

When American leaders came up with the idea of putting World War II's winners in charge of the UN, it apparently didn't occur to them that the U.S. and the Soviet Union might be locked in a Cold War for the next four decades.

The Berlin Wall (pictured here in 1975) was the most iconic symbol of U.S.-Soviet antagonism. Luckily, it was torn down before they installed the Berlin Roof and the Berlin Carpeting.

Think about it: two enemies each with veto power on the same committee? It's a recipe for grief.

The first clear sign that the UN might not be all the U.S. dreamed it would be came just two days after the first New York meeting of the Security Council in 1946—in a gym at Hunter College in the Bronx. UN headquarters in Manhattan had not yet been built. The U.S. pushed for a Security Council vote to help nudge Soviet troops out of northern Iran.[45] The Soviet ambassador refused to debate and stormed out of the meeting.

This pattern repeated itself, um, repeatedly for several years. The Commies were all-the-time storming off.

Honestly, though, this was fine with American leaders. With the Soviets absent from Security Council meetings, the U.S. was able to push through its proposals without fear of a Soviet veto.

The best example of this was the Korean War.

When North Korea invaded South Korea in 1950, the UN Security Council was able to give official backing to the U.S.-led counterinvasion of the Korean Peninsula because the Soviets boycotted the vote. If the phrase "U.S.-led UN counterinvasion of the Korean Peninsula" sounds unfamiliar to you, you might know it by its other name: the Korean War.

General Douglas MacArthur, in Korea, unintentionally created ace material for one of the most popular TV shows ever.

---

44. A 2007 Pew Research Center poll showed just 48 percent of Americans had a positive impression of the UN. In a related study, 92 percent of Americans we asked think it's funny that there's a polling outfit called Pew.

45. Iran was a crucial supply route by which the U.S. helped arm the Soviets against the Nazis during the Second World War.

As the century progressed, the Soviets wised up. They began using their veto power more and nurtured relationships with the dozens of countries in Asia and Africa that gained independence from European colonizers during the 1950s, '60s, and '70s. By the time the 1970s rolled around, countries unfriendly to U.S. and Western European foreign policy began to dominate UN discourse, particularly in the General Assembly.

Zaire's former dictator and all-around Fly Guy Mobotu Sese Seko (left), a frequent topic of discussion in the UN during the tumultuous 1970s (No, the fur cap is not faux.)

In the 1980s, when political conservatives became the majority in DC, they began to snipe at the UN for its perceived hostility. In a particularly petty gesture, the U.S. delayed payment of its UN membership dues. As the organization's biggest contributor, this was crippling to the UN. Nonpayment also denied the American people the free tote bag and thermal coffee mug that come with every paid UN membership.

Although the U.S. won the Cold War as Communism collapsed at the turn of the 1990s, U.S. animosity toward the UN continued. As the world's lone superpower, we don't seem to have a lot of time for a roomful of African, Asian, and European diplomats telling us what we can't or shouldn't do. In 2008,

46. It originally stood for United Nations International Children's Emergency Fund. The name was shortened in 1953, but the acronym was retained.

Republican candidate John McCain said he supported the formation of a rival to the UN called the League of Democracies. It'd be like the UN but would exclude non-democracies like Russia and China.

But honestly, does anyone think China, Sudan, Russia, and Iran are suddenly going to be more cooperative with a League of Democracies that excludes them than they are with the UN? Where did McCain get this wacky idea, anyway? From his good friend Joe the Plumber?

The bottom line is this: Americans love the UN when it does what we want (e.g., enacting and maintaining economic sanctions on Saddam Hussein's Iraq). But we hate it when it balks at our proposals (e.g., not supporting the U.S. invasion of Iraq in 2003). The rest is noise.

AN INCOMPLETE LIST OF THE UN'S GREATEST ACHIEVEMENTS

The U.S. paid $453 million in dues to the UN in 2008. That's $1.50 per American. What do we get for the equivalent of a Snapple?

The UN is the most successful humanitarian organization in the world. We would say "Period. End of sentence," then move on to the next chapter, but book publishers demand examples. So bossy.

★ The best-known humanitarian project of the UN is UNICEF[46] (which, puzzlingly, stands for United Nations Children's Fund). UNICEF promotes and protects children's welfare. It is active in 190 countries promoting education and nutrition and rescuing children from abuse and exploitation.

A child in Congo receives a measles vaccine from UNICEF.

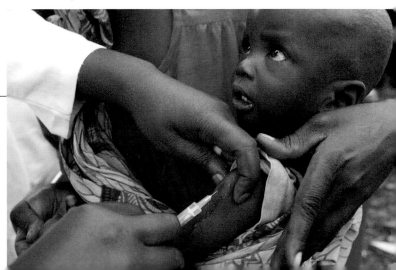

★ Have you ever contracted smallpox from eating at the breakfast buffet at Shoney's? Us neither. You can thank the people who make those see-through buffet cough-guard thingies for that . . . and you can also thank the WHO.[47] The WHO is the World Health Organization, the arm of the UN devoted to improving health around the globe.

Pieces of an Iraqi "supergun" found and dismantled by UN weapons inspectors before it could be used against U.S. troops

Representatives of the WHO—well, close enough

★ With a staff barely large enough to fill a downtown office building, the Office of the United Nations High Commissioner for Refugees (UNHCR) protects nearly thirty-three million people driven from their homes by war, oppression, or natural disaster. Refugee camps aren't pleasant places, but in undeveloped parts of the world, they beat the heck out of wandering by yourself. And each year the UN finds new homes for tens of thousands of refugees—helping them resettle in well-off, peaceful countries.

★ The International Atomic Energy Agency (IAEA) is the arm of the UN that monitors nuclear programs around the world. Countries that have signed the nuclear Non-Proliferation Treaty (NPT) have to allow IAEA inspectors to rummage through their nuclear facilities. The IAEA's track record is pretty good. Of all the countries that have signed on to the NPT, only North Korea has managed to develop a nuke. So, not a perfect record, but not bad.

You may recall, when the U.S. went into Iraq in 2003 (ostensibly to find WMD), there was widespread fear that Saddam Hussein's forces would hit U.S. troops with chemical or biological weapons. Well, he didn't—in part because he couldn't. For that you can thank UN inspectors, who spent much of the 1990s finding, cataloging, and destroying Saddam Hussein's WMD.

Altogether, not bad for the price of a Snapple.

---

47. Not the seminal rock group that brought the world such classics as "My Generation" and "Baba O'Riley."

I SHOULD KNOW WHAT NATO IS, BUT WHY DON'T I?

Probably because its acronym isn't nearly as catchy as WHO. NATO, or the North Atlantic Treaty Organization, is, in its own words, "an alliance of 28 countries from North America and Europe committed to fulfilling the goals of the North Atlantic Treaty signed on 4 April 1949." The treaty stated that if any country in the organization were attacked, all the member countries would fight back on its behalf. For the first forty years of its existence, the specific goals of the treaty could be summed up in three words: "No Commies allowed!" NATO flexed its muscles against its Commie counterpart, the Warsaw Pact, so that neither side would resort to an all-out nuclear war. Having hundreds of missiles pointed at each other also helped. After the collapse of the Soviet Union in 1991, NATO poached a few countries from the old Warsaw Pact (former Commie stalwarts including Poland and the Czech Republic) and focused its efforts on peacekeeping missions in the Balkans as well as providing support and training in Afghanistan and Iraq.

ARE THE GOLDEN ARCHES A MORE EFFECTIVE SYMBOL OF PEACEKEEPING THAN THE UN'S BLUE HELMETS?

The New York Times columnist and author Thomas Friedman wrote in his 2000 book *The Lexus and the Olive Tree*: "No two countries that both had McDonald's had fought a war against each other since each got its McDonald's."

Was Friedman suggesting that foods like deep-fried apple pie and reconstituted onions contain sedatives that suppress mankind's aggressive impulses? Perhaps. Goodness knows the first thing we like to do after a Big Mac, large fries, and soda is nap.

But Friedman's point wasn't gastronomic. It was economic.

Countries with McDonald's restaurants, he was arguing, have market economies that are more integrated into the world economy than their non–Mickey D-havin' counterparts. Integration into the world economy, or globalization, reduces the likelihood of war because the cost of warfare is too high to citizens. When a country's powerful business leaders stand to lose bundles of cash if their nation goes to war, the nation is less likely to go to war.

Friedman has a good point. Countries with extensive economic ties tend not to go to war as often as countries with few economic ties.

Unfortunately, Friedman's McDonald's example is untrue.

★ In 1989, the U.S. invaded Panama and overthrew its government. Panama had a McDonald's at the time.

★ NATO, which is made up of countries chock-full o' McDonald's, bombed Serbia in 1999—which also had a McDonald's.

★ Israel and Lebanon went at it in 2006. Both countries have McDonald's.

★ India and Pakistan have lobbed artillery at each other for decades and have even gone to the brink of nuclear war. Pakistan got the first of its twenty McDonald's in 1998. India also got its McDonald's franchises in the 1990s—although one could argue that McDonald's India, which shuns beef in favor of chicken and vegetarian items like the Chatpata McAloo Tikki Burger, isn't even a real McDonald's.

DISCUSSION QUESTIONS (OPTIONAL)

1 Why is there war, and what can we do to stop it— or at least reduce its likelihood? Will it ever be possible just to hug it out?

2 Have you ever asked foreigners what they think of the United States? What did they say? Did you cry afterward or high-five them?

3 Every previous dominant world power eventually faded. Do you think the U.S.'s power will fade? If so, is that a good or bad thing? (After all, the British standard of living sharply increased as the British Empire fell apart.)

4 Which country is more dependent on the other, China or the U.S.? Why?

5 Is this the best book ever written, or merely the best book ever written in English?

CHAPTER 5

GOD BLESS THIS MESS

Peaceful Religions and Why They Fight

INTRODUCTION

Explaining the Unexplainable
(with the Help of the Puritans)

★ **AMERICA'S FIRST WITCH HUNT**

LIVING WITH MONO(THEISM)

★ **ACT I**
Judaism

★ **ACT II**
Christianity

★ **ACT III**
Islam

★ **ABRAHAM**
Father Figure to All and Star of Genesis (Pre–Phil Collins)

★ **JUST A LITTLE MO'-MO'-MO'**
A Fuller Understanding of the Big Three Monotheisms with the Help of Their Three Biggest Players

★ **JERUSALEM**
It's Mine, Mine, Mine!

★ **ISM-SCHISM**
Religious Denominations within the Big Three

CHECK "OTHER" ☑

Religions Celebrities Know About

★ **HINDUISM**
Oh, My Gods!

★ **BUDDHISM**
Sure He's Fat and Happy—That's Enlightenment!

★ **CHINESE TRADITIONAL RELIGION**
The Tao of Being Pronounced "Dow"

★ **INDIGENOUS OR TRIBAL RELIGIONS**
Putting the Spirit Back in Spiritual

★ **OFF-OFF BROADWAY**
A Fun Glance at Some of the Smaller Faiths

INTRODUCTION
Explaining the Unexplainable
(with the Help of the Puritans)

Philosophy is questions that may never be answered. Religion is answers that may never be questioned.

—Anonymous

For something to qualify as a religion—at least as far as this book goes—we can say the following:

1. It promotes the idea that there is a higher power (or powers) in the universe.
2. It involves activity that recognizes and honors this higher power (or powers).
3. It provides rules for how to live, inspired by this higher power (or powers).

Take the chapter's opening phrase: "We swear to God." If taken literally, it illustrates our definition of religion in a nutshell. We're making an oath in the presence of God that what we're saying is true—so the hypothetical assumption is that we believe in God (#1). Hence, the act of swearing is a religious activity (#2). Finally, by performing this little religious ritual, we're showing you that we adhere to an ethical code: we tell the truth and we want you to believe it (#3). And just so you know, we also swear not to use the word "hence" anymore in this chapter. It's annoying.

Defining the word "religion" is relatively simple; it's a lot harder to approach the practice of religion in a calm, detached, scientific way. Faith is *so* deeply personal, so bound up with how we define ourselves . . . Maybe it's impossible to look at it objectively—or, for that matter, without getting mad at someone who disagrees with our view of it.

And that brings up a host of other questions. (Yikes.) To name one: are science and religion mutually exclusive? Albert Einstein—esteemed brainiac and bad-hair guy—didn't think so,

We swear to God: saying right off the bat that religion is unexplainable isn't meant as a clever dodge. From the moment we ("we" in this case meaning humanity as a whole) first began to record our thoughts, and probably long before that, we've been asking the same questions. Why are we here? How are we supposed to live and get along? Do these kinds of questions even matter? Religion—in all its varieties—says yes. But why are there so many varieties of religion? The existence of religion itself is difficult to explain, even for the faithful. Forget the explanation; is there even a single definition for the actual word?

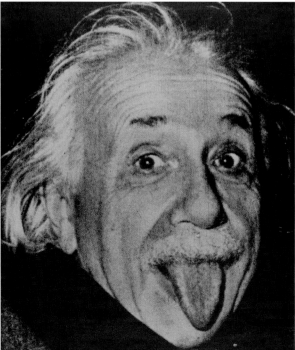

and he was a devout Jew. "God is clever, but not dishonest," he once said, meaning that the outrageous discoveries he made about time, space, and the nutty fabric of the universe didn't disprove God's existence, but demonstrated God in action.[1]

On the other hand, Einstein didn't believe in an afterlife. He didn't believe that God judged people based on their behavior, either. Here he differed from many of his fellow Jews, who believe that upon death, the righteous will be reunited with loved ones and the wicked will be punished for eternity. Not only was there no heaven or hell for Einstein, there wasn't even a purgatory.

EINSTEIN AND BUDDHISM

Here's a quote that is attributed to Einstein but never proven to be his: "If there is any religion that could cope with modern scientific needs it would be Buddhism." Buddhism, as we'll see, is the one major world religion that does not promote the worship of any deity or deities. Yet it still promotes belief in a higher power, which is why we can define Buddhism as a religion. It does not, however, explain the yoga craze that has swept the nation in the last decade.

Of course, we're not here to judge or insist upon the truth of any religious beliefs. We're here only to take a brief look at *what* different people believe. As we'll see (and as Einstein well knew) judging others' religious beliefs or insisting upon the truth of one's own can lead to misunderstanding (at best) or catastrophe (at worst)—often in ways we can't imagine or anticipate. If you want a classic example, you don't have to look any further than our nation's founding: specifically, at the Puritans.

AMERICA'S FIRST WITCH HUNT

In spite of their noble intentions—pursuing religious freedom and escaping tyranny—the Puritans are still probably best known for massacring suspected witches.[2] This is too bad,

Puritans, perhaps on witch patrol

1. At least that's what we think he meant. Like religion itself, a lot of what Einstein said is subject to interpretation.
2. Well, that and for their pointy black hats, which, come to think of it, look a lot like witches' pointy black hats.

because before 1692, they lived for more than sixty years in relative tranquillity (a bare-bones tranquillity, but it was scandal free) as the largest population of European settlers in the New World. Having set up shop in the Massachusetts Bay Colony in 1630—a mere ten years after the famous *Mayflower* Pilgrims landed at Plymouth Rock—British Puritans began sailing to America by the thousands during the mid-1600s[3] for pretty much two reasons: they thought the Reformation was a crock, and they believed the Church of England was doomed.

At the time, the Church of England was, for all intents and purposes, Great Britain's state religion. That meant that if you didn't buy into it, you didn't really belong in Great Britain in the first place. This was a bum deal for the Puritans, who were definitely *not* on board with how the Church of England preached that British royalty was chosen by God to rule. They also disapproved of the Church of England's big, gaudy churches, the gaudy rituals it borrowed from the Roman Catholic Church, and how its gaudy clergy made up laws that didn't come straight from the Bible.

The Puritans were sticklers for the Bible. Their name, taken from the word "pure," says it all. They wanted to practice Christianity the way Jesus himself practiced it. Jesus didn't talk about "the divine right of kings" in the gospels (see Monotheism, Messiah-Style, pages 157–159). Nope, that was Church of England talk. And since the Church of England refused to listen to anyone else, the Puritans saw England as beyond reform, even in light of the Reformation. It was time to start fresh in *New* England.

WHAT WAS THE REFORMATION, ANYWAY?

The Reformation was a power-to-the-people revolution to change Christianity, which, until 1517, was dominated by the Roman Catholic Church. (Yep, the word "Protestant" comes from "protest.") What angered the Protestants most was the sale of indulgences: forgiveness of sins and the guarantee of a heavenly afterlife in exchange for cash money in the here and now. If Einstein had lived in medieval Europe and *had* believed in purgatory, indulgences would have allowed him to buy his way out of damnation by paying off Roman Catholic priests. The good news: the Roman Catholic Church hasn't allowed the sale of indulgences since the Council of Trent (1545–1563), a gathering convened by Catholic higher-ups to put a symbolic sock in the Protestants' mouths. A lot of dubious practices were formally abandoned there.

3. This mass ocean crossing was also known as "the Great Migration." Great in terms of numbers, not the ocean crossing itself, which probably wasn't so enjoyable. Nobody could bathe. Keep in mind that toothpaste and stick deodorant wouldn't be invented for another three centuries, either.

Things **NOT** to do in the New World

☆ Take a "booze cruise"
☆ Wear gaudy clothing
☆ Misplace boyfriend's Bible or black hat
☆ Joke about Satan
☆ Speak in gibberish
☆ Eat stale bread

It all started on a cold winter's night. (Seriously, that's when it began, in January 1692. Cue eerie soundtrack here.) Elizabeth Parris, the nine-year-old daughter of the town's reverend, Samuel Parris, fell ill—followed by eight other girls in rapid succession. It wasn't a case of the sniffles, either. This was serious business, marked by convulsions, hallucinations, itchy skin, and, perhaps most frightening of all, gibberish.[4]

"**Welcome to America.**"

"Fiddle-dee-diddle-dee . . ."

Unfortunately, their fear of corruption—and of tyranny, temptation, sin, evil, Satan, and, really, any sort of pleasure, including sex (even if you *weren't* a Puritan, life in seventeenth-century Massachusetts wasn't exactly an MTV Spring Break extravaganza)—started to make them a little paranoid.

Which brings us to the Salem witch trials.

---

4. It's true. Nothing quite frightens like a bunch of little girls caught in a trance, babbling incomprehensibly.

By February, Salem was a mess. Nobody could cure the sickness or determine its cause. Reverend Parris and the town elders began to suspect that something wicked was afoot. It was the only logical explanation. Who but Satan and his minions (witches) would inflict such misery upon innocent girls?[5] And who but Satan could convince minions to become witches in the first place?

Over the next seven months, the witch hunt began in earnest.[6] More than one hundred and fifty men and women were rounded up on other nonexistent evidence. Twenty were executed. Five died in jail.

Of the suspects executed, none ever confessed to witchcraft, though to do so would have spared their lives. Why didn't they? Well, confessing to a crime they hadn't committed would be lying—a sin as bad as murder, they believed, and one that guaranteed them an eternity in hell. They figured it was better to die honest than to live damned. The tragic irony here is so rich on so many levels that it's tough to make jokes.

Finally, on October 29, 1692, governor of Massachusetts William Phips stopped the insanity by declaring the Salem witch trials over. Those in jail were freed. The sickness, too, faded as abruptly and mysteriously as it had appeared.

5. Yes, we're being deliberately overdramatic and silly. Sometimes humor is the only way to cope with a centuries-old tragedy brought on by a lethal combination of overzealousness, ignorance, and fear.
6. Hence the term "witch hunt." Oh, right—we swore we weren't going to say "hence" anymore. Whoops! It seems we aren't so religious after all, at least in terms of our hypothetical example at the chapter's start.

WAS THE TOWN OF SALEM ON DRUGS?

No, this isn't a typo but actually a theory that has gained credence in recent years. The rye bread the Puritans ate might have been contaminated with the ergot fungus, which has almost exactly the same chemical properties as LSD. Symptoms of ergot poisoning include hallucinations, paranoia, rashes, and, yes, the all-terrifying gibberish. Not only would those poisoned have seemed possessed, but their accusers would have been more likely to blame the behavior on witchcraft or Satan because *they* would have been high as kites, too. In many ways, the whole town of Salem would have been like the "bad trip tent" at Woodstock in 1969—only minus the peace, love, and music.

They were crazy for bread back in Salem!

In the three hundred years since the Salem witch trials, lots of people have wrung their hands to the point of clamminess, wondering how the town could have spun so out of control. *Was* there a demonic presence? Or was it just plain old mass hysteria, made worse by a confluence of mundane factors: harsh living conditions, poor sanitation, and a lousy diet? Or can it be traced to the danger that lies at the heart of every religion—that when a group becomes convinced of the truth of their own beliefs at the expense of everything else, they stop being able to think or behave rationally? The Puritans came to America to *escape* evil practiced in the name of God, not to become its poster children.

The real truth is, we'll never know. Much as we can never know the truth about anything we don't experience firsthand . . . which includes everything we accept on faith.

Makes you think, huh? We figured it was important to start off on such shaky footing because the doubt that leads to discovery—and, on a happier note, to plenty of positive and worthwhile endeavors (spiritual and otherwise)—lies at the heart of religion, too. Now if only we could all get along.

LIVING WITH MONO(THEISM)

God made so many different kinds of people. Why would he allow only one way to serve him?

—Martin Buber, religious philosopher, 1878–1965

More than half of all human beings, approximately 54 percent, believe in the same God—a pretty amazing statistic. It's hard to say "more than half" about anything when it comes to the world's population, except for the obvious—"More than half of us pick our noses." But like all things religious, the reality of that 54 percent isn't so simple.

The God of Judaism, Christianity, and Islam can be found in many of the same places. But each of the Big Three[7] perceives God differently—as do denominations within each of the three faiths, as do congregations within those denominations . . . and so on and so on, down to the individual Jew, Christian, or Muslim.

So where can we find this same God?

Luckily, that is simple: in the first line of the Bible. "In the beginning, God created Heaven and Earth." There God is, in text held sacred by all three faiths—which means that no matter what you believe as a Jew, Christian, or Muslim, God's first written appearance is exactly the same. And since this blunt proclamation of monotheism was written by Jews, we'll begin with them. They started it.

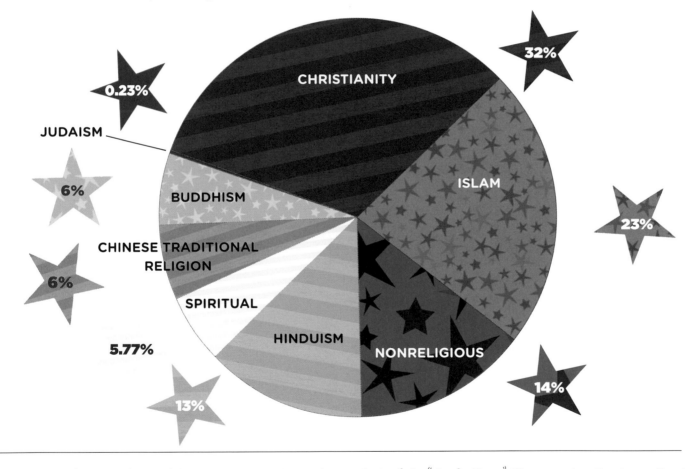

7. As far as we know, nobody actually calls the three major monotheistic faiths "the Big Three." This is our less-than-clever attempt at shorthand.

ACT I *Judaism*

As the poet said, "Only God can make a tree"—probably because it's so hard to figure out how to get the bark on.
—*Woody Allen*

In many ways, Jews consider themselves to be part of one big, lively family. For that reason, being Jewish is as much a personal brand identity as it is a religion. Three thousand or so years ago, members of this family began to write stories about one another—mostly about their laws, their homeland of Israel, and why they felt they were pretty darn special. They had a good reason to think they were special: they were the only tribe around who had a unique relationship with God, thanks to the special bond God had with Sarah and Abraham, the tribe's ancestral mom and pop.

Over the next several centuries the Jews cobbled these stories together, put them in order, edited them, added some inspiring new ones—and eventually produced what became the Tanakh.[8] In some ways, the Tanakh is not unlike a religious-themed family scrapbook or photo album, only without the photos.

WHAT MAKES A PERSON JEWISH, AND DOES MADONNA COUNT?

Good question. Most Jews subscribe, either literally or symbolically, to the "Laws of Moses"—rules and guidelines for how to live, as laid down in the Tanakh. And every Jew believes, either literally or symbolically, that he or she is descended from Sarah and Abraham. So in theory, all Jews are related—"members of the tribe." This has actually caused problems in recent years. Not in any sort of inbred hillbilly way, but in terms of proving who's a Jew and who isn't. Judaism is matrilineal. In other words, you need a Jewish mother to be a Jew. Today, Jews who want to become Israeli citizens must provide evidence that they have Jewish mothers; otherwise they will most likely be denied. While it's possible to convert, many religious Israelis don't recognize converts as "truly" Jewish. Only people with Jewish mothers make the cut.

Wait—what about Madonna? No, seriously. Does she qualify as a Jewish mother, given her recent (and very public) dabbling in the kabbalah? And what is the kabbalah, anyway? That's a question for our next sidebar. But in answer to the Madonna question: no, dabbling in the kabbalah does not make a person Jewish, any more than, say, eating a kosher hot dog does.

(LEFT) *"My personal take on Judaism is every bit as authentic as my late 90s/early 00s techno."*
(RIGHT) *Marilyn Monroe converted to Judaism to marry Arthur Miller, who wrote the play* The Crucible *about the Salem witch trials! It's almost like God is deliberately connecting the dots.*

8. A Hebrew acronym: T for Torah (the books of Moses), N for nevi'im (the prophets), and K for ketuvim (writings). Nowadays, TNK is also an acronym for a Russian oil company. It's probably best just to view this as an odd coincidence and not read any apocalyptic symbolism into it.

WHAT'S WITH THE RED STRING?

The kabbalah is a set of two-thousand-year-old teachings that concerns itself with the mystical aspects of Judaism: specifically the nature of God (who and what is God?), the nature of the human soul (who and what are we?), and the nature of heaven (where is it, and am I invited?). Traditionally the kabbalah wasn't even taught to people under the age of forty because it was considered to be too difficult for a young person to understand. It has gained popularity in modern times among Jews and non-Jews alike because—like the mystical teachings of many other religions—it purportedly enables its practitioners to receive divine enlightenment. ("Kabbalah" is, in fact, the Hebrew word for "receiving.") For example:

As in Christian and Islamic mysticism, the kabbalah teaches that humans can experience the divine through miraculous dreams and visions.

As in Hindu mysticism, the kabbalah breaks down God into different essences. (Not to be confused with high-end fragrances such as Fendi Life Essence.) In the kabbalah, these are known as the Ten Sefirot (the Hebrew word for "enumerations"); in Hinduism they are known as "avatars" (see Hinduism: Oh, My Gods!, pages 169–170).

As in Buddhist mysticism, the kabbalah helps its practitioners eliminate suffering through meditation (see Buddhism: Sure He's Fat and Happy— *That's* Enlightenment!, pages 170–171).

As in Taoist mysticism, the kabbalah suggests that the divine has no beginning and is without end (see Chinese Traditional Religion: The Tao of Being Pronounced "Dow," page 172).

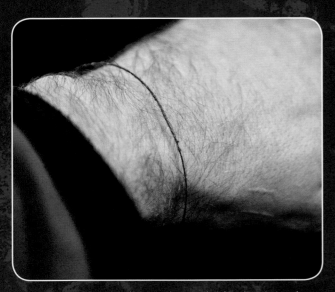

In case you were wondering, wearing a red string does not make a person Jewish either.

FAMOUS KABBALAH FANS

MADONNA

WINONA RYDER

DEMI MOORE

JEFF GOLDBLUM

ASHTON KUTCHER

VICTORIA BECKHAM

BRITNEY SPEARS

DAVID BECKHAM

ELIZABETH TAYLOR

GWYNETH PALTROW

ACT II *Christianity*

Roughly five hundred years after the Jews finalized the Tanakh (see page 145, footnote 8), Jesus was born into the tribe. He studied what his ancestors had written and dug a lot of it—particularly that very first line of Genesis, and the parts about being nice to others, and how we should all try to make the world a better place. But he didn't think you had to be a fellow Jew to have a unique relationship with God. He took the Facebook and MySpace approach: as long as you signed up and friended *him*, he automatically considered you part of God's extended network.

---

fakebook | Search 🔍 | Home   Profile   Account ▾

Jesus Christ It's not easy having such a successful father. I mean Father. on Sunday

Wall   Info   Photos   Notes

Add to My Page's Favorites
Suggest to Friends
Subscribe via SMS

4,358,175 People Like This

Peter   Matthew   Mary

Jesus Christ Did you watch the Heat game last night? LeBron thanked me for that dunk, but it was really all him.
Yesterday at 10:36am · Like · Comment

👍 24,604 people like this.

💬 View all 1,224 comments

Write a comment...

Jesus Christ Good Friday? It wasn't so good for me.
Yesterday at 10:36am · Like · Comment

👍 8,719 people like this.

💬 View all 7,773 comments

Write a comment...

Jesus Christ Mel Gibson made, like $600 million off Passion of the Christ. Not even a thank you note.
Saturday at 10:03am · Like · Comment

👍 22,523 people like this.

💬 View all 1,142 comments

Write a comment...

Jesus Christ What's heaven like? It's life's afterparty!
Saturday at 10:02am · Like · Comment

👍 6,634 people like this.

👤● Chat (57)

Home, James?

IS THERE ANY HISTORICAL EVIDENCE THAT JESUS LIVED?

Well . . . you sort of have to take this on faith, too. As of this writing, no concrete historical evidence has been found to prove that a Jew named Jesus lived in Roman-occupied Palestine in the first century CE. (The closest archaeologists have come is the 2002 discovery in Jerusalem of the supposed ossuary—a limestone coffin—of Jesus' brother, James. Its inscription, "James, son of Joseph, brother of Jesus," was later determined to be a forgery. Oh, well.) And while the gospels are supposed to be firsthand historical accounts of his life by the apostles, no concrete evidence has been found to prove this, either. The apostles might not have even written the gospels; they might have only gotten the credit for them. Sort of like how the Mings got credit for the vases they didn't make.

A lot of Jews didn't agree. Neither did the Romans who occupied Israel (or Palestine, as it was known at the time). The Romans eventually got so fed up with Jesus' talk about how the kingdom of heaven was the only kingdom that mattered (meaning Rome didn't) that they decided to send him there.

Crucifying Jesus didn't prevent his word from getting out, though.[9] His followers and a few close pals, the apostles—particularly Matthew, Mark, Luke, and John—jotted down everything they remembered about his life, death, and resurrection. These writings eventually became the New Testament. It was a lot like a scrapbook, too, only with a different message: Jesus didn't just have a unique relationship with God; he was God, in the flesh.

Over the next several centuries, people all over the Roman Empire read or heard about Jesus.[10] The vast majority of them weren't part of Jesus' original family, the Jews, but they wholeheartedly subscribed to the idea of having a unique relationship with God. By the time the Roman Empire fell apart, in the late sixth and early seventh centuries CE, most of its population had converted to Christianity, including its emperors—a sweet (if slightly late) feather in the cap for those who were fed to lions or otherwise persecuted for believing in Jesus at the start.

Early Christianity was no walk in the park—or day at the zoo.

---

9. From the Romans' perspective, you might even argue that the Crucifixion was the most colossal backfire in human history.

10. The early Christians were experts at what we now call word-of-mouth or "viral" marketing.

Ευαγγέλιο

IT WAS ALL GREEK TO THE APOSTLES

The New Testament was written entirely in Greek, mostly between the years 70 CE and 140 CE. Thanks to Alexander the Great, Greek was the common language of the eastern Roman Empire. Sort of like how, thanks to fifteenth-century conquistadors, Spanish is the common language of South America and, by extension, large chunks of New York City and Los Angeles. Also semirelated: the word "gospel" has become a synonym for "truth," even though each of the four gospels tells a slightly different version of Jesus' story. A good rule of thumb: any sacred text will have lots of inconsistencies.

Once the gospels had made the rounds all over Europe and the Middle East, the Christians translated their God-themed texts into Latin[11] and combined them into one hefty new book, which included the Tanakh, under the title the Old Testament. Jesus was a Jew, so much of what he preached, taught, or spoke of came straight from the Tanakh.[12] His words in the New Testament wouldn't make much sense if people didn't get the references to material from the Old Testament.[13]

Please pass the matzoh to the Host.

APOCRYPHA: THE BIBLE'S OUTTAKES

Did you know that there's a Gospel according to Judas? Yes, *that* Judas. It's true. It was ghostwritten on his behalf at the same time as the other gospels and then lost for centuries.

In it, Jesus and Judas are in cahoots. Jesus secretly asks Judas to betray him so Jesus can fulfill his own prophecy about the Crucifixion. Needless to say, this doesn't exactly jibe with the Bible's account, where Judas acts alone and sells out Jesus for thirty pieces of silver. As Judas (or his ghostwriter) tells it, Jesus longed to be free of his earthly existence. He told Judas that he wanted to be sacrificed and needed help—and Judas, being a good friend, agreed to go along with the plan. Not only does this version of events let Judas off the hook for the betrayal, but it also suggests that he actually did Jesus a favor by turning him over to the Romans. On an unrelated note, Jesus giggles a lot in this text (seriously), another possible reason why those who finalized the Bible chose not to include it.

Jesus and Judas (Priest)—still crazy after all these years!

---

11. Latin was the pope's language and the official language of the Catholic Church. Pig Latin, not so much.
12. Funny, people often forget that Jesus was a Jew. Did you know that the Last Supper was a Passover seder? Jesus was celebrating the holiday that commemorates the Israelites' freedom from slavery in Egypt. And here's an interesting tidbit: the Last Supper also explains why Catholic communion wafers are so thin. The "body of Christ" was originally matzo, unleavened bread.
13. Much like how The Godfather: Part II can't be fully appreciated unless you've also seen The Godfather.

As far as the Tanakh goes, anything written after the prophet Ezra (somewhere around 514 BCE) didn't make it, either. This includes the Book of the Maccabees, which tells the story of Hanukkah. It's not that Jews don't value these texts. They liked a good Hanukkah party as much as anyone. It's just that they were written after ancient Jewish rabbis decided that the Tanakh wasn't like Wikipedia, so it shouldn't be constantly updated. The pre-Ezra edition was final.

Enter Mohammad.[14] Yes, it was during this same tumultuous period in human history—when the Bible was first formalized, and when the Roman Empire finally disintegrated—that the revered founder of Islam lived in what is now Saudi Arabia.

At the age of forty, Mohammad received a visit from the archangel Gabriel, a major player in both the Old and New testaments. According to Gabriel, Mohammad had been handpicked to be God's last prophet on earth.

GABRIEL, WON'T YOU BLOW YOUR HORN?

Gabriel is *the* original old-school herald angel. In the Tanakh, he announces the coming apocalypse by appearing before the prophet Daniel to explain his psychedelic vision of a ram and a goat. (Gabriel's explanation: the animals represent fallen kingdoms at the end times, from whose ruins an evil king will rise up and make everyone's lives miserable.) In the New Testament, Gabriel announces the births of both John the Baptist and Jesus. Many Christians also believe he'll appear to announce the Second Coming. It's safe to say that if you hear his trumpet blowing and you aren't among the righteous, the jig is up.

Hipster artist's rendition of the archangel Gabriel, riffing hard and blowing the sweet sounds of the apocalypse on his trumpet

14. Also spelled "Muhammad" and "Mohammed." Given the human race's tendency to make things more complicated than necessary, no single non-Arabic spelling of Mohammad is correct. We've decided to go with the "Mo" MO to keep with the alliterative flow of "monotheism."

This was kind of a surprise to Mohammad, as he wasn't Jewish or Christian. He hadn't read the Bible, either. He couldn't read—not even Arabic, according to Islamic lore, anyway. Which makes sense: it's all the more miraculous that Mohammad wrote down God's words in the Koran if he couldn't actually *write*. (This also validates the Islamic beliefs that Arabic is a holy language and that the Koran can only truly be understood in its original tongue.) As God's last prophet, Mohammad was simply a messenger.

The message, in brief: it was time to graduate from Judaism and Christianity and to submit to God through Islam. (The word "Islam" literally means "submission" in Arabic.) Sure, God had inspired parts of the Bible, like its very first line. And sure, God had enjoyed a nice relationship with many Jewish prophets, as well as Jesus. But now it was up to Mohammad to spread the final word on God, period.

Mohammad didn't have much of a choice but to submit to God himself, seeing as God had called upon him personally. So he took down all of what God had to say, word for word. The result was the Koran,[15] which isn't so much a scrapbook as a transcript. In this way, the Koran is exactly like the Torah (the first five books of the Tanakh). Jewish tradition holds that God dictated the Torah in its entirety—including that very first line—to Moses on Mount Sinai (see Moses: The First Jewish Comedian, pages 155–156).

So we've come full circle. Transcript to transcript. "Words, words, words!" as Shakespeare wrote. It's a handy way to view how the world's Big Three monotheisms came to be: book by book by book. Muslims even refer to Jews and Christians as "People of the Book," a nod to the words, prophets—and Patriarch—all three faiths share.

Over the next few hundred years, Islam spread west across the Middle East and North Africa, much the same way Christianity had spread west across Europe. One religion traveled north of the Mediterranean; the other traveled south of it. In the ninth century, the two met up at the sea's most

The Koran

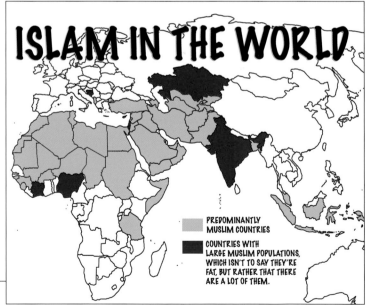

ISLAM IN THE WORLD

PREDOMINANTLY MUSLIM COUNTRIES

COUNTRIES WITH LARGE MUSLIM POPULATIONS, WHICH ISN'T TO SAY THEY'RE FAT, BUT RATHER THAT THERE ARE A LOT OF THEM.

15. "Koran" loosely translated means "read" or "recite." Similarly, many Christians refer to God as "the Word" and Jesus as "the Word made flesh." Monotheism is as word-centric as a vocabulary test.

western point, where Spain meets Morocco . . . and their respective believers have had a hard time getting along ever since.

It's nobody's fault. Blame it on the natural and all-too-human tendency to judge others' religious beliefs and insist upon the truth of one's own. But it is too bad. After all, more human beings worship the God of Abraham than not.

ABRAHAM
Father Figure to All and Star of Genesis
(Pre–Phil Collins)

For Abraham shall surely become a great and mighty nation, and all the nations of the earth shall be blessed through him. For I have singled him out, that he may instruct his children and posterity to keep the way of the Lord by doing what is just and right.

—*Genesis 18:18–19*

The punch line? Neither the Bible nor the Koran ever says *why* God singled out Abraham. The belief shared by all three faiths, however, is that Abraham was the first human being since Noah to revere *God*, singular and capitalized. The post-Flood trend was to revere *gods*, plural and lowercase.

Noah, while righteous, wasn't exactly patriarch material. One of the very first things he did after the Flood was get fall-down drunk. Abraham was both reverent and upstanding, something God appreciated. Besides, God figured it was about time decent people like Abraham showed some respect, seeing as God had created the universe.[16] The lowercase gods didn't create anything except trouble.

Case in point: Abraham's dad, Terah, actually sold gods for a living—in the form of idols. One day while Terah was out, Abraham smashed all but one of the idols with an axe and then placed the axe in the remaining idol's hand.

Noah Almighty!

When Terah returned, he was understandably upset. Smashing merchandise wasn't just bad for business; his customers worshipped the goods. Abraham blamed the destruction on the last idol standing. Terah didn't buy it. Abraham didn't expect he would, which proved his whole point: the idols were worthless to begin with. They *couldn't* smash each other. Abraham was trying to show his dad that a person might as well worship a chamber pot or a pair of underwear—any old thing that could be created or destroyed by another person. The God Abraham worshipped had created *him*.

16. Frankly, God is a little testy after he creates the universe. Throughout Genesis he repeats himself often, demands props when he isn't getting any, and even destroys wicked cities (Sodom and Gomorrah, the Vegas of the Old Testament).

IS ALLAH REALLY THE GOD OF ABRAHAM, TOO?

Short answer: yes. But more than a few non-Muslims would tell you that Muslims aren't part of the 54 percent of all human beings who worship the same God (see Living with Mono(theism), page 144). According to these naysayers—and in spite of what's written in the Koran—Allah is not the God of Abraham but "the moon god of Mecca." This is their not-so-subtle way of claiming that Islam has no relation to Christianity or Judaism. To be fair, the pre-Islamic god of the moon *was* probably called Allah at times, because "Allah" means "the God" in Arabic. But that's sort of like claiming that certain people aren't really people but entities called "ignoramuses," because they have been referred to as such.

Neither the Bible nor the Koran tells how Terah reacted to his son's lesson or if he switched careers, but both texts make clear that God wanted Abraham to pack up and move out of Terah's house, pronto. God even gave Abraham a new name. Until then, he was known as Abram. After he relocated, however, God formalized their relationship by adding the extra syllable "ha." Furthermore, God instructed Abraham to get circumcised, to circumcise his offspring,[17] and to make sure all future generations would be circumcised as the symbol of their new covenant.[18] Finally, God told Abraham to get cracking on his great and mighty new nation by impregnating Sarah, his wife.

All of this was a little hard for Abraham to swallow. He was ninety-nine years old.[19] Sarah was in her nineties, as well. Plus, she was infertile. She didn't see how she could have a child at all, much less become the mother of offspring as numerous as "stars in the sky." And, no offense to her husband, but she doubted she'd even enjoy the sexual intimacy given how old he was. In fact, she couldn't help but laugh at the whole idea. Not surprisingly, her laughter annoyed God. "Is there anything too wondrous for the *Lord*?" (Genesis 18:14) he demanded. She didn't have to answer. It was a rhetorical question.

"Honey, are you as freaked out as I am?"

---

17. Perhaps the "ha" was added to make sure Abraham laughed a little in spite of being ordered to circumcise himself and his child. "Ha! Ha . . . ha . . ." Maybe not.

18. The Hebrew word for circumcision is <u>bris</u>, which comes from <u>brit</u>, the Hebrew word for covenant. Why the covenant between God and Abraham needs to be symbolized by male circumcision for all time is never explained in the Bible, although the nice part is that male circumcision has proven to have health benefits. So has the avoidance of bacon and other pork products. These are just some instances of the Bible's being ahead of its time, health-wise.

19. Most of the Tanakh's patriarchs were well past retirement age when at their most active, an astonishing feat considering there were no gyms, golf courses, or Viagra.

YOU'RE NEVER TOO OLD TO ROCK AND ROLL

The members of Genesis (above), like Abraham, never allowed age to slow them down. The band's original lead singer, Peter Gabriel,[20] left in 1975. (Author Jodi Anderson hadn't even been born yet.) Perhaps you'd think the other members would have taken the hint and thrown in the towel, too. Instead, Phil Collins stepped out from behind the drum kit to take over lead-vocal duties, bringing us hits such as "Invisible Touch" and "Tonight, Tonight, Tonight." Genesis continues to tour in this millennium, as do many other wrinkled old men: Foreigner, Styx, REO Speedwagon, and, of course, the Rolling Stones. Abraham would be proud.

A young Phil Collins, perhaps trying to look like Abraham

Mick Jagger of the Rolling Stones: older than God, bless him

Sure enough, God made good on his promise, and Abraham and Sarah bore a son, Isaac. Later, God asked Abraham to sacrifice Isaac as the ultimate proof that he took their covenant seriously. Abraham was about to kill Isaac when God called off the sacrifice at the last second.[21] (When we mentioned that God was testy in Genesis, we weren't kidding.)

Other highlights from Abraham's post-covenant life include:

★ Accusing God of overreacting in the case of Sodom and Gomorrah, two very wicked cities that God vaporized. Apparently, not a single righteous person lived there, other than Lot, whom God spared. Lot's wife wasn't so lucky; she looked back at the destruction after having been specifically instructed not to, and she turned into a pillar of salt. D'oh!

★ Fathering another son, Ishmael, by one of his slaves, Hagar—and promising Hagar that Ishmael would also father a great nation.[22]

★ Making a fuss over where Isaac and his wife settled with their kids, because Abraham promised God that his mighty nation would stay close to home.

This is all that's left of Lot's wife. That's one big pillar of salt—when it rains, it pours!

20. No relation to the archangel.
21. This is where the expression "putting someone to the test" comes from. Really, it's in the Bible (Genesis 22:1).
22. Muslim tradition holds that Mohammad was descended from Ishmael, which would fulfill this prophecy. Muslim tradition also holds that Abraham built the Kaaba, the sacred tent in the center of the Great Mosque at Mecca, facing which all Muslims pray five times a day.

At first glance, these highlights may not appear to have very much in common. They don't really, but they do demonstrate that Abraham behaved ethically[23] and expected everyone else to, as well—including God. The covenant between Abraham and God was a two-way street. It wouldn't do much good to blindly serve an unjust God, would it?

JUST A LITTLE MO'-MO'-MO'
A Fuller Understanding of the Big Three Monotheisms with the Help of Their Three Biggest Players

Just as every great band has a great front man (or front woman, and, yes, Genesis *was* better with Peter Gabriel), so the three big monotheisms each have a single legendary figure at their centers. Moses and Mohammad were different from Jesus in that they weren't actually God—merely mortals, as you'll see. But divine or not, all three laid down the rules and set the bar for what it means to be a Jew, a Christian, or a Muslim.

 ## MOSES
THE FIRST JEWISH COMEDIAN

Abraham may be the Jews' foremost patriarch,[24] but Moses is by far the Jews' foremost prophet. Even the Bible says so: "There has not arisen a prophet since like Moses" (Deuteronomy 34:10). More than any other Jew, Moses served as God's go-to middleman in dealings with planet Earth.

Even before he became a prophet, Moses led a pretty charmed life—at least compared to his fellow Israelites, who were enslaved in Egypt at the time. Egyptian law required all Israelite firstborn males to be drowned in the Nile. Luckily Moses' mother defied the law and plopped him into the river, hidden in a reed basket. Downstream a little ways, he was discovered by Pharaoh's daughter and raised as an Egyptian prince, setting an uncanny precedent both for evading death and for being in the right place at the right time.

He later rejected his Egyptian upbringing: when God decided it was time for the Egyptians to set the Israelites free after four hundred years of oppression, God picked Moses to stand before Pharaoh and shout, "Let my people go!" Later, God picked Moses to part the Red Sea, a scene made famous by Charlton Heston[25] in the 1956 epic *The Ten Commandments*. And after Moses had spent forty years wandering the desert—when God finally announced he would make a new covenant with the Jews and give them both the Torah and the promised land—God picked Moses to climb Mount Sinai and take down the Torah, word for word.

---

23. Well, aside from owning slaves and having a child with his wife's handmaiden. But, hey, given the moral standards of the time, he behaved ethically. Besides, his wife set up the whole relationship and was the one who originally wanted Abraham to be Hagar's baby-daddy.
24. The only other patriarchs were Abraham's son Isaac and his grandson Jacob, so competition was slim.
25. In his later years, Charlton Heston (RIP) was perhaps most famous for being a spokesman for the National Rifle Association.

Charlton Heston as Moses

Bad rock! This is the big rock that kept Moses out of the promised land.

God once even threatened to wipe out all the Israelites *except* Moses. Granted, God was particularly irritated at the time: the Israelites had taken to worshipping a golden calf because Moses was taking a little longer than expected up on Mount Sinai. But Moses convinced God to relax, pointing out that if God went on a lethal rampage, the Egyptians could say, "Oh, look how evil God is. He freed his people only to kill them all in the desert." God conceded the point and ended up sending only a plague instead.

This isn't to say that Moses didn't occasionally irritate God, too. Their worst tiff came when he disobeyed God in front of the Israelites. The Israelites were thirsty—and, as usual in Exodus,

complaining about it—so God instructed Moses to call forth water from a rock. Instead of calling to the rock, Moses struck it with his staff.

One might think that this wasn't such a big deal (just a different means to an end, really; the water still gushed out), but God was so angry at Moses' disobedience that he refused to allow Moses into the promised land. So after Moses helped free his people, after forty years in the desert, after everything he'd done on God's behalf . . . he still couldn't reach his final destination—all because he hit a rock instead of speaking to it. Which is kind of funny, although from Moses' perspective, maybe not funny "ha-ha."

IS THERE A CODE HIDDEN IN THE TORAH THAT CONTAINS THE ANSWER TO EVERYTHING?

Zoinks! Well, like all things religious, it depends on what you believe. An eighteenth-century Jewish sage, the Genius of Vilna, proclaimed: "All that was, is, and will be until the end of time is included in the Torah." Most people believe he was speaking symbolically. But if you believe that Moses really did jot down the Torah in its entirety on Mount Sinai, letter by letter, you might argue that it's a fact.

Transcribing a new Torah must be done by hand; it is an exact, painstaking science. The text literally hasn't changed a single letter in almost three thousand years. Some people say that God encoded the original Hebrew. Their theory goes that by mixing up the letters in different ways, you can uncover the story of everything that ever happened in the history of the universe—as well as what will happen in the future. There is even some statistical evidence for the existence of a Bible code. In 1995, an American reporter named Michael Drosnin made headlines when he allegedly used the code to foretell the assassination of Israeli prime minister Yitzhak Rabin.

Of course, there's also a lot of statistical evidence that says that this was just a creepy coincidence. And the people who believe in the Bible code may also be the same types who believe in the Bermuda Triangle, alien abduction, and Atlantis. Which is totally cool. The whole point of this chapter is that we don't judge religious beliefs.[26]

Answers to everything included!

✝ MONOTHEISM, MESSIAH-STYLE

Okay, let's just call it faith in Jesus—and not to sound blasphemous, but any savior who loves his enemies, hangs out with a hooker, and turns water into booze must be onto *something*. For that matter, it takes more than a spiritual revolutionary to raise the dead or feed thousands of people with some fish and a couple of loaves of bread. And what about walking on water? Or healing the sick? But don't take Jesus' word that he was the Messiah. As far as holy scripture goes, he proved it. Some of his biggest miracles involved fulfilling prophecies that were written in earlier parts of the Bible.

---

26. Not even those who claim that the Antichrist—due to appear any day now—will most likely be an American-born Jew. Uh-oh. That means it could be one of the authors of this book!!!

Jewish Prophecies to Fulfill

☆ Call Bethlehem my home
☆ Cure the blind, deaf, and sick
☆ Provide salvation for Jews and non-Jews
☆ Get betrayed for thirty pieces of silver

The prophet Micah foretold that the Messiah would be born in Bethlehem (Micah 5:2). *Check.* The prophet Isaiah foretold that the Messiah would cause the blind to see, the deaf to hear (Isaiah 29:18), and that he would offer salvation to all humankind, not just the Jews (Isaiah 49:6). *Check, check, check.* The prophet Jeremiah even foretold that the Messiah would be betrayed for thirty pieces of silver and that the money would be used to buy a potter's field (Zechariah 11:12–13). *Drumroll, please . . .* In the Gospel according to Matthew, the temple elders use Judas' blood money to buy a potter's field, which they then turn into a burial ground (Matthew 21:3–10).[27]

WHAT DOES THE WORD "MESSIAH" MEAN?

This, too, is a good question. Again, it depends on whom you ask.

In Judaism, the Messiah is a warrior-king who will be sent by God at the end times to vanquish Jewish enemies and restore Israel to its former glory.

In Christianity, he's already appeared—as Jesus—and will appear again during the Second Coming. The word "Christ" actually comes from the Greek word for "Messiah," *Kristos.* Of course, Christians see the Messiah as not so much a human political leader, like a president, but a divine and spiritual one, like . . . well, Jesus. In other words, Jesus' fight isn't about kicking butt on a battlefield; it's about winning souls.

In Islam, there is a kind of Messiah, too. Sunni Muslims talk of the Mahdi, the "restorer of the faith," who will return at the end times to unite humanity under Allah. Shiite Muslims believe that the Mahdi is the "hidden imam," the twelfth successor to Mohammad. Born in 868 CE, the twelfth imam is believed to be still alive, only he's been hidden by God from the rest of the world. When God sees fit to usher in the end times, the hidden imam will make his show-stopping reappearance. Shiite tradition holds that Jesus (yes, *that* Jesus) will appear with the hidden imam to help him out at the end times. Clearly, turning planet Earth into paradise is a tough job. The more divine assistance, the better.

The conclusion? All three faiths agree that you can't talk Messiah without talking apocalypse. The good news is that no matter how the apocalypse goes down, it will be followed by a golden age of peace and perfection. (For the faithful, that is.) Woo-hoo!

---

27. This last one might qualify as less of a miracle and more of a tragedy—unless, of course, you believe Judas' version of the Crucifixion, from the Gospel according to Judas.

It's one thing to fulfill ancient prophecies. However, it's another to be the son of God. This raises an issue that's often come up over the past two thousand years: How can Christianity truly be monotheism if the son is a separate entity from the father? Isn't that two gods? And what about the Holy Spirit? Doesn't that make *three*?

Saint Patrick, the fifth-century Irish missionary, preached that the Holy Trinity is like a shamrock (a three-leaf clover).[28] Viewed this way, the father, son, and Holy Spirit are all equal parts of the same flower. No one leaf can survive or exist apart from the stem.

As far as Jesus viewed himself, he had this to say in the gospels: "I am the way, the truth, and the life. No one comes to the Father except through me" (John 14:6). Which, come to think of it, doesn't really clarify matters on monotheism, although it doesn't leave much doubt as to his divinity. It was also his way of saying that the only covenant that really mattered was the new covenant with him—not the previous covenants with God through Abraham and Moses. So the laws of Moses could pretty much be scrapped. From now on, circumcision and pork avoidance were optional.

Dinner, approved by Jesus

28. Yes, <u>that</u> Saint Patrick, the one associated with leprechauns, Blarney stones, silly green hats, and March 17. Kiss him, he's Irish!

MOHAMMAD: THE MESSENGER OF GOD WHO ALSO GAVE THE WORLD ITS MOST COMMON FIRST NAME

That's right: chances are better than not that if you're a male human being, your name is Mohammad—the most popular name in the world, at an estimated fifteen million. The name's popularity is due in part to Islam's emphasis on Mohammad's humanity. Muslims emphatically do not see Mohammad as divine, the way Christians see Jesus, but as an average Joe.[29] Okay, scratch that; above average, nearly perfect. As a matter of fact, the hadith and sirah—canons of Islamic scripture second only to the Koran—consist entirely of Mohammad's quotes or stories about Mohammad's life and its lessons.[30]

Some highlights from Mohammad's life include:

★ The "Night Flight." Mohammad was the first prophet from any of the Big Three monotheisms to fly from Mecca to Jerusalem first class (well, on a winged horse named Burak), with only two pit stops—one on Mount Sinai, to see where Moses received the Torah, and one in Bethlehem, to see where Jesus was born. On his return trip, he made a brief layover in heaven, where Moses and Jesus congratulated him for being an awesome prophet and told him to keep up the good work.

★ The occasion on which he said: "Shall I not inform you of a better act than fasting, alms, and prayers? Making peace between one another: enmity and malice tear up heavenly rewards by the roots." (He said a lot of stuff about peace, but this is one of the more famous quotes.)

★ His ascent into heaven from Jerusalem. Legend holds he left his footprint in a rock there, where the mosque called the Dome of the Rock was built.

Mohammad is also unique among the major monotheistic prophets in that he had several wives (by varying accounts, either eleven or thirteen)—many of whom he married at the same time, near the end of his life. Since Islam promotes the

BREAKIN' THE LAW, BREAKIN' THE LAW

On a final, irreverent note—and also giving props to an oldie-but-goody Judas Priest song—Moses, Jesus, and Mohammad each fought the authority of their times. Moses defied Pharaoh by demanding that Egypt free its slaves. Jesus defied the Romans and Jewish elders by overturning the tables of the moneylenders in the temple. And, in the tradition of Abraham, Mohammad refused to worship the idols of those who ruled Mecca. It appears that in every great prophet, there is also a victorious rebel.

Cause or no cause, this rebel also had the benefit of great hair products—something Moses, Mohammad, and Jesus did not.

idea of living according to Mohammad's example, polygamy is still legal in many Islamic countries. Needless to say, this raises a lot of questions and eyebrows among non-Muslims. But it's worth mentioning that Mohammad was mostly monogamous, having been married to his first wife, Khadijah, and her alone, for twenty-five years.

---

29. Ironically, not the most popular name in the world. So a better phrase would be "an average Mo."

30. There are no pictures of Mohammad in any of Islam's sacred texts because Muslims believe that it is wrong to try to create a likeness of someone who was perfect (i.e., Mohammad, the messenger of God), in the same way that it is wrong to worship an idol or painting that represents God. This explains why Muslim extremists get so angry when someone draws a cartoon of Mohammad and, tragically, why the most extreme have even gone so far as to murder the offending cartoonist in protest, as in the case of Dutch filmmaker and artist Theo van Gogh, on November 2, 2004.

JERUSALEM
It's Mine, Mine, Mine!

Given all that the Big Three monotheisms have in common, it's no wonder their believers fight over a small dusty city, conveniently sandwiched between the desert and the Dead Sea, a sea with no fish.[31]

What makes Jerusalem so special, anyway?

 For Jews the city has been their spiritual capital dating all the way back to King David, who ruled there during Judaism's golden age. One of Judaism's most cherished beliefs is that the Messiah, a direct descendant of King David, will rule from Jerusalem again someday.

These days most Jews regard this messianic Jerusalem as an *idea* rather than as a real *future place*, something to aspire to by living a righteous life. That's why "Next year in Jerusalem!"—the ceremonial cry that concludes every Passover celebration—isn't meant to be taken literally. It's a symbolic declaration of hope for better times, like when Barack Obama said, "If you're walking down the right path and you're willing to keep walking, eventually you'll make progress."

Until only very recently, however, the actual city of Jerusalem has been occupied by a succession of foreign powers. In other words, Jews *had* to get used to the idea of thinking of it as only an idea, because for the most part the place itself has been beyond their control . . . which in turn makes the idea of it all the more precious and elusive and, according to some, worth fighting for.[32]

For Christians, Jerusalem is also a spiritual center. It's the place where Jesus confronted Roman and Jewish authorities, where he preached and performed miracles, where he gave his life to save mankind . . . and where he'll return on Judgment Day.

For going on nearly two thousand years, Christian pilgrims have flocked to the city to walk in Jesus' footsteps and to visit the Church of the Holy Sepulcher, built on Golgotha, where he was crucified. For a good chunk of that time, they believed that spot to be the center of the earth.

For Muslims, Jerusalem remains Islam's third holiest city after Mecca and Medina—not only the place where Mohammad ascended to heaven but also the place where the Mahdi will ultimately defeat the enemies of Islam. And, like the early Christians, Mohammad once believed Jerusalem to be the center of the earth. He even used to pray in the direction of Jerusalem before he started praying toward Mecca.

To quote Shakespeare again: "There's the rub." All three monotheisms have legitimate reasons for claiming Jerusalem as their own. Many within those faiths continue to view Jerusalem as a past, present, and future battleground—which doesn't exactly make for warm and fuzzy dialogue about, say, sharing.

On the other hand, some people have floated the idea of turning Jerusalem into a separate entity, like the Vatican,[33] but governed by special representatives of all three faiths. Realistically, it's doubtful this will happen any time soon. It is a nice idea, though. Then again, no matter what you believe, so is peace and redemption, right?

---

31. The situation in Jerusalem would almost be funny, if it weren't. The Dead Sea is pretty funny, though, in that a person can't help but float in it. The high concentration of salt makes everything naturally buoyant and almost impossible to sink, like Utah's Great Salt Lake.

32. Since the late nineteenth century, this figurative torch has been carried by the Zionists: Jews who believe that Jerusalem—and by extension, all of Israel—belongs to Jews alone, as their rightful homeland.

33. According to The Guinness Book of World Records, the Vatican is the world's smallest sovereign nation, occupying 0.44 square miles, with a population of 911 (as of the 2003 census). As a real-life country, its vote in the United Nations has the same power as the vote of any other nation.

2,500+ YEARS OF THE BATTLE FOR JERUSALEM

DATE	EVENT
586 BCE	After a twenty-year siege, the Babylonians conquer Jerusalem. King Nebuchadnezzar destroys the First Temple, built by King David's son and successor, King Solomon.[34] The ark of the covenant is also lost or stolen, laying the groundwork for the billion-dollar *Indiana Jones* film franchise.
175 BCE	Seleucid king Antiochus IV sacks Jerusalem, plunders the Second Temple, and erects a statue of Zeus in the middle of it.
70 CE	Roman emperor Titus destroys the Second Temple and burns most of Jerusalem during the First Jewish-Roman War.
135	Roman emperor Hadrian forbids any Jewish presence in Jerusalem.
365	Roman emperor Julian allows Jews to return to Jerusalem, only to be persecuted.
614	Persian general Shahrbaraz conquers Jerusalem and burns the Church of the Holy Sepulchre.
1009	Muslim caliph al-Hakim orders the destruction of all synagogues and churches in Jerusalem.
1099	In the First Crusade, Christians seize Jerusalem, slaughter most of the city's Muslims and Jews, and convert the Dome of the Rock into a church.
1187	Syrian leader Saladin conquers Jerusalem and takes it from the crusaders, slaughters most of the Christians, and turns the Dome of the Rock back into a mosque.
1541	Muslim extremists seal the Golden Gate—the entrance to the Old City—just in case the Jewish Messiah appears and tries to sneak in.
1517–1917	The Ottoman Turks, who are Muslim, rule Jerusalem in relative peace, tolerating the presence of both Jews and Christians—except for an eight-year period beginning in 1832 when the Egyptians briefly conquer Palestine.
1946	Zionist terrorists blow up the King David Hotel in Jerusalem, killing ninety-one people.
1951	Arab terrorists assassinate King Abdullah I of Jordan on the Temple Mount.
1967	Israeli security forces take the Temple Mount from Jordan during the Six Day War and eventually open its holy sites to people of all faiths—which should have solved a lot of problems, except that so many people have been extremely unhappy with the terms of the Israeli occupation ever since.

DATE	EVENT
1973	Egypt and Syria launch a surprise attack against Israel on Yom Kippur—the Jewish Day of Atonement and one of the holiest days in the Jewish calendar—hoping to reclaim territory lost in the 1967 war. After two weeks of fighting, the United Nations brokers a cease-fire, and Jerusalem remains in Israeli hands.
1978	In September, the Camp David accords mark the first time that Egyptians and Israelis officially try to make a lasting peace—under the watchful eye of the thirty-ninth U.S. president, Jimmy Carter. It doesn't last.
1987–1993	The first intifada, or the "War of the Stones." Palestinians rebel against the Israeli occupation in the West Bank, Gaza, and East Jerusalem. The uprising claims more than 1,100 Palestinian and 160 Israeli lives.
1993	The Oslo accords—a peace settlement organized in part by forty-second U.S. president Bill Clinton—are signed in Oslo, Norway. It marks the first time an Israeli leader (Yitzhak Rabin) and a Palestinian leader (Yasir Arafat) ever meet face-to-face. This should have solved a lot of problems, too, except that militants on both sides believe it to be a cop-out.
1995	Israeli prime minister Yitzhak Rabin is assassinated—for signing the Oslo accords—by a radical right-wing Orthodox Jew named Yigal Amir, in Tel Aviv.
2000	The second intifada, or Palestinian uprising, begins. Also called the Al-Aqsa intifada—named for the Al-Aqsa Mosque, or Dome of the Rock, in Jerusalem—the rebellion has to date claimed more than 5,300 Palestinian, 1,000 Israeli, and 64 foreign lives.
2006	Hamas—a radical Palestinian organization formed in 1987 during the first intifida, and considered a terrorist group by the United States for its use of suicide bombers and stated policy calling for the destruction of the State of Israel—wins a majority of seats in the Palestinian Authority parliament.
2007	The Annapolis peace conference marks the first formal call for a "two-state solution" in the Middle East: the creation of a separate Palestinian state to exist side by side with Israel. Part of the solution calls for the division of Jerusalem, with East Jerusalem going to Palestine. The conference ends in a stalemate. As of this writing, no further concrete steps have been taken toward the establishment of a fully independent Palestinian state or a shared Jerusalem.
2008–2009	Israel invades Gaza in retaliation for Hamas rocket attacks; after a month-long war, a cease-fire is agreed upon.

King Solomon—smarty-pants of the ancient world.

ISM-SCHISM
Religious Denominations within the Big Three

Trying to present an overview of *all* the different denominations within Christianity, Islam, and Judaism—and telling why they've often been at one another's throats—would easily take up another book (or several), so we're going to keep things relatively simple here. Consider these charts more of a religious cheese platter, something to sample from in occasionally bitter but sometimes hopeful bite-size portions.

WELCOME TO FIGHT CLUB . . .

✡ JUDAISM

DENOMINATION	WHAT IT MEANS AND WHY—AND IF ITS MEMBERS FIGHT
ORTHODOX Approximately 7.5 million. This includes Hasidic Jews and other observant Jews who adhere to a strict dress code, one that generally includes *kippot* (head coverings) and *talis* (prayer shawls).	Orthodox Jews strictly follow *halacha,* or Jewish law, as it has been practiced for over three thousand years. Historically, Orthodox Jews have fought to protect their homeland, Israel, from Persian, Roman, Christian, and Muslim invasion and occupation (in that order). In modern times, Orthodox Jews have fought with Conservative and Reform Jews over what it means to be "Jewish," though thankfully mostly with words as opposed to weapons. And, as pictured, not a few Orthodox Jews are fed up with fighting, period.
REFORM AND SECULAR Approximately 5.5 million— including Jon Stewart (previously known as Jonathan Stuart Leibowitz).	In the mid-nineteenth century, many Jews in the U.S. and UK sought to abandon some of the stricter tenets of Orthodox Judaism in order to assimilate into their largely Christian societies. Reform Jews believe that the Torah was inspired by but not written by God. They have come under fire from both Orthodox and Conservative Jews for being the least observant.
CONSERVATIVE AND RECONSTRUCTIONIST Approximately 1 million.	Formally organized by American Jews in 1913, the Conservative movement was formed to strike a balance between Reform and Orthodox Judaism. Semirelated: Senator Joe Lieberman (left), a Conservative Jew, has often tried to strike a balance between hawkish Republicans and progressive Democrats, sometimes pissing off members of both parties.

DENOMINATION	WHAT IT MEANS AND WHY—AND IF ITS MEMBERS FIGHT
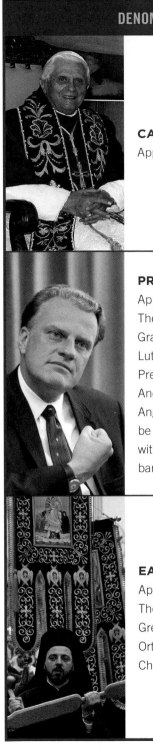**CATHOLICS** Approximately 1.2 billion.	Catholics are the first and oldest Christian denomination. They consider the pope to be head of the Christian church. Until recently, its members have fought Jews (in an effort to convert them, often going to extreme lengths, such as during the Spanish Inquisition[35]), Muslims (for the same reason, and to retake the Holy Land during the Crusades[36]), and pretty much every other kind of religious believer who wouldn't be converted to Catholicism. In the past fifty years, however, they've taken great strides to stop fighting and make peace with everyone, most of all fellow Christians. This peace process is known as the "ecumenical movement."
PROTESTANTS Approximately 500 million. These include Reverend Billy Graham (left) and Baptists, Lutherans, Methodists, and Presbyterians, among others. And WASPs, of course (White Anglo-Saxon Protestants, not to be confused with the insect, or with the mid-1980s heavy metal band).	Protestantism, as we've seen, traces its roots to the word "protest." The original Protestant, Martin Luther, was fed up with the fact that he couldn't argue with the pope, who was infallible. In 1517, Martin Luther nailed a list of 95 complaints to a cathedral door and then started his own movement to worship God as he saw fit: very simply. Not surprisingly, a lot of Protestants eventually ended up disagreeing with *him*, too. Historically, and to this day, Protestants have fought with Catholics over what it means to be a true Christian. Northern Ireland, for example, continues to be a hotbed of Protestant-Catholic conflict; the majority of those fighting for independence from Great Britain are Irish Catholics.
EASTERN ORTHODOX Approximately 225 million. These include the Russian and Greek Orthodox, the Oriental Orthodox, and Armenian Churches.	Eastern Orthodox Christians officially became a separate denomination when they were excommunicated, in 1054, from the Catholic Church for not recognizing the authority of the Roman Catholic pope, in what was called "the Great Schism." Like Catholics, they have also fought with members of different faiths in an effort to convert them—including Catholics themselves. In 1965, the Roman Catholic Church officially apologized for the Great Schism. Its leader, Pope Paul VI, and the leader of the Eastern Orthodox Church, Patriarch Athenagoras of Constantinople, issued a joint statement revoking the excommunication. (Hey, a nine-hundred-year-late apology is still better than none at all.)

35. The Spanish Inquisition was a state-sponsored effort to convert the Jews and Muslims in Spain to Catholicism—by any means necessary (most notably, gruesome torture). Begun in 1478, it wasn't officially abolished until 1834, after nearly 45,000 Jews and Muslims had been killed.

36. The Crusades were a series of religious wars fought between the years 1095 and 1272 to free the holy Land (especially Jerusalem) from Muslim occupation. These days, the word "crusade" connotes any struggle that's religious in nature—much like the Islamic word "jihad." This probably explains why people get so upset or confused when you mention either.

DENOMINATION	WHAT IT MEANS AND WHY—AND IF ITS MEMBERS FIGHT
PENTECOSTALS AND CHARISMATICS Approximately 405 million. This is one of the fastest growing groups in the Protestant tradition. The Assemblies of God is the largest Pentecostal Church, with 51 million members.	Pentecostals believe in a direct, personal experience of God. They also believe that Jesus desires to fill their followers with the holy spirit—which can lead them to spiritual healing through the laying on of hands (see left) and speaking in tongues, also known as glossalalia. One of the essential Pentecostal beliefs is that literally every word of the Bible is true. They fight (over doctrine) with traditional churches that believe in infant baptism, since only adults, who have knowingly been saved by Jesus, can be baptized in this faith.
ANGLICANS AND EPISCOPALIANS Approximately 78 million. Anglicans and Episcopalians consider themselves Protestants, tracing their origins to the Reformation.	Anglicans, also known as The Church of England, officially separated from the Roman Catholic Church in 1534, when Henry VIII (see left) decided he wanted a divorce from Catherine of Aragon so he could marry Anne Boleyn. (Catholicism forbids divorce.) Anglicans and Catholics have had a testy relationship ever since, although there are a great many similarities in their practices and tenets. Episcopalians are the American branch of the Church of England.
ANABAPTISTS Approximately 4.5 million. Anabaptists include Mennonites, Hutterites, Brethren, and Amish.	Anabaptists strive for the most primitive form of Christianity, in the vein of the Puritans. Many are pacifists, so they don't fight at all, even in times of war—which sometimes gets them in trouble.
OLD CATHOLICS Approximately 3.5 million.	Ironically, these are the "newest" Christians. They fight mostly with fellow Catholics who accept the rulings of the Second Vatican Council. Vatican II was convened in 1959 by Pope John XXIII in large part to absolve Jews of the charge of deicide. Until then, and for nearly two thousand years, most Catholics took it as an article of faith that Jews had murdered Jesus—which is why they fought with Jews so violently. Old Catholics also believe that a Catholic mass must be performed in Latin.[37]
NONTRINITARIANS Approximately 1.25 million. These include "rationalist" Christians such as Universalists, Unitarians, and Quakers. (The Universalists and Unitarians merged in 1961 to form the Unitarian Universalist Association of Congregations.)	Nontrinitarians are those Christians who reject the idea of a Holy Trinity. For the most part—because they value being rational as much as they value being Christian—they've made a concerted effort not to fight with anyone. Nontrinitarians, particularly Quakers (such as Susan B. Anthony, left), have historically been at the forefront of nonviolent civil rights battles, from abolitionism to women's suffrage.

37. Mel Gibson's father, Hutton Gibson, is an Old Catholic. In addition to believing that Jews murdered Jesus Christ, he also believes that the 9/11 attacks were an inside job by the American government and that the Holocaust was exaggerated. Thankfully, he lives in Australia. Amen.

☪ ISLAM

DENOMINATION	WHAT IT MEANS AND WHY—AND IF ITS MEMBERS FIGHT
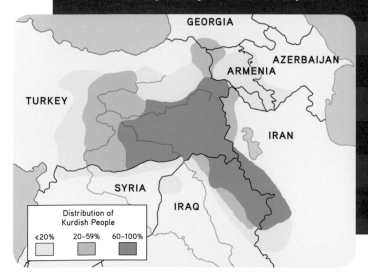 **SUNNI** Approximately 1 billion.	Sunni Muslims believe that the leader of Islam—called a caliph—should be elected by the *umma*, the entire Muslim community. The first caliph was Mohammad's closest advisor, Abu Bakr. In modern times, militant Sunni Muslim extremists have fought with anyone who is not also a militant Sunni Muslim extremist. The vast majority of Sunnis, however, do not fight with anyone. Unless, of course, they are professional boxers, such as famous Sunni Muslim (and pacifist) Muhammad Ali (left).
SHIITE (ALSO SHI'A) Approximately 180 million. The majority of Shiite Muslims can be found in Iran, Iraq, Lebanon, and southern Turkey.	Shiite Muslims believe that the leader of Islam—called an imam—should be a blood relative of Mohammad. As such, they believe Mohammad's cousin and son-in-law, Ali ibn Abi Talib, was Mohammad's rightful successor—not Abu Bakr. There hasn't been a Shiite imam since 874, when the eleventh imam died. Many Shiites (such as Iranian president Mahmoud Ahmadinejad, left) await the return of the twelfth, or the "hidden" imam. Traditionally, extremist Shiite Muslims have fought with Sunni Muslims over what it means to be a true Muslim. Because Ali's son Hussein was martyred in 680 CE trying to wrest control of Islam from Yazid I, the third caliph, Shiite Muslims place a premium on martyrdom.

WHO ARE THE KURDS, AND HOW DO THEY FURTHER CURDLE THE MESS IN THE MIDDLE EAST? (NO OFFENSE, KURDS!)

Contrary to popular belief, Kurds are not members of a separate religion or denomination of Islam. They are a non-Arab, mostly Sunni Islamic ethnic group that inhabits parts of Turkey, Syria, Iraq, and Iran. Kurds have been in the news recently because they are one of the three largest ethnic or religious groups currently battling for control of Iraq—the other two being the Sunni Arabs and the Shiite Arabs. Twenty-three percent of all Kurds live within Iraq's borders, and many Kurds have fought in the Iraq war with the (unsuccessful) hope of creating a separate, autonomous Kurdistan.

GEORGIA

AZERBAIJAN
ARMENIA

TURKEY

IRAN

SYRIA

IRAQ

Distribution of
Kurdish People

<20%   20–59%   60–100%

THE MORMONS:
AMERICAN HISTORY MAY NOT BE QUITE WHAT YOU THOUGHT IT WAS

While members of The Church of Jesus Christ of Latter-day Saints (the official name of the Mormon church), the Mormons also consider themselves Christians—though not all other Christians agree. This raises a tricky question: should Mormonism be considered a Christian denomination? Many Mormon beliefs and practices are just a little too fringe for some Christians. These include the sainthood of Mormonism's founders and presidents (which is where we get the term Latter-day Saints) and, until 1890, polygamy. The suspicion has run both ways. Until recently, Mormons preferred not to be associated with other Christians, whose non-Mormon beliefs its founders deemed "abominable."

According to Mormonism, founder Joseph Smith received a visit from a "heavenly being" named Moroni in 1823, who four years later directed him to ancient metal plates buried in a hill near his home in Palmyra, New York. The plates, translated by Smith with divine guidance, detail the history of a group of ancient Israelites who escaped from Jerusalem just before the Babylonian conquest and sailed to the promised land, America.

Over the next several centuries, descendants of these Israelites built a huge civilization, which split into two warring tribes. Shortly after Jesus was resurrected, he appeared before them and encouraged them to make peace. He also invited them to feel the wounds he sustained during the Crucifixion—mostly to spread the message that salvation lay through him and that warring was a bad thing.

Sadly, the message didn't take. Eventually these tribes annihilated each other and, in the process, destroyed almost all evidence of their existence. (Except for Native Americans such as the Cree and Navajo, who are believed to be the descendants of these tribes, though they don't know it.) Fortunately, Jesus will return to America on Judgment Day to prove that an ancient American civilization did exist—and, of course, to save all those who believed from the get-go.

Today, Mormons number over thirteen million worldwide, including 70 percent of the state of Utah and former U.S. presidential candidate Mitt Romney. Other famous Mormons include Democratic Majority Leader Senator Harry Reid, professional snowboarder Torah Bright, and novelist Stephenie Meyer, author of the bestselling Twilight Saga.

CHECK "OTHER" ☑

Religions Celebrities Know About

In this day and age—when nearly a fifth of the planet watches the Super Bowl in 170-some-odd countries every year—it's sometimes easy to forget that the U.S. isn't the center of the universe. Along these lines, not everyone shares a Judeo-Christian or Islamic heritage the way most Americans do, either. Imagine: wouldn't it have been a surprise if New York Giants quarterback Eli Manning had thanked Vishnu or Shiva in celebration of his Super Bowl XLII victory?

Maybe Eli Manning should reach out to Jesus, Vishnu, and Shiva next season.

HINDUISM
Oh, My Gods!

Almost 900 million people consider themselves Hindus—making it the third-largest religion after Christianity and Islam. But it's a little more complicated to define what makes a Hindu than, say, a Christian ("faith in Jesus"), a Muslim ("submission to Allah"), or a Jew ("obeys the laws of Moses").

Unlike the Big Three monotheisms, Hinduism does not have a common founder or patriarch, or even a set of common beliefs. It's more of a catchall for the loosely related religious ideas that began to take shape in India four thousand years ago. These ideas stem from a group of texts known as the Vedas, which include hymns, incantations, and rituals aimed at preserving dharma: perfect balance in the universe.

If you ask Hindus if they consider themselves monotheists, they may say yes—in that they are devoted to Brahma: the principle that a single divine entity unites and transcends all reality.[38] Many believe Brahma can be perceived as a kind of trinity, similar to the Catholic idea of the Holy Trinity:

★ Brahma, the creator (see below). He's the god who made the universe and who constantly remakes it.
★ Vishnu, the preserver. Whenever dharma is threatened, he's the four-armed god to call.

---

38. *Pretty deep and heady stuff, which is why luminaries such as the late Beatle George Harrison are attracted to Hinduism.*

With Vishnu's help, George Harrison was one of the most famous Western advocates of Hinduism.

deities. And almost all Hindus believe in samsara, the eternity of the soul. So if you have ratlike qualities in this lifetime, chances are good you could be an actual rodent in the next.[40]

As far as fighting goes, Hindus have traditionally fought against Muslims seeking to convert them to Islam. The Muslim invasion of India during the eleventh century was among the bloodiest invasions in history, with a death toll in the millions. After declaring independence from Great Britain in 1947, India split along religious lines when Pakistan declared its independence, largely so that India's Muslims could have their own country. Today, the territory of Kashmir, home to both Muslims and Hindus, is still under fierce dispute between Pakistan and India—which isn't very reassuring considering that both countries have nuclear weapons.

BUDDHISM
Sure He's Fat and Happy—That's *Enlightenment!*

Buddhism is by far the least "religious" religion: there are no gods or god involved. So does it count? The Boy Scouts of America say yes. They won't allow atheists ("God does not exist!") or agnostics ("I'll believe in God when I see God!") to join, but they do allow Buddhists.[41] One might argue that the universe itself is Buddhism's higher power, in that the essential idea is to eliminate all suffering and become one with the universe.

Like many other major religions, Buddhism's origins can be traced to a single, miraculous founder. The Buddha was actually born a Hindu, sometime during the sixth century BCE in either Nepal or India. (Buddhists share a lot of the same beliefs as Hindus, chief among them reincarnation and karma: the idea that what goes around comes around.) Immediately after he was born, the Buddha supposedly took seven steps and announced, "I am chief of the world."[42] But for him, world domination was never about power or superstardom; it was about seeking the Truth, with a capital *T*.

★ Shiva, the destroyer. He's the god who meddles most with human affairs; considered by Hindus to be physically most attractive.

All three of these gods have multiple avatars, or incarnations,[39] which is probably where Westerners get the Western idea that Hinduism is polytheistic. So is Hinduism polytheistic or monotheistic? Good question. As with most matters of any religion, there is no right or wrong answer. In a way it is both—which is contradictory and impossible. To complicate matters further, there can be a hierarchy, too. Some Hindus see Vishnu as supreme, while others side with Shiva. Regardless of who is biggest and baddest on the spiritual block, however, most Hindus do also worship a variety of lesser and more local gods, so they're comfortable with the idea of multiple

39. One of the most famous is Krishna, avatar of Vishnu and star of the Bhagavad Gita—a sacred text often given away for free by proselytizing Hindus at events such as Earth Day.
40. A bad cowlike person would probably not come back as a cow, however, as Hindus consider cows sacred animals.
41. The Boy Scouts of America won't allow openly gay people to join, either, so perhaps they still have progress to make on the path to enlightenment.
42. Clearly he didn't lack in the self-esteem department, which was a good thing, considering his eventual girth.

Until he was twenty-nine, the Buddha—known as Siddhartha Gautama ("Siddhartha" loosely means "the one who gets what he wants"; Gautama was the family name)—led a pretty cushy life. After his first son was born, however, he went on a series of journeys marked by visions of misery and death, capped off by a vision of a serene monk. Whatever inner peace that monk had, Siddhartha wanted—and Hinduism wasn't getting him there.

For the next six years he meditated, hung out with holy men, and ate next to nothing, hoping to achieve the monk's calmness and contentment. Finally, while he was sitting under a tree one night, it happened: nirvana.[43] From now on, he no longer had to worry about anger, pain, doubt, sickness, hunger—or even being reincarnated again. He'd reached the end of the line and saw "four noble truths":

1. All life is suffering.
2. Suffering is caused by desire.
3. Suffering can be overcome by ridding oneself of desire.
4. There is a path that leads to zero desire, and therefore zero suffering.

Like Jesus and Mohammad, the Buddha devoted his post-revelation life to spreading his message across a continent. (In his case, Asia.) And like the other major world religions, Buddhism took root in different ways, developing into hundreds of different practices and schools of thought. But all 360 million Buddhists do share a core belief: as long as you subscribe to the four noble truths, you can reach nirvana.

THE DALAI LAMA, THE PACIFIST ROCK STAR OF BUDDHISM

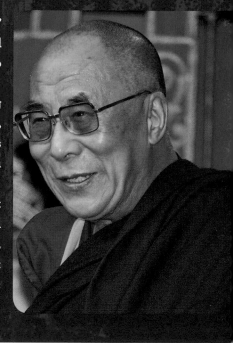

Face it: if you've been photographed with His Holiness Tenzin Gyatso, you're "somebody." This bespectacled A-lister has graced more magazine covers than Britney Spears, and deservedly so: he is the fourteenth incarnation of the Dalai Lama, the spiritual leader who has presided over Tibet in a succession of lifetimes for more than five hundred years.

In 1959, Tenzin Gyatso was ousted from Tibet by the Chinese government for insisting upon Tibet's freedom from Communist Chinese rule. Forced to rule in exile ever since, his fight to return home has turned into a cause célèbre among famous human rights activists. As he's said himself: "Our prime purpose in this life is to help others. And if you can't help them, at least don't hurt them."

One would think that the followers of such a peaceful, mellow man wouldn't make anyone angry. But the tragic fact is that Tibetan Buddhist monks have suffered persecution at the hands of the Chinese military—including imprisonment, torture, and secret executions—for going on fifty years. (For more information on the plight of Tibetan Buddhists, the nonprofit group Human Rights Watch is a great resource: www.hrw.org/wr2k1/asia/china.html.)

43. The Buddhist term for enlightenment, from which the seminal early 1990s grunge band took its name.

CHINESE TRADITIONAL RELIGION
The Tao of Being Pronounced "Dow"

Nearly 400 million people subscribe to some form of belief that can trace its origins to the *Tao Te Ching*, a sacred text reputedly written by the Chinese philosopher Lao-tzu (who may not even have existed, like many great religious figures you've read about in this chapter) during the third century BCE. In a nutshell, the Tao means "the Way." But according to Lao-tzu, assigning any meaning at all to the Tao puts limits on it, which is impossible because the Tao *has* no limits.

Taoism holds that the entire universe is governed by two opposing forces: the named and the nameless, fullness and emptiness, MC Skat Kat and Paula Abdul.[44] The trick, as in Hinduism and Buddhism, is to achieve balance between these two—and reach a perfect, harmonious whole.

Yin and yang, overused tattoo and Taoist symbol of balance

Above all, Taoism recognizes that nothing is permanent but change itself. This makes it a kindred spirit of other Chinese systems of belief, such as Confucianism (responsible for the pithy proverbs found in fortune cookies) and the I-Ching, whose primary tenet is that everything is constantly in flux. All three fall under the rubric of "Chinese Traditional Religion." The idea is that if you practice what they teach, you'll be far better prepared to deal with life's zany curveballs.

INDIGENOUS OR TRIBAL RELIGIONS
Putting the Spirit Back in Spiritual

Not all religions include complex sacred canons, leaders or founders responsible for entire philosophies, or even clear boundaries between the everyday and the sacred. Nearly a half billion people—primarily in sub-Saharan Africa, Siberia, and parts of the Amazon—subscribe to beliefs that have been passed on by word of mouth for thousands of years, predating any of the texts found in other religions. In short, if your religion doesn't come with a reading list, it probably falls into this category.

Some common traits of indigenous religions:

★ Your ancestors may be dead, but they continue to live on as spirits, often quite actively. So treat them with respect! (Songs, dancing, and sacrifice help.)

★ Shamanism: most problems can be solved or cured by an in-house mystic with supernatural wisdom and a close relationship with the spirit world.

★ Most natural phenomena are controlled or can be influenced by these spirits.

★ Be a part of nature, not apart from nature.

Bigger gods also play a role in tribal or indigenous religions. They tend to be associated with universal issues: fertility, the seasons, war, that sort of thing. They also tend to have very human personalities, so they can be seduced, bargained with, appeased—even hoodwinked.[45] The health of both the individual and the tribe depends on how happy the unseen world is with the seen.

A shaman, rocking out with the unseen world

---

44. The duo responsible for the 1989 hit single "Opposites Attract."
45. In a lot of ways, the paganism practiced by ancient Greeks and Romans could qualify as an indigenous or tribal religion—it's just that the tribe was the size of an empire (or two).

OFF-OFF BROADWAY
A Fun Glance at Some of the Smaller Faiths

Part of the beauty of America, aside from its vibrant and wacky independent theater community, is that we can worship as we please. And while one person's religion might be another person's belly laugh (to paraphrase the famous novelist Robert Heinlein), everybody can find his or her way to the divine and not worry about being locked up—or worse. After all, a person can go see *The Lion King* on Broadway and start snoring. Another person can see a one-man show in a ten-seat theater in Omaha and have a "religious experience." There was a point to this paragraph, honestly. Maybe it's just best to sum up with the tried-and-true sentiment: all religion is theater to some extent.

ZOROASTRIANISM

Did you know that Freddie Mercury was a Parsi?[46] The Parsis are the last surviving remnant of Zoroastrianism, the religion of ancient Persia. Today, most Parsis can be found in northern Iran.

The religion's founder, Zoroaster, was a mystic who lived around the same time as Confucius and Lao-tsu, during the sixth century BCE. Like other mystics of the time, he compiled his teachings into a collection of sacred texts, known as the Avesta. Most of these concern his belief that the world was a battleground between good and evil. Good was represented by Ahura Mazda, giver of light and creator of all things. Evil was represented by Angra Mainyu, whose sole purpose was to destroy the universe.

Little is known for certain about Zoroaster's life, but he did have a lot in common with the founders of other major religions. He received a vision; he was enlightened; he traveled and preached; and, of course, he is associated with miracles. The ancient Romans claimed he was the only human being ever to laugh at the moment of his birth.

Freddie Mercury, arguably the world's most famous Zoroastrian

If most Persians hadn't converted to Islam, Zoroaster could have been a contender, right up there with the likes of the Buddha, Moses, and Mohammad. As it stands, there are only 200,000 left today. We can thank Zoroaster in part for Friedrich Nietzsche's *Thus Spake Zarathustra*,[47] which gave us one of the most famous and controversial quotes concerning religion of all time: "God is dead."

---

46. *Different question you may have: who was Freddie Mercury? As lead singer of the rock band Queen, he wrote and performed such classics as "Bohemian Rhapsody" and "We Will Rock You" before tragically dying of AIDS in 1991.*

47. *Zoroaster is the Greek pronunciation of "Zarathustra." Don't blame us for the confusion; blame Alexander the Great for conquering Persia.*

"I feel you, bro. Everyone thinks I'm Muslim, too."

SIKHISM

Aside from their turbans (worn to keep their long hair out of their faces), Sikhs are probably best known in the West for being the world's only other true monotheists outside the Big Three. Sikhs believe in one god, Waheguru, thanks to the teachings of Nanak, a fifteenth-century Indian guru who broke with Hinduism and Islam but drew upon elements of both. As Nanak and his fellow gurus saw it, a person's ultimate goal should be to abandon a state of manmukh (self-centeredness) and achieve a state of Gurmukh (God-centeredness).

Haircuts and shaves are strictly prohibited as a sign of Sikhs' acceptance of God's will and because Sikhs believe that the human body is divine handiwork and shouldn't be tampered with. God made hair, so who are we to cut it off? In keeping with the belief that the body is divine, Sikhs are forbidden to consume anything unhealthy, such as cigarettes, alcohol, and meat. Things that are bad for the mind are also prohibited, such as gossip and superstition. Premarital sex is frowned upon, too. So is wealth, for that matter. In this and many other ways (such as the lack of a formal priesthood or church hierarchy), Sikhs are to Islam and Hinduism what Nontrinitarians are to Christianity—they are the simple, bling-free denomination.

Historically, Sikhs have fought both Hindus and Muslims (Christians, too), mostly in self-defense. (Like the practitioners of many other faiths, Sikhs have had a hard time worshipping in peace for most of their existence.) Unfortunately, 23 million Sikhs have also fought with each other, over differing religious practices within Sikhism.

WICCA

Formalized in 1954 by a retired British civil servant named Gerald Gardner, Wicca draws upon elements of English witchcraft and pre-Christian European paganism. It puts nature above all else in its various rituals and practices. And yes, Wiccans do practice magic, mostly in the form of spells for love, health, and self-protection. Number of practicing Wiccans: about a million.

A pentagram, the symbol of the Wiccan faith. And no, it is not a symbol of Satanism! (When it is used by Wiccans, that is. When it is used by Satanists, then the pentagram is a symbol of Satanism. Oh, well.☹ No wonder there's been some misunderstanding.)

WHAT ABOUT SCIENTOLOGY? IS THAT A RELIGION?

Well, celebrities definitely know about it, so that counts for something. And Scientologists themselves consider it to be a religion. In their own words (from the official Scientology website): "Scientology is the study and handling of the spirit in relationship to itself, others and all of life. The Scientology religion comprises a body of knowledge extending from certain fundamental truths." These truths include the idea that humans are immortal beings (called "thetans") with unlimited ability—the trick is to unleash their potential.

Scientology has been criticized for a variety of reasons (not just because Tom Cruise freaked out on Oprah's couch when gushing about Katie Holmes). Its leaders have been rumored to threaten those who want to leave the church; it is a for-profit business whose financial practices have come under suspicion by the U.S. government, and its members are encouraged to sever ties with family members and friends who don't join.

But in answer to the question "Is Scientology a religion?" . . . Probably not—at least as far as this book goes—unless you define its founder, bestselling science-fiction novelist and philosopher L. Ron Hubbard, as a "higher power."

Some of the world's more famous thetans

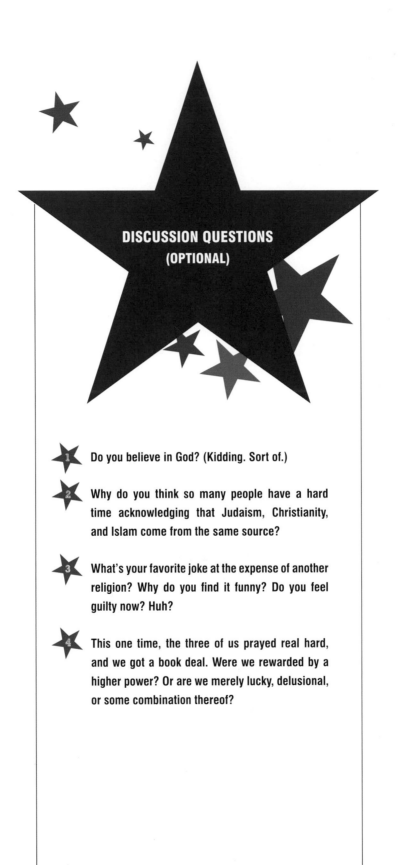

DISCUSSION QUESTIONS
(OPTIONAL)

1. Do you believe in God? (Kidding. Sort of.)

2. Why do you think so many people have a hard time acknowledging that Judaism, Christianity, and Islam come from the same source?

3. What's your favorite joke at the expense of another religion? Why do you find it funny? Do you feel guilty now? Huh?

4. This one time, the three of us prayed real hard, and we got a book deal. Were we rewarded by a higher power? Or are we merely lucky, delusional, or some combination thereof?

CHAPTER 6

HOT BUTTONS

The Issues Americans Like to Yell about Most

INTRODUCTION
Pushing Each Other's Buttons

Americans love to get angry. We're the country that spawned Bill O'Reilly and a song that goes "We'll put a boot in your a**, it's the American way."

Often our most heated debates are not about foreign policy or the economy but about moral issues, like who can get married, how we should go about tackling AIDS, or at what point a fetus should be considered a living human. Elections have been won and lost on issues like these, influencing people on both sides of the debate, with name-calling and overgeneralizations. Seeing things in black-and-white instead of shades of gray is as American as apple pie. Here, we try to look at both sides of the issues we fight over most.

THAT'S LIFE. OR IS IT?
ABORTION

The abortion debate in the U.S. hasn't been so much a discourse as a screaming match. We like to yell as much as the next person, but we thought, rather than rehash the ideological debate, we'd give you a bunch of interesting and relevant info.

WHO WAS ROE? WHO WAS WADE?

"Jane Roe" was the alias used by the court in the 1970–1973 case of a pregnant woman named Norma L. McCorvey, who wanted an abortion and had been denied one by the state of Texas. The defendant was Dallas County District Attorney Henry Wade. The case took so long that it was too late for McCorvey to have an abortion by the time it was decided. She gave birth to the child—a girl—who was given up for adoption. In the mid-1990s, McCorvey had a change of heart about the abortion issue and became a pro-life activist.

Norma McCorvey, now a born-again Christian

WHAT DID THE *ROE V. WADE* CASE DECIDE?

The court decided that it was illegal for states to deny a woman's right to abortion, because it meant violating our constitutional

The Supreme Court

"Right to Privacy." What does privacy have to do with abortion? The court decided that the emphasis on personal liberty in certain constitutional amendments could include a woman's freedom to decide whether to end her pregnancy. The ruling has been hotly contested ever since.

WHAT WOULD HAPPEN IF *ROE V. WADE* WERE OVERTURNED?

Contrary to popular belief, abortion wouldn't be illegal on a national level. Overturning the law would basically allow each state to restrict abortions if it chose, which would make the abortion debate hot in state elections. Abortion would end up being legal in some states and illegal in others.

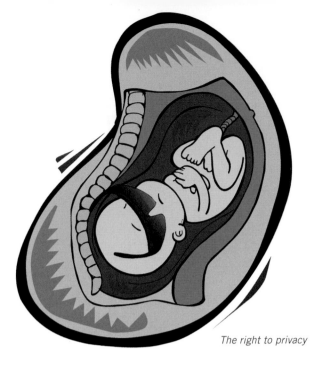

The right to privacy

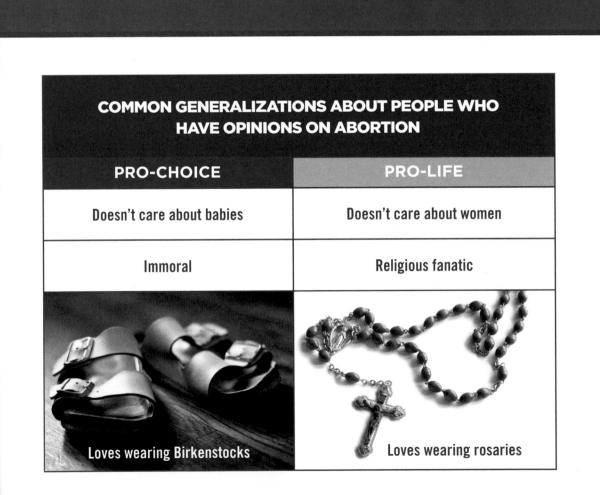

COMMON GENERALIZATIONS ABOUT PEOPLE WHO HAVE OPINIONS ON ABORTION	
PRO-CHOICE	**PRO-LIFE**
Doesn't care about babies	Doesn't care about women
Immoral	Religious fanatic
Loves wearing Birkenstocks	Loves wearing rosaries

SO WHAT ARE THE ABORTION LAWS NOW?

States are allowed to put some restrictions on abortion:

INFORMED CONSENT

A woman has to be given information about the development of the fetus and be counseled in the alternatives to abortion.

PARENTAL CONSENT

If the woman is under eighteen, her parents have to consent to the abortion.

PARENTAL NOTICE

If the woman is under eighteen, her parents have to be told . . . but they don't have to give their consent.

VIABILITY

If the fetus is viable, or able to survive outside the womb, it can't be aborted. Viability happens after about five months.

To see what restrictions apply in which states, you can go to the State Center at www.guttmacher.org.

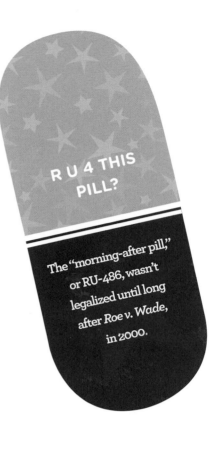

R U 4 THIS PILL?

The "morning-after pill," or RU-486, wasn't legalized until long after *Roe v. Wade*, in 2000.

TALKING IN NUMBERS

According to the Guttmacher Institute, 1.21 million abortions were performed in the U.S. in 2008, down from 1.31 million in 2000. More recent data is not available at the time of printing.

Abortion rights have been sparking protests and debates ever since the Roe v. Wade *court decision on January 22, 1973.*

HOW DOES THE U.S. STACK UP AGAINST OTHER COUNTRIES WHEN IT COMES TO ABORTION LAWS?

MATCH THE ABORTION LAW WITH THE COUNTRY:

1. Only allowed in cases where it's necessary to save the life of the mother

SPAIN

2. Only allowed when necessary to save the life or the physical or mental health of the mother

UK

3. Allowed when necessary to save the mother's life or health, or for social or economic reasons

FRANCE

4. Allowed upon request, with no stated reason required

IRELAND

1. Ireland 2. Spain 3. UK 4. France

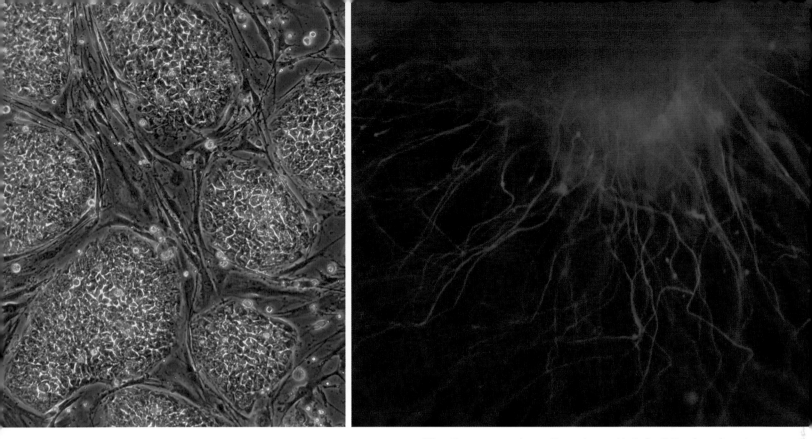

When they grow up, stem cells can be any kind of cell they (or we) want.

THE STEM CELL DEBATE

A century ago, Americans could expect to live for just fifty years. Today that number's closer to eighty (and would probably surpass that if not for all the rock stars and rappers OD'ing so young and screwing up our averages). By and large, we owe our longer lives to relatively uncontroversial medical advancements like antibiotics, X-rays, and advanced surgeries. But not all medical advances have been so universally embraced. Stem cell technology has many people wondering if medical science has pushed too far.

WHAT *ARE* STEM CELLS?

Stem cells are the blank Scrabble tile of cells. They can develop into any type of cell in the body—heart cells, nerve cells, whatever. Scientists hope that by growing these cells they can repair all sorts of diseases, like Alzheimer's, Parkinson's, and diabetes. That's because stem cells inserted into the body can potentially replicate and replace cells that have been damaged by disease.

WHY ARE THEY SO CONTROVERSIAL?

To work their magic, stem cells need to be retrieved early, while they're young and adaptable—before they have "differentiated," or become set in their ways. In the past that has meant removing them from human embryos. And up until recently, nobody's been able to do that without destroying those embryos. Abortion and stem cells are interconnected, because where better to get stem cells than from aborted embryos?

It's only in recent years that researchers have figured out ways to get stem cells without destroying or possibly even using embryos, by modifying skin cells to behave like embryonic stem cells or extracting cells from amniotic fluid. But stem cell research is still controversial. Why?

Good ol'-fashioned cloning. Stem cell research—already used to clone the cells of animals—paves the way for the cloning of human embryos for medical use. There could be embryo "farms," harvested for stem cells. Many people see that as an ethical dilemma, or even as morally wrong. Others argue it's ethically wrong to let people suffer from illnesses we have the technology to cure.

Andy, cloned

IS STEM CELL RESEARCH AGAINST THE LAW?

Nope. It's legal under the Obama Administration, and it was legal under Bush, too. But Bush favored policies that limited federal funding for stem cell research (for the ideological reasons just described). Shortly after Obama came to office, he overturned those policies and increased federal funding while vowing to develop "strict guidelines" to ensure that such research "never opens the door to the use of cloning for human reproduction."

Naturally, countries have different policies toward stem cell research—opening up a Pandora's box of possible moral takes on the issue. The UN put in its two cents in 2005, calling on member states to "adopt all measures necessary to prohibit all forms of human cloning in as much as they are incompatible with human dignity and the protection of human life."

THAT'S SO GAY!
Gay Marriage in America

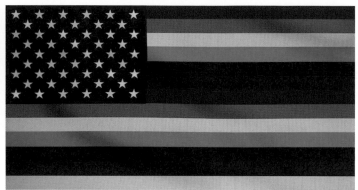

Contrary to myth, homosexuality was not invented during the counterculture 1960s as a way of cultivating future cast members for not-yet-created programs on HGTV and Bravo. Lesbians and gays have been around since, well, pretty much forever.

It's not a lifestyle. It's a sexual orientation and it's as immutable a personal trait as skin color. Just as heterosexuals don't choose to be straight, homosexuals don't choose to be gay. The modern gay rights movement has indeed made great strides for lesbian, gay, and transgendered equality since the 1960s. The movement's marquis battle at the moment is over marriage rights.

I'M CONFUSED. IS GAY MARRIAGE LEGAL, ILLEGAL, AN AMENDMENT TO THE CONSTITUTION, OR WHAT?

Thanks to something called the Defense of Marriage Act (passed in 1996 under Bill Clinton), the federal government doesn't recognize same-sex marriages. But states are allowed to decide on their own whether to recognize them or not—and whether to recognize them as "marriages" or as "civil unions."

AT THE TIME OF PRINTING:

Connecticut, Iowa, Massachusetts, New Hampshire, Vermont, and Washington DC allow gay marriage.

California, Colorado, Hawaii, Illinois, Maine, Maryland, Nevada, New Jersey, New York, Oregon, Rhode Island, Washington, and Wisconsin recognize some alternative form of same-sex union, though some are under fire.

Delaware, Indiana, Minnesota, New Mexico, North Carolina, Pennsylvania, West Virginia, and Wyoming neither recognize nor ban same-sex marriages or civil unions.

Twenty-four states have an anti-gay constitutional amendment.

WHAT HAPPENED IN CALIFORNIA?

The latest battle in California was sparked in May 2008, when the California Supreme Court overturned laws restricting marriage to heterosexual couples, essentially comparing them to the laws restricting interracial marriage that existed well into the 1960s.

INTERRACIAL MARRIAGE: DECLARE YOUR LOVE AND PISS OFF YOUR GRANDPARENTS

Yep, marriage has been controversial before. Back in the day, it was illegal for interracial couples to marry in many states, even if it was obvious they'd have really gorgeous children.

Heidi and Seal would have been denied the right to create more supernaturally beautiful humans.

In response, Proposition 8 was put forward by the opposition, giving Californians the opportunity to vote on a constitutional amendment that would define marriage as between a man and a woman. It passed. How, considering California leans liberal? Well, largely with religious backing, particularly by the Mormons, who mobilized people of faith to show up at the polls.

There's a movement under way to repeal Proposition 8, but it is only in the beginning stages at the time of this writing. To see an interactive map on gay marriage laws state by state, go to www.freedomtomarry.org/states.

COULD GAY MARRIAGE EVER BE ILLEGAL NATIONWIDE?

Recently, there have been proposed amendments to the U.S. Constitution that would redefine marriage as a union of one man and one woman, meaning no state would be able to recognize a marriage between a man and a man, a woman and a woman, a hobbit and a hobbit, and so on. The most recent vote was in 2006 and it failed. But similar amendments can be proposed until the cows come home.

SO WHERE DO WE STAND TODAY?

Gay people can't marry in most states, and in the states where they can marry, they live with the possibility that if federal laws change, their existing marriages could be legally dissolved.

Married couple Ellen DeGeneres and Portia de Rossi

EVEN THOUGH MARRIAGE IS A PROVEN WAY TO GET COUPLES TO STOP HAVING SEX,
Why Do So Many Social Conservatives Oppose Gay Marriage?

Arguments against gay marriage range from religious to economic. Some say that marriage is a religious right, not a civil right; that homosexuality is unnatural and should not be supported by law; and that marriage is for having children. Many worry that allowing gay marriage will further erode the institution of marriage, which, they argue, is already in crisis. And, economically speaking, some feel that gay couples shouldn't be entitled to the legal and financial perks that straight couples have.

Supporters of gay rights argue that marriage is a contract and that its spiritual meaning is private, personal, and up to the couple getting married. A lot of these same supporters also believe that gay people should be allowed to serve openly in the military. At the end of 2010, the U.S. government agreed, ending seventeen years of "Don't Ask, Don't Tell"—a policy that we'd like to call "Shh!" Supporters argue that outlawing gay marriage contradicts one of our nation's founding principles: the separation of church and state. They argue that two committed partners marrying is not an erosion of marriage as a whole, and that—as far as marriage for having children goes—many married straight couples decide not to conceive while many gay couples do have or adopt children. Finally, they assert that homosexuality is natural, genetically determined, and also adorable. Just look at these gay penguins!

SOME OF OUR FAVORITE GAY ANIMALS
Bonobos (left), dolphins, and these two penguins at the Central Park Zoo are just some of the critters known to engage in homosexual activity, sometimes on and on till the break of dawn.

LAWMAKIN' WITH LEVITICUS

Quotes from Leviticus (in the Old Testament, or Torah) are often cited to justify legislation limiting the marriage rights of homosexuals. What else does Leviticus say in his list of 613 laws? What you'll learn about menstruation, polyester, and slave ownership may surprise you!

QUÉ PASA WITH IMMIGRATION?

Plus Some Helpful Clichés about Mexicans!

According to the Pew Hispanic Center, there are about twelve million illegal immigrants (sometimes called illegal aliens)—people without permanent-resident cards or visas—living in the U.S. Recently, how to deal with this has been one of the most heated issues in American politics.

In 2005, President George W. Bush called for a big overhaul of immigration laws. His proposal focused on creating a guest-worker program, through which Mexicans could legally temporarily fill American jobs. It was supposed to be a win-win situation: workers got employment, and employers got to fill empty spots. But Congress rejected the plan and responded by passing a bill that called for deporting all illegal immigrants and making it a felony for anyone to offer them assistance. Illegal immigrants didn't like that much, and neither did their friends. There were huge protests in the Latino community and among its supporters.

The latest big controversy of note on immigration law centered on Arizona in April 2010, when Arizona governor Jan Brewer signed a bill that aims to pinpoint, arraign, and deport illegal immigrants. The bill made the failure to carry immigration documents a crime and gave police more power to detain suspected illegals, spurring nationwide protests and drawing criticism from President Obama. Arizona isn't the only state passing these kinds of laws, but its bill was especially controversial because it mandated that police check a person's immigration status during traffic stops and arrests—which many said encouraged racial profiling. That portion of the bill was later struck down by a federal judge.

WHY IS IT SO DIFFICULT FOR US TO AGREE ON IMMIGRATION?

People feel strongly about immigration for a few reasons. Some argue that illegal immigrants are a major part of our economy, filling an economic void by doing jobs Americans don't want to do, either because they don't pay enough or are too unappealing. On the other hand, many believe that if it weren't for

The first unwelcome immigrants

illegal immigrants, who offer a cheap, unlimited source of labor, employers would be forced to pay better wages to Americans for these jobs.

Some people believe that illegals put a burden on our education and health-care systems, using public services without paying taxes. (Illegal immigrants qualify for emergency medical care and K–12 education.) Surprisingly, though, a growing number of illegal immigrants pay taxes on their earnings using ID numbers issued by the IRS just for them, in the hopes of proving that they are eager to be upstanding American citizens who pay their fair share.

Guest-worker programs are controversial for people on both sides of the issue. On the one hand, it's a legal way to pay Mexicans less than minimum wage for what, a lot of the time, is very arduous work that most American citizens don't want to do, while giving them few rights. On the other hand, guest-worker jobs are said to "take" jobs from American citizens.

And finally, there's good ol'-fashioned racism. Just visit a few chat boards about immigration and watch how long it takes for arguments to turn to name-calling and stereotypes. The small percentage of illegal immigrants involved in gangs—like the gang MS-13, which originated in Central America—adds fuel to the fire, much like it did when Irish and Italian gangs fanned anti-immigrant feelings in the 1800s.

But let's go on the assumption that people who make dangerous border crossings in order to work physically demanding jobs so they can send money home to their families are, for the most part, okay people. Still . . .

Racism toward immigrants wasn't any prettier in 1860 than it is now. Except they did have better hats.

WHY ARE SO MANY PEOPLE FLEEING MEXICO, ANYWAY?
Did Somebody Cut the Cheese?

Over the past few years, between 385 and 420 people died annually while crossing the border from Mexico—mostly from heat exposure and drowning. Why are Mexicans willing to risk their lives in order to come here? Is it because they don't like Mexican food?

Nope. It's because they're living in poverty.

While Mexico has the highest income per person in Latin America, the wealth is concentrated in the hands of very few. About half of all Mexicans are impoverished. With the promise of better prospects just over the border, most Mexicans go north at some point in their lives to seek higher paying jobs, whether for a few years—to save up money before coming back home—or for good.

Mexicans cross the border in different ways, often with the help of smugglers called "coyotes," who charge them thousands of dollars for their services. Being "smuggled" involves hiding in secret compartments of cars going through customs, or crossing on foot at especially wild and arid parts of the desert, where there is less supervision.

SO WHY DON'T THEY APPLY FOR PAPERS AND COME HERE LEGALLY?

The process for getting a permanent-resident card in the U.S. is long, difficult, expensive, and sometimes—because of immigration quotas—impossible. Due to a major backlog, the process takes years, not to mention a staggering number of lost work hours, due to lines and paperwork.

A march for immigration rights

WHAT DOES MEXICO THINK ABOUT IT?

The Mexican government isn't overly concerned about losing some of its residents to the U.S., since those immigrants tend to send a lot of money back home. Generally, officials look the other way. They're also none too happy about more fencing along our borders. They see being fenced out as sort of insulting.

ASK A MEXICAN

Started in 2004 by Gustavo Arellano, this column (www.ocweekly.com/columns/ask-a-mexican) encourages people to ask off-limits questions about racial stereotypes (like, "Why do Mexicans wear clothes while they're swimming?") and inquire about real stuff (like immigration reform).

WHERE DOES IT ALL STAND NOW?
And What Are the Possible Solutions?

For now, immigration policy in the U.S. continues to be a mass of contradictions, with the law saying one thing but officials enforcing another. According to law, illegal immigrants should be deported but, in reality, police and government officials turn a blind eye more often than not. This leaves everyone involved with uncertainty, and illegal immigrants with very few rights. Meanwhile, thousands of people sneak across our borders every year.

Stabilizing Mexico's economy would give people less reason to leave, and this could be an issue in upcoming proposals. As for the illegal immigrants currently in the U.S., people continue to debate whether it's better, for all involved, to give them a path to legalization or to go through the costly process of finding and deporting them.

Felipe Calderón, president of Mexico, sort of looking the other way

DRUGS, GUNS, AND MONEY

There's another big problem with Mexico we haven't mentioned yet: they smuggle us drugs and we smuggle them guns. Upon coming to office, President Obama met with President Calderón, and they vowed to create comprehensive reform on both immigration and drug trafficking across the border. We'll see.

AIDS

The Biggest Ongoing Pandemic in History That You Don't Hear Much about Anymore

While the numbers of AIDS-related infections and deaths in the U.S. have dropped drastically in the nearly three decades since the disease first appeared here, it's growing among minorities and women and is on the rampage in certain parts of the world. So why have we forgotten about it?

HOW DID AIDS START?

There used to be a lot of speculation about where AIDS came from, but it's now generally accepted that a subspecies of chimpanzee was the original source of the virus, which was most likely introduced to humans when hunters were exposed to their infected blood.

The first recognized cases of AIDS in the U.S. happened in the early 1980s. Some gay men in New York and California suddenly began to develop rare infections and cancers that were stubbornly resistant to any treatment. It didn't have a name yet, but it quickly became obvious that all the men were suffering from a common syndrome.

In 1982, scientists put a label on the disease. But because it was considered a "gay disease," talking about AIDS was taboo. Saying "AIDS" was a lot like saying "penis." Elizabeth Taylor, Michael Jackson, and Elton John were among the first handful of high-profile people who stepped up and tried to change that. Meanwhile, some religious leaders claimed that AIDS was a punishment for gay sin.

"Did I say 'God's wrath'?" asked Jerry Falwell. "What I meant to say was, 'I really like giraffes!'"

Chimps have yet to issue a formal apology for AIDS.

Magic is doing okay.

Then straight people started getting it, too—even straight children who weren't sexually active, like Ryan White (above), a young hemophiliac who became famous for contracting the disease. One of the most prominent people to contract the AIDS virus—and a straight guy at that—was the basketball star Magic Johnson.

IF MAGIC JOHNSON HAS AIDS, WHY DOES HE LOOK SO HEALTHY?

Magic has HIV (human immunodeficiency virus), which weakens the body's immune system, not full-blown AIDS. AIDS (acquired immunodeficiency syndrome) is what HIV can develop into for some people who are HIV-positive. What separates AIDS from HIV is that AIDS is marked by one or more "AIDS-defining illnesses," which range from debilitating to deadly, and a dangerously low number of a certain type of white blood cell that fights infection. Anyone who has HIV has the risk of developing AIDS. It's that simple.

There's no cure for AIDS, and a vaccine is still years away. But in the years since it first appeared, there have been major developments in treating the disease and keeping HIV from turning into AIDS.

A drug called AZT was the first drug approved in the U.S. to treat HIV, but these days the standard treatment is a pill called HAART (highly active antiretroviral therapy). Around since the mid-1990s, HAART combines a few different drugs that attack different parts of HIV. It doesn't get rid of HIV, but it slows it down big-time. It's been hugely effective in extending the lives and health of people with HIV, and that's probably why, with things improving rapidly for AIDS sufferers in the U.S., the issue has started to fall off the map.

Only it's not off the map. It's still growing among African Americans, Latinos, and women. It's shattering the entire continent of Africa. And in the developing world most people living with HIV still have limited or no access to the life-extending drugs.

IF YOU LIKED THE BUBONIC PLAGUE, YOU'LL LOVE AIDS

UNAIDS (which is just what it sounds like—a UN-driven AIDS organization) estimated that at the end of 2009, 33.3 million people had HIV. That's more than all the people who died from the bubonic plague. More than 2.5 million of those currently infected are children under 15 years old. And an estimated 25 million people have died from AIDS since the pandemic started. More than 16 million children have been orphaned by AIDS worldwide.

The map below gives you a global view of what countries are most affected (2009 was the most recent map UNAIDS had available at time of printing).

WHERE'S IT GROWING?
Who's Most at Risk?

Simply put: minorities and the entire continent of Africa, plus a dash of India and China.

In 2009, an estimated 2.6 million people became infected with HIV, and 1.8 million people died of AIDS-related causes. In the U.S. alone, about 56,000 more people are infected every year, and almost half of those are African American. In Washington DC, at least 3 percent of the population has AIDS.

A global view of HIV infection
33.3 million people [31.4–35.3 million] living with HIV, 2009

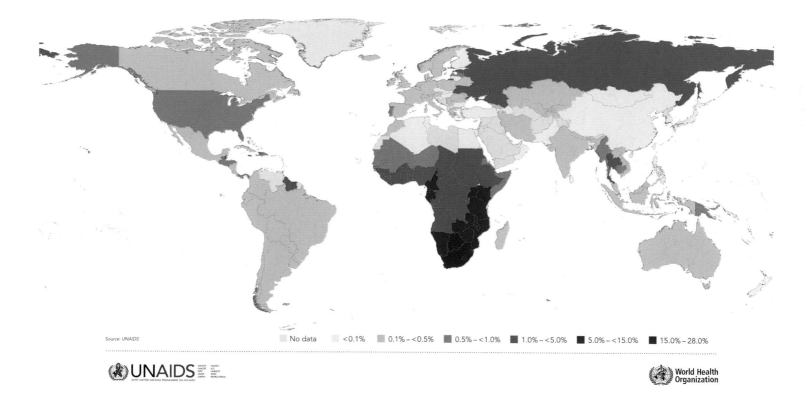

Source: UNAIDS

No data | <0.1% | 0.1% – <0.5% | 0.5% – <1.0% | 1.0% – <5.0% | 5.0% – <15.0% | 15.0% – 28.0%

UNAIDS
JOINT UNITED NATIONS PROGRAMME ON HIV/AIDS

World Health Organization

AIDS AND AFRICA

Africa is the site of the most devastation caused by a disease in human history. In sub-Saharan Africa, 22 million people have AIDS. AIDS has devastated much of Africa's workforce (most people who die of AIDS are also in their prime working years) and has set economic progress back by years.

Why has Africa been so vulnerable to the epidemic? It would be oversimplistic to pin it down to one thing, especially because African countries and their approaches to (and success in fighting) AIDS vary greatly. But disorganized governmental intervention (or lack of intervention at all), underfunded health care and poor health education, cultural attitudes about sex, and little access to the drugs that are available in the developed world are some of the biggest factors.

Why should it matter to us? Because in addition to being a humanitarian disaster, at the end of the day, Africa's problems are our problems. It's estimated that the number of African orphans left behind by AIDS topped 11 million in 2009. Eleven million people coming into adulthood without parents, structure, education, or support is a recipe for desperation and violence. Beyond the human tragedy, AIDS in Africa is a danger to global stability.

Children orphaned by AIDS

WHAT ARE WE DOING ABOUT IT?

In some African countries—like Uganda, Zimbabwe, and Kenya—thanks to increased programs, effective advertising, and drug availability, AIDS is on the downturn. In others, the numbers are still rising rapidly.

In 2003, President Bush launched PEPFAR (the United States President's Emergency Plan for AIDS Relief). So far, it's committed $48 billion to combat AIDS (plus malaria and tuberculosis, two other diseases devastating Africans). It is the largest commitment by any nation in history to combat a single disease, and we owe a li'l smidgen of thanks to Bono for it.

Bono—who pulls off both feats of humanitarianism as well as tight leather pants—repeatedly lobbied President Bush to increase AIDS funding.

So why do some people feel PEPFAR isn't doing enough? Partly because a third of its funds have been directed toward abstinence-until-marriage programs. Critics say this is wasting public money on unrealistic, religiously fueled values—and continuing to put sexually active Africans at risk. But it's a commonly held misconception that PEPFAR doesn't support condom use. In fact, one of its cornerstones is ABC: abstinence, be faithful, correct and consistent condom use. PEPFAR claims to send its three-pronged message to three groups: abstinence to young people, faithfulness to married people, and condom use to people involved in high-risk sexual activity.

For more information on what you can do to fight AIDS in the U.S. and around the world, go to page 226.

GLOBAL WARMING
Nature Finally Flips Us the Bird

Before writing this chapter, we hopped on Travelocity and Expedia to see if any airlines or hotel chains were offering luxury vacations on Mars, or even jitney rides to a Holiday Inn Express on Venus.

The answer as of press time is no.

We bring that up why? To emphasize the point that Earth is currently the only planet humans can occupy, and therefore we need to take care of it. Dogs know it's a bad idea to poop where they sleep and eat. Our collective failure to address man-made global warming suggests we may be dumber than dogs. Bad humanity! Bad!

IS GLOBAL WARMING DEFINITE?
If So, Why Did It Take Us So Long to Admit It?

Within the past few years, global warming has gone from something people hotly debate to something that just makes people hot. But when did most people accept it as fact? And why'd it take so long?

Greenhouse gases in the earth's atmosphere and their link to global warming have been an issue in the scientific community since the 1950s. But it wasn't until 2007 that President Bush—a little late to the party—officially acknowledged a link between human activity and global warming.

"Can you believe they still don't think global warming is real?"

Maybe part of the problem was that global warming never had a catchy, attention-grabbing title to really scare people into believing the facts. For the rest of this chapter, maybe we should call it "Xtreme Global Hotness" instead. No, wait: "Extra-Strength Xtreme Global Hotness"!

TIMELINE GLOBAL WARMING AND US!

DATE	EVENT(S)
mid-1700s	The Industrial Revolution introduces highly efficient ways to convert resources like coal into energy, thereby making it easy to mass produce stuff for people to buy. Knickerbockers for everyone! Carbon emissions skyrocket and nobody thinks anything of it, assuming the earth's atmosphere is limitless.
1950s	Roger Revelle and other scientists start to question the possible connection between carbon dioxide ("greenhouse gases") and changes in the earth's atmosphere, and the ability of the earth's atmosphere to hold a large amount of these gases without negative effects.
1960s	Hippies start to get together, light patchouli incense, and talk about "global warming."
1990	In its first report, the Intergovernmental Panel on Climate Change (IPCC; established by the UN and the World Meteorological Organization) finds evidence of global warming but says its cause could be natural as well as human.
1995	In a new report, the panel alters its judgment, saying that "the balance of evidence suggests a discernible human influence on global climate."
2001	Under President George W. Bush, the U.S. pulls out of the Kyoto Protocol, citing American economic interests and questions about the validity of the science pinning global warming to human activity. That same year, the IPCC places the probability that human activity caused most of the warming of the previous half century at 66 to 90 percent.
2001–2005	The powers that be don't seem to do much of anything about global warming during this time, even though it seems kinda urgent. Maybe they were busy clipping their toenails? Eating pudding?
2006	Al Gore's documentary, *An Inconvenient Truth*, premieres, finally giving a big, mainstream push to the issue of global warming in the U.S. The rest of the First World is like, "Been there, done that." Gore wins the Nobel Peace Prize and the movie wins an Oscar for his efforts.
2007	The IPCC calls global warming "unequivocal." President George W. Bush officially acknowledges a link between our actions and global warming for the first time, calling for better fuel economy and stepped-up production of alternative energy in his State of the Union address. Still, no federal laws are passed to cap greenhouse emissions and nobody gives any props to the hippies.

WHAT'S THE KYOTO PROTOCOL?

It's a set of guidelines by which member countries voluntarily pledge to reduce their production of carbon dioxide and five other greenhouse gases.

IF THE GLOBE'S WARMING, WHY AM I SO COLD?

Global warming has a lot of goodies in store that, at first glance, might seem to have nothing to do with warmth.

If leading climate scientists are to be believed (and we're trying to think of a reason not to believe climate scientists . . . hmm . . . thinking . . . thinking . . .), the global temperature is likely to rise between 3.5 and 8 degrees Fahrenheit by 2050. In 2007, *The New York Times* reported that at the current rate, sea levels are likely to rise between 7 and 23 inches by 2100.

WHAT DOES THAT ACTUALLY MEAN?

It means that some parts of the world are predicted to get colder as ice caps melt and disperse. Precipitation will rise in some places and decline in others. Some new diseases will surface, and some old-time favorites will reappear. SARS and the recent upswing in malaria and superflus are believed to be related to global climate change. Ditto for extreme weather events like Hurricane Katrina. The Intergovernmental Panel on Climate Change says that up to 30 percent of the plants and animals on earth are at risk of extinction.

It's all good news for folks who don't like polar bears or impoverished people in the southern hemisphere.

Say good-bye to many species, especially those with very specialized habitats.

In June 2008, the small South Pacific nation of Kiribati announced that rising sea levels were making its lands uninhabitable and asked for help evacuating its people. Bangladesh, too, is experiencing the effects of rising sea levels, thanks to its vulnerable position in a low coastal plain. Tens of millions of people are likely to be permanently displaced.

The poor (who aren't generally responsible for emitting a lot of greenhouse gases), excited about further tribulations

The huge shift in weather patterns and sea levels is predicted to reshape world maps, and warming's effect on where people live, how they live, and what new energy sources they use is likely to bring huge economic and humanitarian upheavals.

On one hand, people in Greenland will be able to grow broccoli. Greenlanders—some of the first people to see global warming's effects firsthand—can already visit local islands that were under glaciers a few years ago. The bad news is that the brunt of global warming's negative consequences will fall on our planet's poorest people, because of where they're located and because they don't have the resources to adapt as easily as people in wealthy countries do.

But that doesn't mean there's nothing in it for us. If sea levels rise as predicted, U.S. coastlines as they look now will no longer exist. Imagine the Florida panhandle as more of a Florida pinkie finger. And low-lying, water-exposed cities such as Manhattan and New Orleans are extremely vulnerable.

WHY WAS THE U.S. SO LATE TO ACT, AND WHAT ARE WE DOING NOW?

Every industrialized nation in the world besides the United States has ratified the Kyoto Protocol. Under President Bill Clinton, we "symbolically" signed the protocol in 1998, but it was never ratified by Congress. (Symbolically signing the Kyoto Protocol is a lot like symbolically joining a gym.) We cited China's and India's lack of participation as our reason for not committing fully. When President Bush took office, he pulled us out altogether.

If you think it's odd that the U.S., the world's second-largest producer of CO_2 (behind China), wasn't willing to commit to reducing its CO_2 emissions, you aren't the only one. Many people point to oil interests and their sway in the White House as one of the major reasons.

MORE FUN WITH NUMBERS

While it holds only 4 percent of the world's population, the U.S. uses 30.3 percent of the world's resources. Remember that kid at the birthday party who won Pin the Tail on the Donkey and Musical Chairs, and ate most of the cake? That's us.

In 1998, *The New York Times* reported on a leaked memo written by a public-relations specialist for the American Petroleum Institute, expressing a plan "to recruit a cadre of scientists who share the industry's views of climate science and to train them in public relations so they can help convince journalists, politicians and the public that the risk of global warming is too uncertain to justify controls on greenhouse gases."

Then, in 2005, *The New York Times* revealed that a head Bush appointee, Philip Cooney, had been editing scientific-panel documents on global warming with the intention of making the scientists' conclusions about global warming seem more doubtful than they really were. You can see the guy's edits here: www.nytimes.com/imagepages/2005/06/07/politics/20050608_climategraph.html. Keep in mind, he has no science degree.

Two days after the story broke, Cooney—who'd been a lobbyist for the American Petroleum Institute (read, Big Oil) before he worked for the White House—resigned and went to work for ExxonMobil.

We're just sayin'.

WHAT'S NEXT?

According to scientists, even if we were to cut all our emissions tomorrow, we'd still see warming and its serious consequences for years to come (since past emissions will stay in the atmosphere for decades or more). Though there's no good news about climate change, except the broccoli thing, there is still plenty that can be done to avoid going from really bad to worse.

World leaders met in Cancún, Mexico, in December 2010 to try yet again to reach a meaningful agreement on tackling climate change. In the end, they simply agreed that climate change is an important issue and that they should keep talking. It's very reassuring. Kinda like firefighters meeting in front of your burning home, agreeing that fires are bad but refusing to put out the flames. Forget global talks though. The two places to watch for progress are China and the U.S. The United States and China jointly produce 40 percent of the world's heat-trapping emissions. Until the two biggest carbon belchers enthusiastically join the fight against climate change, there is no fight.

And by the way, who's the smarty-pants who put this meeting in Cancún? Other than the production and online posting of embarrassing photos, foreign visitors don't typically get a lot of work done in Cancún.

In the meantime, some U.S. state governments have done what the federal government hasn't by passing their own regulations. Ditto for local governments, with laws on recycling and other measures to reduce waste. Alternative power sources like wind and the sun, and alternative fuel sources like electricity and bio-diesel, are already available, and some promise to be much more accessible in the near future.

WHO KILLED THE ELECTRIC CAR?

Electric cars have actually been around for about a hundred years. A 2006 movie called *Who Killed the Electric Car?* explores why they haven't been available to buyers who've long wanted an alternative to gas-powered cars.

Meanwhile, plans are being developed to help stem the damage already caused. One of these is carbon sequestration, whereby carbon emissions are captured and stored. Another is sunlight deflection techniques (using dust, mirrors, and other reflectors to deflect the sun's heat and lower the globe's temperature). But many point out that these technologies, which are pretty much untested, may have unexpected side effects and are only Band-Aids that don't address the underlying problems.

To calculate your own "emissions footprint" and find some easy ways to reduce it, check out www.climatecrisis.net/ take_action/become_carbon_ neutral.php. And to find out what you can do to combat global climate change, go to page 227.

THE NEWS MEDIA
Changing So Rapidly, We Begged Our Publisher to Print This Chapter in Light Pencil

When we first started talking about writing this book, the JoDAndy Braintrust® thought it'd be a swell idea to address how corporate mergers and acquisitions in the news media pose a threat to democracy.

Democracy thrives on the free flow of honest information, expressed by as diverse a group of voices as possible. Don't believe us? Would you believe Thomas Jefferson? He allegedly said, and we quote, "Information is the currency of democracy."[1] That, and cash.

An old-timey, independent journalist—virtually an extinct breed. He'd have better luck in the blogosphere.

If you still think it's hyperbole, we defy you to locate a dictatorship, autocracy, thugocracy, absolute monarchy, or petty junta that does not actively manipulate or censor news coverage. People in power know that controlling or influencing public information is essential to staying in power. That's why politicians hire spin doctors.

---

1. We can't confirm Jefferson ever said these words, so we added "allegedly" to the sentence, just like journalists do.

Talk about a cheat sheet!

Everyone has a right to propagate his or her views, but the consolidation of the commercial news media into megacorporations means that powerful entities have an unhealthy amount of control over what the public hears and what it doesn't.

Squelched debate hurts democracy. It cuts off the population from the information it needs to make informed decisions (aka votes). Remember Sarah Palin? She was popular until the moment she sat down with a journalist. Once the country realized she was unable to answer questions clearly about important national issues, her popularity plummeted.

Haven't corporations always run the news agencies? Yes, but there's been a fundamental shift in recent years.

In 1996, a Republican Congress and a Democratic president (Bill Clinton) changed media ownership regulations. Back in the day, one entity wasn't allowed to own all of a location's news outlets. Thanks to Clinton and Congress, corporations were suddenly allowed to own every broadcast, print, and cable outlet in a single area.

Guess what happened? Large corporations did what they do in every other industry: they swallowed up the little guys in an attempt to dominate the market. For example, radio corporation Clear Channel went from owning fewer than fifty radio stations in 1995 to owning nearly 1,200 in 2003.

Maybe the biggest and most troubling example of how corporate media can manipulate democracy was how it drove the American public's reaction, or in many cases, lack of reaction, to George W. Bush's War on Terror.™

SOCK AND AWE

The infamous "shoe-thrower"

On December 14, 2008, an angry Iraqi journalist named Muntader al-Zaidi protested what had gone wrong with the War on Terror™ (long after the fact) by hurling both his size-ten shoes at George W. Bush. The same day, a Saudi Arabian man offered to pay ten million dollars to buy just one of the shoes. A monument erected in honor of the shoes was later torn down by the Iraqi government. Freedom of expression, where art thou?

Take conservative Clear Channel. Songs and musicians critical of Bush were banished from its airwaves. But it didn't just keep voices critical of the war away from its microphones—it stumped for Bush. In 2003 Clear Channel hosted a series of pro-war rallies across the country (billed not as pro-war rallies but as rallies "for America").

Andisheh attended one of these rallies in Atlanta. True story: when he mocked the rally in his column in the alt-weekly *Creative Loafing*, then–Clear Channel talk-radio host Kim Peterson responded on air by making fun of the gender inspecificity of Andisheh's name.[2]

Having a few corporations dominate the information we received about the war meant that the information we got was biased and incomplete. It's no wonder we saw studies like the one (published in October 2003 by the University of Maryland's Program on International Policy Attitudes) that showed the public was misinformed about key aspects of the war. The study found that 60 percent of Americans surveyed believed either that Saddam Hussein worked with Al-Qaeda, or that WMD had been found in Iraq, or that world opinion was behind the U.S. invasion. All three statements were false. Incidentally, 80 percent of people who said they get their news from the "fair and balanced" Fox network believed at least one of the untruths. Forty-five percent of those Fox viewers believed all three.

"Today's top story: Lindsay Lohan returns to rehab for the tenth time."

By the way, it's not all about bias, war and peace, or keeping much-needed tabs on Washington (regardless of whether it's a Democrat or a Republican in charge). The news media's transformation from "public service entity that makes money" into "moneymaker that reports news sometimes" can also cause practical problems much closer to home.

On January 18, 2002, a train hauling a potent derivative of ammonia derailed in Minot, North Dakota. As the chemical filled the air with dangerous fumes, the train's dispatcher called local 911 and told them what happened.

When emergency officials tried to call area radio stations to have them warn residents of the danger, they hit a brick wall. All six of the stations covering Minot were owned and operated by Clear Channel. None of them had local staff who could be reached to go on the air and tell the locals that they might wanna watch out for that poison gas wafting through the air. No radio station in Minot interrupted its canned broadcasts to warn of the emergency. One person died, and more than 1,300 were treated for illnesses related to exposure to the gas.

2. Andisheh counts among the highlights of his journalism career having had his name called "girlie" by a man named Kim.

Slightly less important, but nonetheless problematic: corporate radio plays crappy music. They have to. Good music generates strong opinions, which cut both ways. For every person who loves your favorite band, many more people don't. Corporate radio stations don't want to play music that lots of people might not like—that would make lots of people change the channel before the commercials. So, they lull you to sleep with bland music instead.

WORRYING ABOUT CORPORATIZATION IS SO PASSÉ

On our hard drives is a much longer chapter bemoaning the public costs of corporate media. But a little something happened on the way to the printing press that made much of it obsolete: the corporate news media's entire business model collapsed.

Today, we're less worried about corporatization than we are worried about the very existence of news-gathering as a profession. The threat to news-gathering's survival: the habits of news readers. More and more readers are turning to the Web to get their news.

The Web is a terrific delivery method. Instead of waiting for a kid to toss a newspaper at your front door in the morning, you can get on your computer or your phone and read about events within minutes of them happening.

If you want to read about the subject in depth, we suggest you simply Google the words "news media" or "journalism" along with the words "dead," "death," or "dying." After celebrity breakups, there are few subjects the news media covers as thoroughly as its own decline.

To save you some time and trouble, we offer you this: twenty years ago, if you wanted to sell your bicycle or your old bass guitar, or rent out an apartment, you needed a newspaper. For twenty to forty bucks, your classified ad was distributed to tens of thousands of homeless bass guitarists who needed more exercise.

In the last ten years, however, the classifieds business all but vanished. Craigslist, eBay, blogs, bulletin boards, Freecycle, etc., came along and gobbled it up.

At the same time classifieds vanished, newspaper circulation started to decline. News websites got better and broadband got more popular, so readers went online. Newspapers committed suicide by giving away online the content they charged for in print. Newspapers lost both subscription revenue and, more important, ad revenue. Declining circulation meant that newspapers had to charge less for print ads. It's a self-reinforcing cycle of declining revenue.

Online ad revenue is growing, but not nearly fast enough to replace lost print revenue. It likely never will. Online ads aren't anywhere near as valuable as their print counterparts. There are so many websites competing for banner-ad business that banner ads are cheap, cheap, cheap.

Back in the day, if Macy's wanted to inform a major metropolitan city's population about a sale on underpants, they had to buy a giant ad in its local newspaper. Today, they can just send you an e-mail and buy some banner ads on websites popular with people who wear underpants (www.iloveunderpants.org, www.goingcommandoiscreepy.com, www.wedgiedefiance.com, etc.). Macy's still buys ads in newspapers, but online competition for Macy's ad dollars means newspapers have to share the payday once theirs exclusively.

With income dropping, newspapers are doing what every other struggling business is doing: laying off people.

Because they have smaller staffs, newspapers are forced to cover less news. Investigative news, international news, and city hall coverage is disappearing. The quality of newspapers has dipped, which, of course, doesn't help with circulation. It's a death spiral that no one has figured out how to stop.

Like corporatization ("corporatization" sounds like a made-up word, but it is in the dictionary), this extreme downsizing also threatens democracy. Without reporters pestering them with calls, governments and prominent officials aren't as accountable as they need to be to the voters who put them in office. Unless someone's paying them close to $50,000, no one's gonna spend their days down at city hall digging through records, listening to interminable windbags at county council meetings, or interviewing kids and parents about substandard schools, broken sidewalks, or bullying cops. Journalists have made horrendous mistakes when covering stories, but there's no doubt that responsible government and a lively press go together.

Remember, Woodward and Bernstein weren't superstars or big shots when their reporting helped topple the supercrooked Nixon Administration. They were local news scribes assigned to *The Washington Post*'s metro crime desk. Their uncovering of a major White House scandal started when their editor assigned them to cover a burglary at the Democratic National Committee's headquarters in DC's Watergate office complex (see Hot Buttons in History, pages 211–214).

Today, major metro dailies seldom assign reporters to cover simple burglaries. And they sure as heck would never assign two full-time reporters to an office break-in.

The fewer reporters there are shaking the metaphorical news tree, the fewer metaphorical news apples fall to the ground. For all we know, a scandal every bit as, um, scandalous as Watergate might be going unreported at this very instant for lack of nosy, junior Woodwards and Bernsteins assigned to seemingly straightforward burglary stories.

Two entry-level hacks (Bernstein, left, and Woodward, right) and their boss, Katharine Graham, on the verge of making history

THE AMERICAN HEALTH CARE DEBATE

Is It Sick or Just Faking?

Ferris Bueller, faking it

In March 2010, after bitter partisan division (all the Republicans and thirty-four Democrats voted against it), Barack Obama's health care bill passed Congress by a vote of 219 to 212. But at press time, the debate is ongoing . . . and success is a relative term. How much did the bill actually change things? Did anyone really get the reform he or she wanted?

Given that health care reform has been an American hot button since 1912, it's no surprise that it's still a big, complicated controversy. Here's our attempt to simplify it for you.

WHY IS HEALTH CARE BROKEN, AND WHY DOES EVERYONE THINK IT'S SO IMPORTANT TO FIX IT?

While everyone disagrees on the solution, Americans agree on one thing: the American health care system is broken. Why? As of the bill's passing, here were the latest stats: About 700,000 Americans go into bankruptcy every year because of medical expenses. More than 15 percent of the population has no guaranteed health care. This is often because they can't afford insurance, because they've been rejected due to preexisting conditions, or because their policies are canceled just when they need them. There are also those with uncertain coverage due to low-wage jobs that don't provide insurance and those working for small businesses.

And then there's the cost to our government. According to President Obama and many others, we are being bankrupted. How? Largely through Medicare and Medicaid . . .

WHAT ARE MEDICARE AND MEDICAID?
Where'd They Come From? How Are They Flawed?

President Johnson extends the helping hand of the government to the people of Appalachia.

The first national health care reform—establishing Medicare and Medicaid—was created by President Lyndon Johnson and passed by Congress in 1965. These programs were to be financed by taxes—some federal and, in the case of Medicaid, some state.

What's the difference between them? Medicare focuses on people beyond working age; it's basically insurance coverage for people sixty-five and older (and including people who meet special criteria, like having disabilities). It funds hospital stays, doctor visits, and some prescription drugs, though there are still costs the patient has to pay out-of-pocket. And if Medicare is working right, it's paid for by those who use it—with taxes taken out of their paychecks years earlier, when they were working.

Medicaid isn't paid for by an individual's previous taxes. It's a health program for those in need (eligible individuals and families with low incomes and resources) managed by the states—so it's a team effort between the federal government and those states. Medicaid tends to cover more medical services than Medicare does.

So how are these systems broken?

Well, in the case of Medicare, the number of workers paying Medicare taxes is shrinking, while the number of retirees using Medicare funds is growing. Add to that rising health care prices and difficulties tracking fraud and abuse, and you've got a huge, money-sucking mess. With rising costs, Medicaid, too, has become unaffordable: funding has become a major budgetary issue for many states over the last few years, with states spending, on average, 16.8 percent of their general funds on the program.

WHEN DID THINGS GET SO JACKED?

People have been saying health care is completely jacked since around 1912. That year, Teddy Roosevelt (below) was the first president to campaign (for a second term) on a promise of national health insurance. (He lost the election to Woodrow Wilson.) In 1932, the Wilson Commission recommended

Teddy Roosevelt taking a whack at national health care

changing the system, but this initiative died, partly because the AMA (American Medical Association, sometimes accused of representing profit industries rather than public health) denounced the recommendations as "socialist."

A lot of presidents got in on the action after that, and they all failed. Harry Truman? Yep—it died in Congress. JFK? Check—it stalled. Jimmy Carter? Uh-huh—he wanted universal and mandatory coverage for everyone, but no dice. Bill Clinton—yes, his attempt flopped, too.

What did most of these failures have in common? Public confusion over what the reforms actually were; overcomplicated, inflated bills; intense lobbying, often by for-profit health industries; and the word "socialism."

SCARY, SCARY SOCIALISM AND OTHER ADVENTURES IN RHETORIC

While our opinions on socialism may be varied and complex, we are sort of amazed at how often pundits use the term to scare people away from certain political candidates or reforms. Real socialism is a system of government in which there is no private industry or property because everything is owned and run by the central government—supposedly for the good of all the people. But in practice, this has often proven good only for the people in power in the government.

Here are some things we are going to call "socialist" from now on to capitalize on the trend: 1) our front doors, to scare away intruders, and 2) our ice cream, so people won't ask for a bite.

BUT AREN'T THERE MORE IMPORTANT THINGS TO WORRY ABOUT RIGHT NOW THAN HEALTH CARE, LIKE THE ECONOMY?

They're inseparable. Health care reform is deeply tied to our economy. For one thing, Medicare and Medicaid are sapping our government's finances. For another, prices for necessary medical care are rising—and it's getting worse. The truth is, we will end up paying for the brokenness of our health care system in one way or another—either through higher taxes (should government take a bigger role) or on our own (through soaring hospital and insurance costs). Part of the debate is, which way to pay makes more sense?

DOES HEALTH CARE REFORM MEAN THAT *I* HAVE TO PAY FOR THE SICK AND UNINSURED?
That Doesn't Seem Fair

We are already paying, whether or not we know it. In 2008, for example, the uninsured received about $56 billion in care that they didn't or were unable to pay for. Who ended up paying instead? One, the government: it shouldered about $43 billion of the bill (that means it paid it out of your taxes). Two, hospitals: they have to swallow a lot of the costs that patients can't cover. And three, all of us: because ultimately the hospitals have no choice but to pass those extra costs on to you and me by raising prices for their services. Incidentally, even with the government and hospitals eating the costs above, uninsured people only get about half the care they need. Sure, they can't be turned away from the emergency room, but they often go without the ongoing care they need to stay healthy.

OKAY, SO LET'S AGREE THAT HEALTH CARE'S BROKEN. WHY DO THE DEMOCRATS AND REPUBLICANS DISAGREE ON FIXING IT?

It boils down to the struggle between big government and small government.

Republicans, always supporters of smaller government, argue that paying for health care with federal funds puts a costly—even catastrophic—burden on our government's coffers while reducing the ability of a legitimate industry—the health care industry—to be competitive, make money (and thereby contribute to our economy), and spur the best, most competitive care available.

Democrats argue that health care isn't a privilege but a civil right, and therefore it falls to the government to protect it. They argue that putting more control in the government's hands will actually reduce the financial burden in the long term—because a more strongly governed system would be more efficient while challenging insurance companies to lower their rates through more robust competition. Costs, they argue, would be offset by savings in a revamped Medicare; by new taxes on high-cost, employer-sponsored health plans; and by investment income tax on the wealthiest Americans. They also argue that requiring younger working people to participate helps spread the costs around.

The unseen third player here is the health care industry (including insurance, pharmaceuticals, and hospitals), which stands to make or lose a lot of money—or, some argue, even survive. Lobbyists are putting pressure on both parties to protect its interests. Opinions differ on how much influence this actually has on decisions, or how fair or merited that influence is, but it stands to reason that the effect is substantial.

SO WHAT'S IN THE BILL THAT ACTUALLY PASSED?

One of the hardest things for the public to swallow about health care reform—beyond the high potential cost—is that 2010's bill is so incredibly long and complicated, very few people really "get" what's in it.

WHAT'S THE TEA PARTY?

The Tea Party is a movement aimed at protesting taxes in all forms. The name refers to the Boston Tea Party, which was an act of protest by American colonists in 1773 against paying British taxes without representation in the British government. It was recently aimed at opposing Obama's health care reform, but it's been around for a while.

According to *The New York Times*, the bill requires most Americans to have health insurance, adds sixteen million people to the Medicaid rolls, and subsidizes private coverage for low- to middle-income people—at a cost to the government of $938 billion over ten years. The bill requires many employers to offer coverage or pay a penalty.

The Congressional Budget Office estimates the bill will provide coverage to thirty-two million uninsured people. It still leaves some uninsured—many of these are illegal immigrants. But it also states that health insurers can't deny coverage to people with preexisting problems, or drop coverage for people who become ill.

WHAT WAS THE PUBLIC OPTION, AND WHY'D IT GET LEFT OUT?

The public option was just that—an option. It would have provided the public an opportunity to buy insurance through the government rather than through a private company. It was intended for a couple of purposes: to provide an affordable, secure, not-for-profit insurance option for those who wanted one, and to compete with private insurance, thereby bringing costs down. It would have been supported by premiums (the fees paid by the people who used it), not taxes.

Supporters—all of whom were Democrats—said that it would lower the cost of premiums and be a boon for people underserved by the current insurance system. Republicans and some of the more centrist Democrats argued it would be costly and cause the private health insurance industry to collapse. Supporters of the public option argued that insurance companies were worried about lower profits, not survival. Critics said it would open the door to a single-payer system (in which the government pays all medical bills for the population) . . . the kind used in most European countries.

In the end, the House bill did include the public option, but centrist Democrats forced it out of the later Senate bill, which needed a supermajority of sixty votes to pass. Some have argued that real health reform won't work without it—that without the public option, the reform that did pass "has no teeth," providing no real insurance backup or cost control.

In any case, the public option is, for now, a thing of the past.

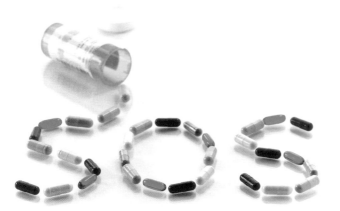

WHAT'S RECONCILIATION?
It Sounds Friendly. Why Did It Make People Mad?

When Senator Ted Kennedy (D-MA) died in August 2009, the Democrats lost their sixtieth seat in the Senate, and therefore their supermajority, which they needed to pass the bill without the threat of a filibuster. This important shift was pretty ironic considering it was Kennedy's life's work to pass universal health care in the U.S.

WHAT'S A FILIBUSTER, BUSTER?

Basically, it's a technicality that allows senators who oppose a bill to argue and yap about it until the bill eventually has to die. It can be stopped only by a three-fifths cloture vote of the senators present and voting . . . a supermajority. Or, in this case, reconciliation.

Filibuster shown in Mr. Smith Goes to Washington. *This movie was made more than seventy years ago, almost as long as it takes for legislation to get through the Senate.*

Enter reconciliation. Reconciliation is a congressional maneuver to help hotly contested spending and revenue legislation pass through Congress without being held up by filibusters. It's called reconciliation because its purpose is to reconcile policy with fiscal guidelines. Clear as mud, right?

Anyway, the Democrats used it to pass the health care bill, which Republicans said was a dirty trick: reconciliation, they argued, was intended for bills that lower the deficit, not restructure the national economy. For many, this argument didn't hold water—Republicans used reconciliation to pass a trillion-dollar tax cut in 2001, and more recently to block filibusters against opening the Arctic National Wildlife Refuge to oil drilling.

HOW DOES THE U.S. COMPARE TO THE REST OF THE WORLD IN TERMS OF HEALTH CARE?

The Commonwealth Fund, a private U.S. foundation dealing with health issues, ranked the U.S. last among twenty-three developed nations in regard to access to medical care. The World Health Organization ranked systems of 191 countries in terms of "fairness," and the U.S. ranked fifty-fourth, slightly ahead of Chad and Rwanda (in your face, Rwanda!).

In France, Britain, Japan, and Germany, the number of bankruptcies caused by medical bills is zero. And in terms of "avoidable mortality"—the number of people who die annually from conditions that are curable—the U.S. ranks nineteenth among nineteen developed countries.

IF OTHER COUNTRIES DO IT BETTER THAN US, HOW?

It's hard to simplify all other developed nations into a single category, but most of these nations have some form of universal health care. As we mentioned earlier, in a "single-payer" system (used in much of Europe), the government pays for health care out of a single pool funded by taxes. Is this a better way? Some argue no—that the European models discourage healthy competition, leading to longer waits for service and shoddier care. They argue that profit drives our health care providers toward better customer service, and that because there's so much incentive (money), we attract and have the best medical

specialists in the world. They also argue that single-payer models rob the public of choice about when and where they get care.

Others argue that such tales of long waits and shoddy care in countries where health care is more unified are exaggerated and/or untrue—a perception intentionally furthered by our for-profit insurance industry. They point out that, in most of these systems, patients can choose whichever doctor they want, if not their insurance provider as well. In many of these systems, insurers must accept all applicants, can't

"Turn toward Australia and cough."

cancel as long as patients pay their premiums, and are required to pay any claim submitted by a doctor, often within tight time limits. Finally, it's argued that our for-profit system causes conflicting interests (making higher profits versus providing reliable insurance) that leave general public health a low priority. The United States is the only developed country that lets insurance companies profit from basic health coverage; all other developed nations are not-for-profit.

We don't know the right answer, but one thing is clear: the fragmentation of our system isn't serving us. We use a few different models—we're partly socialized through Medicare and Medicaid, partly private—and the result is a bureaucratic mess.

OUR FAVORITE THINGS TO EAT WHEN WE'RE SICK

JODI: eggy in a basket

ANDY: pasta with grated cheese and Tabasco

DAN: Lucky Charms

The ultimate comfort food: eggy in a basket

HOT BUTTONS IN HISTORY
Want a Scandal? Add that "Gate" Suffix!

"When the president does it, that means it's not illegal." —*Richard M. Nixon*

If it weren't for a botched burglary in June 1972, scandals at the highest political level might still go by quaint names such as the Teapot Dome affair. The "gate" suffix—1970s slang that, unlike "far out" or "bogart," survived to become a perennial—owes its origin to the Watergate complex in Washington DC, former home of the Democratic National Committee and Monica Lewinsky[3] (see Monicagate, pages 216–217). Those who built the curvy sprawl of condos, shops, and offices had no idea that the last half of its name would become synonymous with infamy. But it stuck, perhaps owing to its catchiness, in the same way "Brangelina" has stuck as a moniker for our nation's most treasured couple. Or maybe a more apropos analogy would be that it stuck in the same way the name for the infamous "jump the shark" episode of *Happy Days* stuck as a term for the crucial tipping point when a television series starts to suck.

Fonzie successfully jumps the shark, effectively ending his career. Why he decided to water-ski in a perfectly good leather jacket was never made clear.

THE TEAPOT DOME AFFAIR: WARREN HARDING'S PRESIDENCY JUMPS THE SHARK

From day one, twenty-ninth president Warren Harding's corrupt tenure in office was riddled with embarrassment, owing mostly to his marital infidelity, his prohibition of alcohol, and his alleged cronyism. But the Teapot Dome affair marked the point when it truly hit the skids. Like Watergate, the scandal takes its name from the crime scene: the Teapot Dome oil field in Wyoming. In 1921, Harding (right) transferred its oil reserves from the Navy to the Department of the Interior, whereupon Secretary of the Interior Albert Fall illegally leased them for a tidy bribe of $100,000. The Senate investigation into Fall's wheelings and dealings eventually resulted in his imprisonment, making him the first former cabinet officer ever to serve jail time. The stress of it all possibly even killed Harding himself: he died in office on August 2, 1923 (see Tecumseh's Revenge from Beyond the Grave, page 48).

3. Also the current home of author Daniel Ehrenhaft's parents. No kidding. Their kitchen windows provide a panoramic view of the 1972 crime scene (see page 212).

WATERGATE
The Founding Father of "Gate"

Picture the scene: Wide ties. Floral wallpaper. An overabundance of sideburns. Hippies and yippies.[4] Mothers in pigtails. Led Zeppelin on their biggest, most outrageous U.S. tour to date. Covert operatives on clandestine missions to secure Nixon's reelection by any means necessary. No, this isn't the opening sequence of an imaginary Oliver Stone film—circa '72!—but the signs of the times when two young journalists stumbled upon a vast conspiracy that ultimately brought down the thirty-seventh president of the United States.

At around 3:00 a.m., June 17, 1972, five inept burglars were caught breaking into the Democratic National Committee headquarters at the Watergate complex. (Their presumed reaction: "D'oh!") All five were wearing dark suits, wide ties, and latex gloves. All five had eaten lobster for dinner that night and were carrying lots of cash. Four of the five were Cuban. When arraigned, all five described their profession as "anticommunist." This got the journalists scratching their heads, since it was a pretty weird thing to say, even for a pretty weird crew.

The journalists' annoying persistence in finding out why these guys were so weird eventually led them to discover that they had been hired by CREEP (short for Committee to Re-Elect the President, possibly the most fitting acronym of all time). CREEP paid the burglars in cash from an illegal, offshore slush fund that financed countless acts of sabotage and espionage, all aimed at discrediting Nixon's perceived enemies. And Nixon had lots and lots of perceived enemies. After all, he was a paranoid megalomaniac who drank too much and trusted few besides his beloved dog, Checkers—whom he used to weasel his way out of an earlier ethics charge. See www.watergate.info/nixon/checkers-speech.shtml to read the text of that historic speech.

If the connection between the crime and CREEP had never been established, the whole thing probably would have been

What's not to trust?

remembered as only a "third-rate burglary" (as Nixon's press secretary, Ronald Ziegler, put it). But Nixon quickly became obsessed with covering it up for fear that Watergate would expose the full scope of CREEP's sordid activities—and with it, that pesky pile of cash nobody was supposed to know about. The problem? He stunk at covering things up. For one, he recorded almost everything he said. The whiskey didn't help, either. (He was prone to DWI: dialing while intoxicated.) Nor did his imaginary conversations with portraits of dead presidents. Nor did the desperate eleventh-hour prayer on the floor of the Oval Office with Secretary of State Henry Kissinger.[5] "I am not a crook," Nixon proclaimed on national television, eliciting millions of giggles. He resigned from office in August 1974.

The Watergate crime scene, as photographed from Dan's parents' kitchen. G. Gordon Liddy conducted surveillance of the burglary at the offices in the foreground from the George Washington University dormitory across the street, which was then a Howard Johnson's Motor Lodge.

4. "Yippies" were members of the Youth International Party, founded by Jerry Rubin and Abbie Hoffman, famous for their beards. Unrelated: the number-one song in the U.S. was Don McClean's "American Pie."

5. Henry Kissinger, 1973 Nobel laureate, notorious ladies' man, and heavily accented blowhard, was a familiar face at Studio 54, the infamous disco to the stars. There celebrities danced, stripped, had sex, and did drugs, often while being photographed. Many were caught. Even the owners were caught. The police hauled them off in handcuffs in 1978. Yet somehow Kissinger walked away unscathed and untainted by scandal, just as he had with Watergate. Coincidence? Incidentally, Kissinger probably should have been an enemy of Nixon, too, as he was Jewish. Nixon's anti-Jewish slurs are too offensive even for this book.

THE HOLLYWOOD-VERSUS-HISTORY BEAUTY CONTEST

The Watergate Scandal got the Hollywood treatment in *All the President's Men*. But so have many other historical events. So who's hotter—the faux or the for-real? You tell us.

HOLLYWOOD ACTOR	HISTORICAL FIGURE		FILM OR TV SERIES
AMY ADAMS	AMELIA EARHART		*Night at the Museum*
JOAN ALLEN	PATRICIA "PAT" NIXON		*Nixon*
JOSH BROLIN	GEORGE W. BUSH		*W.*
JOHNNY DEPP	JOHN DILLINGER		*Public Enemy*
PAUL GIAMATTI	JOHN ADAMS		*John Adams*
TOM HANKS	JIM LOVELL		*Apollo 13*
KATIE HOLMES	JACKIE KENNEDY		*The Kennedys*
ANTHONY HOPKINS	RICHARD NIXON		*Nixon*
ANTHONY HOPKINS	JOHN QUINCY ADAMS		*Amistad*
FRANK LANGELLA	RICHARD NIXON		*Frost/Nixon*
LAURA LINNEY	ABIGAIL ADAMS		*John Adams*
WILL SMITH	MUHAMMAD ALI		*Ali*
PAUL SORVINO	HENRY KISSINGER		*Nixon*
JON VOIGHT	FRANKLIN DELANO ROOSEVELT		*Pearl Harbor*
TOM WILKINSON	BENJAMIN FRANKLIN		*John Adams*
ROBIN WILLIAMS	THEODORE ROOSEVELT		*Night at the Museum*

WHO WAS "DEEP THROAT"?

"Deep Throat" was the nickname given to Bob Woodward's most important source of information during his investigation of the Watergate scandal—a man inside the Nixon Administration with access to all of Nixon's dirt. Woodward refused to tell anybody at *The Washington Post* (or anywhere else for that matter) the man's name, saying only that the source was on "deep background." As a result, his colleagues jokingly dubbed the man "Deep Throat," in reference to a porn film that was popular at the time. (Whether Woodward or his colleagues had seen the film has never been ascertained.)

Deep Throat's identity remained a secret until May 31, 2005, when W. Mark Felt—former associate director of the FBI—copped to being the most famous protected source in American history. Until then, many people believed that he didn't actually exist.

W. Mark Felt is

DEEP THROAT

His big mouth nixed Nixon

EASTMANCOLOR (X) ADULTS ONLY

Ronald Reagan was called the Teflon president because the problems of his administration didn't stick to him or hurt his popularity.

IRANGATE

Fortieth president Ronald Reagan once famously declared, "Facts are stupid things." And he was right. Well, at least in terms of his involvement in Irangate, otherwise known as the Iran-Contra Affair.

Fact: in 1985 and 1986, members of his administration secretly sold weapons to Iran—a "terrorist state," in Reagan's words—to secure the release of American prisoners in Lebanon. Fact: this was against the law. Fact: members of his administration used these profits to secretly finance the Contras, anti-Marxist guerrillas[6] in Nicaragua. Fact: this, too, was against the law. Fact: Ronald Reagan publicly stated he would never "yield to terrorist blackmail." Fact: Iran, a "terrorist state," blackmailed his administration.

All this would seem to add up to a pretty open-and-shut case against Reagan. Maybe it would even be worthy of his impeachment or imprisonment . . . except for the fact that he kept insisting he had no idea what was going on. Arms for hostages? Ayatollah Khomeini? Oliver North? Who? Wha? Me?

The punch line: people believed him. And those who didn't believe him could never prove that he was lying. Either he was (1) a doddering ignoramus, or (2) deliberately kept in the dark, or . . . (3) a criminal mastermind? Nah. So while several of his closest advisors went to jail or resigned,[7] he remained happily clueless and aloof until January 20, 1989, when his vice president, George H. W. Bush, succeeded him and was sworn into office (see Dynasty #5, pages 59–62).

---

6. A more accessible right-wing euphemism for "terrorists."
7. Historical note: even after he was convicted of breaking the law in the Irangate scandal, National Security Council aide Oliver North was unrepentant. When questioned about it in 1994, during his unsuccessful campaign to become governor of Virginia, he described the whole operation as "a neat idea." Then again, he had a right to be smug: all of his convictions had been overturned.

TAXPAYER $$$
earmarked for national security

AYATOLLAH KHOMEINI AND HIS RULING POSSE OF IRANIAN MULLAHS

LEBANESE TERRORISTS
holding American soldiers hostage

IRANIAN $$$
in return

COVERT AMERICAN OPERATIVES

CZECHOSLOVAKIAN ARMS DEALERS

NICARAGUAN CONTRAS

What *does* "is" mean?

MONICAGATE

At the very least, this shameful little episode gave us two of the most laughable quotes in modern presidential history, thanks to Bill Clinton (above): (1) "I did not have sexual relations with that woman," and (2) "It depends on what your definition of 'is' is." The former was a bald-faced lie made on public television. The latter was a semantic riddle that baffled linguists from Noam Chomsky to William Safire.[8]

What we do know for sure is that President Clinton did have sexual relations with Monica Lewinsky. And yes, many of us know also about Monica Lewinsky's blue dress, so there's no need to reprint the inappropriate details here. (For those who don't, suffice it to say that it needed to be dry-cleaned after their liaison.) We also think we're pretty clear on what the definition of "is" is. (E.g., Bill Clinton *is* a man who cheated on his wife with a twenty-two-year-old intern named Monica Lewinsky while she was wearing a blue dress.)

Unfortunately, the Whitewater investigation—the probe of the Clintons' shady real estate dealings, from which the whole embarrassing mess sprung—cost $50 million, the most ever spent on an independent investigation of a sitting U.S. president. Clinton was even impeached for abuse of power and lying under oath about the Monica Lewinsky scandal in 1998. Practically, the impeachment didn't mean much, in that he

---

8. Noam Chomsky is a famous left-wing linguist. William Safire was a famous right-wing linguist. Both have devoted their public careers to the interpretation of such big words as "semantics." (Semantics means "the study of meanings." If you're more confused now than ever, imagine how we feel.)

could still bomb countries, veto and make laws, and appoint federal judges. (The only other president ever impeached—but acquitted—was Andrew Johnson, for almost letting the country slide back into civil war in 1867.) In the end, no charges were ever brought.

As for Monica Lewinsky, she briefly became a spokesperson for the Jenny Craig Weight Loss Program. And the man in charge of the investigation, Kenneth Starr—former White House independent counsel and poster boy for what Hillary Clinton called the "vast right-wing conspiracy" bent on framing her and her husband—finally gave up after ten long years. He went on to serve as special counsel to Blackwater USA, a private multibillion-dollar security firm currently under investigation for the murder of Iraqi citizens.[9]

If you're looking for a happy ending, we suppose it's best to turn to Hillary (right) herself. Her eighteen-month 2007–2008 bid for the Democratic nomination marked the first time in U.S. history that a woman ever had a viable chance of becoming president of the United States. And as of this writing, she is secretary of state. So in spite of all the "gates" that continue to burst open in an endless froth of public humiliation and absurdity, remember: our country *is* still making progress.

Who's laughing now?

---

9. Blackwater is also under investigation for mishandled relief efforts in the wake of Hurricane Katrina. And hey, since this chapter is all about controversy, we've decided to offer a little of our own. Some believe Blackwater isn't, objectively, all that different from Al-Qaeda, Islamic fundamentalism notwithstanding. It's a privately funded mercenary force with training camps on sovereign territory—and it boasts a global military agenda, no less. To learn more about the company (renamed Xe in 2009) and what it offers as the U.S. Training Center, go here: www.sourcewatch.org/index.php?title=Xe.

IRAQGATE

Jon Stewart calls Iraq "Mess O' Potamia." The best we could do is "Iraq-nophobia." Yes: we're scared of the truth about this war. Disregarding the ten-billion-dollar-a-day price tag, it's still quite frightening. Where even to start? Wait—here's an idea. How about we let the politicians (and Jay Leno) speak for themselves?

"We cannot wait for the final proof [on Iraq]—the smoking gun—that could come in the form of a mushroom cloud."

Former president
GEORGE W. BUSH,
October 7, 2002

"We will be greeted as liberators . . . I think it will go relatively quickly . . . weeks rather than months."

Former vice president
DICK CHENEY,
March 16, 2003

"A year from now, I'll be very surprised if there is not some grand square in Baghdad that is named after President Bush . . . The people of Iraq have been liberated and they understand that they've been liberated."

RICHARD PERLE, former chairman of the Pentagon's
Defense Policy Board, September 22, 2003

"We know where [the weapons of mass destruction] are. They're in the area around Tikrit and Baghdad and east, west, south and north somewhat."

Former defense secretary
DONALD RUMSFELD,
March 30, 2003

"Some folks look at me and see a certain swagger, which in Texas is called 'walking.'"

Former president
GEORGE W. BUSH, at the Republican National
Convention, 2004

"The United States does not torture."

September 6, 2006

"More people get killed in New York every night than get killed in Baghdad. The fact of life is that there will never be such a thing as 100 percent security—it doesn't exist."

L. PAUL BREMER III, director of the Coalition Provisional Authority, August 2003

"The likely economic effects [of a war in Iraq] would be relatively small . . . Under every plausible scenario, the negative effect will be quite small relative to the economic benefits."

LAWRENCE LINDSEY, assistant to the president for economic policy and director of the National Economic Council, September 16, 2002

"It is unimaginable that the United States would have to contribute hundreds of billions of dollars [in Iraq] and highly unlikely that we would have to contribute even tens of billions of dollars."[10]

KENNETH POLLACK, former director for Persian Gulf affairs, National Security Council, September 2002

"War continues in Iraq. They're calling it Operation Iraqi Freedom. They were going to call it Operation Iraqi Liberation until they realized that spells 'oil.'"

JAY LENO, April 9, 2003, on *The Tonight Show*

10. As of this writing, America has spent over $1 trillion in Iraq.

FOLEYGATE

This "gate" definitely wins the prize for Most Icky. On September 29, 2006, Republican senator Mark Foley of Florida resigned when it was discovered he'd been sending sexually explicit e-mails to some of his pages—all teenage boys—for more than ten years. That would be creepy enough, but here's the ickier twist: at the time, Foley was chairman of the House Caucus on Missing and Exploited Children, famous for its tough legislation on sexual predators. Shakespeare said it best in *Hamlet*: "The [pervert] doth protest too much." (Okay, we're paraphrasing.)

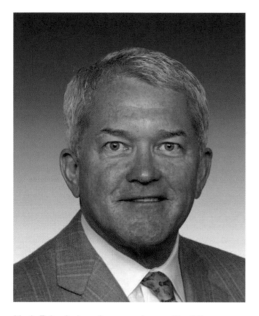

Mark Foley in happier, more hypocritical times

In one e-mail, Senator Foley gushed that a page was "in really great shape." In another he asked a sixteen-year-old boy for a photo of himself and asked what he wanted for his birthday. In yet another he asked for . . . worse. The scandal also brought down Speaker of the House Dennis Hastert (Republican of Illinois), whose close ties with Foley made it impossible for him not to appear creepy by association. After his resignation, Foley announced that he was gay and then checked himself into a treatment facility for alcoholism and other behavioral problems. And it's probably best to leave Foleygate at that.

WE CAN'T POSSIBLY MAKE THIS STUFF UP

You think Foley is icky? Remember former New York governor–turned–paid CNN loudmouth Eliot Spitzer? He built a career as a "letter-and-spirit-of-the-law" prosecutor until it was discovered he was consorting with a $5,000-an-hour call girl. Likewise, former Republican senator Larry Craig of Idaho, famous for his wide stance—sorry, tough stance—on limiting homosexual rights, was arrested on June 11, 2007. The charge: lewd conduct at the Minneapolis-Saint Paul International Airport, where he allegedly solicited an anonymous hookup with the guy in the next stall. The guy turned out to be a cop. Oh, the humanity.

SOME OTHER FAMOUS GATES

LOBBYGATE

This scandal owes its name to DC's once most powerful lobbyist, Jack Abramoff (below). As of this writing, he is currently serving a federal sentence in a minimum security prison in Maryland for fraud and bribery. With a penchant for black fedoras, private jets, steak dinners, and compulsive gambling (mind you, he gambled with actual *casinos*, not poker chips), Abramoff helped ruin the careers of former representative Bob Ney (Republican of Ohio), former deputy secretary of the Interior Steven Griles— and last but not least, former House majority leader Tom DeLay (Republican of Texas).

You're the man now, dawg.

GRANNYGATE

This gate has nothing to do with American politics whatsoever. Nor does it have much to do with grandmothers. It refers to a scandal involving international rugby.

BILL GATE(S)

See Dynasty #10, page 67.

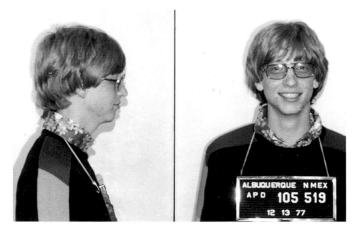

Bill Gates got his scandal out of the way early.

DISCUSSION QUESTIONS
(OPTIONAL)

1 Which hot button issues can you understand both sides of? Which make you feel like one side is crazy? Why do you think the debates are so heated?

2 What stereotypes about your point of view on these issues make you angriest? Why?

3 What do you think is the best way to keep our media fair and informative?

YOU'VE READ THIS BOOK; NOW WHAT?

GANDHI, MARTIN LUTHER KING JR., FRODO, . . . AND YOU?

If you think you are too small to make a difference, try sleeping in a closed room with a mosquito.

—*African proverb*

Economically, politically, and militarily, our nation is one of the most powerful in the world. From our dealings with North Korea and Afghanistan to our nuclear policies to our trading partners, the repercussions of our politics, government, strategies, and programs are felt around the globe. That means that the inner workings of our country—the way we vote, the way our media influences our decisions, how we feed our economy—reverberate everywhere. And it means that as U.S. citizens (and world citizens in general), we impact the planet no matter what we do, whether we like it or not. By shopping, driving,

going to school, talking to each other, and watching Seth Rogen movies,[1] we have an impact, for better or worse.

When we first started writing this book, we didn't call it a "civics" project or a book about our country. We called it our "Take Over the World" book. Why? Because we wanted to enable you to feel informed about your country and to let you know how you can (and do) shape it. We wrote this book to empower you to take over the world. If you feel like it. In a good way.

ACTIVISM

Not Just for Earnest, Patchouli-Wearing College Students Anymore (Though We Do Love Earnest, Patchouli-Wearing College Students)

Learned about something in this book you want to change? Not sure how?

When you think of getting involved, you might think of traditional stuff like sit-ins, protests, letter-writing campaigns, and spelling the word "woman" with a *y* instead of an *a*.

We're not saying these methods aren't great or effective. But rather than rehash stuff you're familiar with, we want to expand, maybe even improve your idea of the word "activism." These are fun, interesting, surprising ideas to get involved with and influence the issues that concern you, whatever they may be and wherever you stand on the political spectrum (even if you're on the end that completely disagrees with us). These are basics you can apply in your own way and in your own style. That way, you can show your patriotism by jumping into the mix.

---

1. Well, okay, maybe not watching Seth Rogen movies.

Have it your way.

MAKE-UR-OWN U.S.A.
Tools for Making Your Country (and Your World) a Better Place

PICK YOUR CHANGE. Consider the issues throughout this book and find one that speaks to you. Or recall something you heard or read about that really pissed you off, or made you sad, or inspired you. Could be anything. Pick one. Pick two. Decide to do something about it. You can. Really.

DO A LITTLE RESEARCH. It could be as little as a five-minute Internet search or as much as reading a bunch of books and calling people for info. Find out what's been done or being done about the issue(s) you're passionate about. Who else is out there working on it (people, groups, Bono?), and what are they doing? Do you agree with their approach, or have you found another you like better?

DECIDE WHAT FITS. Do you want to make a simple change—something local? Or are you more interested in working on "the big picture"? Do you want to reduce illiteracy by heading to a foreign country, majoring in a related field in college, or simply tutoring kids in your neighborhood? Once you know what size is right for you, look into what resources are available: Like-minded friends? Funds for local projects? A national organization with a branch nearby?

CONNECT. Reach out for a network. If you decide you'd like to volunteer for or join a group that already exists, here are a few good places to start:

- ★ WWW.VOLUNTEERMATCH.ORG
- ★ WWW.IDEALIST.ORG
- ★ WWW.NETWORKFORGOOD.ORG

All three have search engines for volunteer opportunities near and far, and you can search by issue (just type in a keyword, like "immigration").

LET THEM KNOW THEY NEED YOU

Don't be afraid to make cold calls, even to places that aren't advertising for volunteers. If there's an organization that you'd love to work with, call or write to make your case. They may need you without knowing they need you.

If the organization you're looking for doesn't exist, or if you're not much of a joiner, why not consider creating your own group or project? You can pull in friends or post for volunteers. It's totally doable. Check out our website to read interviews with and get info on people who've done it. Like Steve Argent, who—thanks to a chance experience in Africa and a dream of helping—founded Orphfund (www.orphfund.org), an organization that serves impoverished children worldwide. Or Chloe Jo Berman, who created a website and weekly newsletter called *Girlie Girl Army* (www.girliegirlarmy.com) that combines her love of insider fashion with insights into animal rights and cruelty-free living.

USE YOUR PASSION.

There are a million ways you can turn your interests, hobbies, and passions into social change.

USEFUL PASSIONS	USEFUL WAYS TO USE 'EM
WRITING	Write op-eds to your local paper.
FRIENDING	Reach out to like-minded world-changers online. For instance, www.idealist.org has an "affinity group" search engine to help find people who share your interests. And, of course, you can join or start a Facebook group.
E-MAILING AND TWEETING	Keep the people in your network informed on the issues that matter to you.
COOKING	Host a brunch or letter-writing party at your house. Maybe even charge a small cover fee that will go toward your cause.
SHOPPING	Harness the power of your dollar by buying only products that line up with your values. Maybe even form a group of like-minded consumers to let retailers know you mean business.
LISTENING TO MUSIC	Reach out to groups that support independent music and radio, like www.downhillbattle.org.
SHMOOZING	Canvass for a candidate you like.

NOT-SO-USEFUL PASSIONS

SLEEPING
CRYING
THE SHOW *PASSIONS*

WANTED: YOUR SKILLS

A few groups can use your skills for change.

Habitat for Humanity always needs people who are handy with tools—or just willing to learn (www.habitat.org).

Know how to sew? Project Linus's volunteers make blankets for ill or traumatized children ages zero to eighteen (www.projectlinus.org). Locate your nearest chapter to learn how to help.

Know how to read? Out loud? Librivox is always looking for volunteers to read and record audiobooks for those who can't read or see (www.librivox.org).

WHAT'S YOUR ISSUE?

MAKE IT YOUR MAJOR OR YOUR JOB. Want to make a living making change? If you haven't yet been to college or are thinking of going back for another degree, there are lots of obvious options—like, say, social work, or public policy, or environmental studies. For a comprehensive list of majors available in U.S. colleges, www.a2zcolleges.com is a good place to look.

But that's only the tip of the iceberg. Many degrees might not seem like an obvious match, but majoring in "good works" isn't a requirement to make a living doing them. You might be surprised at the variety of expertise you can leverage into an ethics-driven job—either on your own or for a business, institution, or organization.

For profiles of more people turning nontraditional skills into do-good careers, check out our website.

Look at a site like idealist.org to get an idea of what kind of degrees or experience nonprofits are looking for and what kind of entry-level positions are available. The site has search engines for nonprofit jobs, internships, and networking groups, and you'll see everything from accounting to computer programming to communications degrees being called for—and sometimes no degree at all. Chances are that, even if you majored in kinesiology or have had a desk job for ten years, there's a way for you to launch a career in do-gooding.

PICK-UR-OWN ISSUE

Not ready to make a big commitment but still want to effect a little change? Here are a few prepackaged, ready-to-serve issues and some ideas and resources for pursuing them. (Please note: all the websites below start with "www." unless otherwise stated.)

MAKE VOTING FAIR, EASY, AND INCLUSIVE.
* **Work to abolish the Electoral College:**
  College Democrats of America (http://partybuilder.collegedems.com/page/group/abolishtheelectoralcollege)

* **Work to keep corporate money out of elections:**
  Reclaim Democracy (reclaimdemocracy.org), Open Secrets (opensecrets.org)

* **Get more people to vote:**
  Particip8 (particip8.org), Rock the Vote (rockthevote.com)

* **Fight gerrymandering:**
  End Gerrymandering (endgerrymandering.com), The Redistricting Game (redistrictinggame.org)

ERADICATE AIDS.
* **Contribute to a major organization:**
  The AIDS Alliance (aids-alliance.org), The AIDS Treatment Activists Coalition (atac-usa.org)

* **Bring meals to AIDS patients in your area:**
  Meals on Wheels (mowaa.org)

VOLUNTEER OVERSEAS.
* **Help families, communities, and wildlife in other countries (if you're sixteen or older):**
  OrphFund (orphfund.org), International Volunteer Program (ivpsf.org), i-to-i Ventures (i-to-i.com), Greenheart Travel (greenhearttravel.com)

JOIN THE IMMIGRATION DEBATE.
* **To link up with a more conservative point of view:**
  The Heritage Foundation (heritage.org), The Center for Immigration Studies (cis.org)

★ **For a more liberal view:**
America's Voice (americasvoiceonline.org), The Center for American Progress (americanprogress.org)

★ **Help spur a thoughtful, fair, measured discussion about immigration:**
National Council of La Raza (nclr.org)

SUPPORT YOUR VALUES IN POLITICS.

★ **To further conservative values in politics:**
Young America's Foundation (yaf.org), Young Republican National Federation (yrnf.com)

★ **To further liberal values in politics:**
People for the American Way (pfaw.org), Young Democrats of America (yda.org)

SUPPORT THE TROOPS.

★ **Write to soldiers overseas:**
Homefront Hugs (homefronthugs.org), United Service Organizations (uso.org)

★ **Send care packages to soldiers:**
Operation Care Package (operationcarepackages.org)

SUPPORT GAY RIGHTS.

★ **Work against stereotypes:** The Gay & Lesbian Alliance Against Defamation (glaad.org)

★ **Find and support fair-minded candidates:**
Gay & Lesbian Victory Fund (victoryfund.org)

★ **Lobby for gay rights by visiting your member of Congress:** The Human Rights Campaign (hrc.org)

★ **Find an LGBT organization near you and get involved:** Good As You (GAY) (goodasyou.org)

COMBAT CLIMATE CHANGE.

★ **Calculate your own carbon footprint:**
carbonfootprint.com/calculator.aspx

★ **Organize your community:**
Don't wait for federal or state laws to curb consumption—work from the bottom up. Create a vow list ("I vow to cut driving by X," "I vow to cut electricity by X," etc.) and get your neighbors to agree. Get your school or business on board.

★ **Join a virtual march:**
Stop Global Warming (stopglobalwarming.org)

★ **Volunteer:** Search votesolar.org for lots of different opportunities.

★ **Invest in alternative energy:**
There are many mutual funds that specialize in "green" energy. Invest and potentially profit—but remember, there are no sure things in stocks these days.

★ **Host a screening:**
Rent some movies on global warming, have a viewing party, and then talk about what you saw. *An Inconvenient Truth* is a good place to start.

SUPPORT A FAIR MEDIA.

★ **Enlist a speaker to come to your school:**
Fairness & Accuracy In Reporting (FAIR) (fair.org)

★ **Make sure there's an Internet for everyone:**
Free Press Action Fund (freepress.net)

★ **Weigh in with an op-ed:**
When you feel a paper (local or national) is being unfair and unbalanced, let them—and their readers—know.

★ **Support independent programming:**
Donate an old clunker or host a party or brunch to raise money for a public radio station.

CREATIVE ACTS OF ACTIVISM

DARFUR IS DYING

Susana Ruiz created a video game called Darfur Is Dying, showing the difficult life of an average Darfuri. Since April 30, 2006, Darfur Is Dying has been played 2.5 million times and is responsible for thousands of letters to the president and U.S. representatives urging action in Darfur.

MUHAMMED YUNUS

Yunus won the Nobel Peace Prize for creating a system for investors like you and me to make small loans—called microloans—that enable the poor to start their own businesses.

BEAD FOR LIFE

This organization creates sustainable ways for women to lift their families out of poverty by giving them a way to sell their handmade jewelry worldwide. You can buy some at www.beadforlife.org.

NEWMINDSPACE

This group organizes creative events like subway parties and massive pillow fights in big cities to help build a sense of community.

A VERY SPECIAL
ANDY, JODI, AND DAN
CONCLUSION
PARAGRAPH

That's it. We're done. Signing out.

And though you may think this book was our excuse to talk about *Dynasty,* make funny photo collages of the Founding Fathers, and show you adorable animals (which, partly it was), we hope you feel like you got a little something valuable from it—maybe even a lot something. We hope it riled you up. We hope you'll come to our website and tell everyone (including us) what's on your mind. That way you can help us all write the course of our giant, crazy (and, now, infused with goji berries!) nation's future history.

We the people wish you the people a great American life.

Sincerely,
Andy, Jodi, and Dan

SOURCES

(Books with stars are also worth checking out for yourself.)

CHAPTER 1: CIVICS, PIMPED OUT

Bacevich, Andrew J. *The Limits of Power: The End of American Exceptionalism*. New York: Holt Paperbacks, 2009.

★Bennett, William J., and John T. E. Cribb. *The American Patriot's Almanac: Daily Readings on America*. Nashville: Thomas Nelson, 2008.

Buchanan, Patrick J. *Day of Reckoning: How Hubris, Ideology, and Greed Are Tearing America Apart*. New York: Thomas Dunne Books, 2007.

Cogliano, Francis D. *Revolutionary America 1763–1815: A Political History*. New York: Routledge, 2008.

★Elliott, Stephen. *Looking Forward to It: Or, How I Learned to Stop Worrying and Love the American Electoral Process*. New York: Picador, 2004.

Foner, Eric. *A Short History of Reconstruction*. New York: Harper Perennial, 1990.

Gallagher, John J. *The Battle of Brooklyn 1776*. Cambridge, MA: Castle Books, 2003.

Goldberg, Jonah. *Liberal Fascism: The Secret History of the American Left, from Mussolini to the Politics of Change*. New York: Broadway Books, 2009.

Hamilton, Alexander, James Madison, and John Jay. *The Federalist Papers*. Edited by Clinton Rossiter. New York: Signet Classics, 2003.

★Hersh, Seymour M. *Chain of Command: The Road from 9/11 to Abu Ghraib*. New York: Harper Perennial, 2005.

Maisel, L. Sandy, and Kara Z. Buckley. *Parties and Elections in America: The Electoral Process*, 4th ed. Lanham, MD: Rowman & Littlefield Publishers, Inc, 2004.

O'Rourke, P. J. *Parliament of Whores: A Lone Humorist Attempts to Explain the Entire U.S. Government*. New York: Grove Press, 2003.

Scala, Dante J. *Stormy Weather: The New Hampshire Primary and Presidential Politics*. New York: Palgrave Macmillan, 2003.

★Stewart, Jon. *The Daily Show with Jon Stewart Presents America (The Book): A Citizen's Guide to Democracy Inaction*. New York: Warner Books, 2005.

Toobin, Jeffrey. *The Nine: Inside the Secret World of the Supreme Court*. New York: Doubleday, 2007.

Vowell, Sarah. *The Wordy Shipmates*. New York: Riverhead Books, 2008.

★Wolf, Naomi. *The End of America: Letter of Warning to a Young Patriot*. White River Junction, VT: Chelsea Green Publishing Company, 2007.

Woodward, Bob. *The War Within: A Secret White House History 2006–2008*. New York: Simon & Schuster, 2009.

★Woodward, Bob, and Carl Bernstein. *All the President's Men*. New York: Simon & Schuster, 1974.

Zelden, Charles L. *Bush v. Gore: Exposing the Hidden Crisis in American Democracy*. Lawrence, KS: University Press of Kansas, 2008.

Zinn, Howard. *A People's History of the United States: 1492–Present*. New York: Harper Perennial, 2005.

CHAPTER 2: DYNASTY

Burns, James MacGregor, and Susan Dunn. *The Three Roosevelts: Patrician Leaders Who Transformed America*. New York: Grove Press, 2002.

★Bush, George. *All the Best, George Bush: My Life in Letters and Other Writings*. New York: Scribner, 2000.

Cleaves, Freeman. *Old Tippecanoe: William Henry Harrison and His Time*. New York: Scribner, 1939.

Margonelli, Lisa. *Oil on the Brain: Petroleum's Long, Strange Trip to Your Tank*. New York: Broadway Books, 2008.

★McCullough, David. *John Adams*. New York: Simon & Schuster, 2008.

★Rubin, Gretchen. *Forty Ways to Look at JFK*. New York: Ballantine, 2005.

Stiles, T. J. *The First Tycoon: The Epic Life of Cornelius Vanderbilt*. New York: Vintage, 2010.

CHAPTER 3: ECONOMICS MADE FUN

Mankiw, N. Gregory. *Principles of Economics*, 4th ed. Mason, OH: Thomson South-Western, 2006.

Meyer, Laurence H. *A Term at the Fed: An Insider's View*. New York: Harper Paperbacks, 2006.

Rubin, Robert E., and Jacob Weisberg. *In an Uncertain World: Tough Choices from Wall Street to Washington*. New York: Random House Trade Paperbacks, 2004.

CHAPTER 4: DIPLO-MESSY

Bacevich, Andrew J. *The Limits of Power: The End of American Exceptionalism*. New York: Holt Paperbacks, 2009.

Chomsky, Noam. *Rogue States: The Rule of Force in World Affairs*. Cambridge, MA: South End Press, 2000.

Cirincione, Joseph. *Bomb Scare: The History and Future of Nuclear Weapons*. New York: Columbia University Press, 2008.

Fallows, James. *Postcards from Tomorrow Square: Reports from China*. New York: Vintage, 2009.

★Hersh, Seymour M. *Chain of Command: The Road from 9/11 to Abu Ghraib*. New York: Harper Perennial, 2005.

Hitchens, Christopher. *A Long Short War: The Postponed Liberation of Iraq*. New York: Plume, 2003.

Klein, Naomi. *The Shock Doctrine: The Rise of Disaster Capitalism*. New York: Picador, 2008.

★Mayer, Jane. *The Dark Side: The Inside Story of How the War on Terror Turned into a War on American Ideals*. New York: Anchor, 2008.

Meisler, Stanley. *United Nations: The First Fifty Years*. New York: Atlantic Monthly Press, 1997.

Morris, Benny. *Righteous Victims: A History of the Zionist-Arab Conflict, 1881–2001*. New York: Vintage, 2001.

★Pipe, Jim (author), and David Antram (illustrator). *You Wouldn't Want to Be an Aristocrat in the French Revolution! A Horrible Time in Paris You'd Rather Avoid*. New York: The Salariya Book Company, 2007.

Rashid, Ahmed. *Jihad: The Rise of Militant Islam in Central Asia*. New York: Penguin, 2002.
Said, Edward W. *The Question of Palestine*. New York: Vintage, 1992.
Staten, Clifford L. *The History of Cuba*. New York: Palgrave Macmillan, 2005.
Suskind, Ron. *The Way of the World: A Story of Truth and Hope in an Age of Extremism*. New York: HarperCollins, 2008.
Wilkerson, Isabel. *The Warmth of Other Suns: The Epic Story of America's Great Migration*. New York: Random House, 2010.

CHAPTER 5: GOD BLESS THIS MESS

Bulliet, Richard W. *Islam: The View from the Edge*. New York: Columbia University Press, 1995.
Cole, Juan. *Engaging the Muslim World*. New York: Palgrave Macmillan, 2009.
Collinson, Patrick. *The Reformation: A History*. New York: Modern Library, 2006.
Drosnin, Michael. *The Bible Code*. New York: Simon & Schuster, 1997.
Krakauer, Jon. *Under the Banner of Heaven: A Story of Violent Faith*. New York: Doubleday, 2003.
Pagels, Elaine, and Karen L. King. *Reading Judas: The Gospel of Judas and the Shaping of Christianity*. New York: Penguin, 2008.
Said, Edward W. *Orientalism*. New York: Vintage, 1979.
Smith, Huston. *The World's Religions*. New York: HarperOne, 2009.
Telushkin, Rabbi Joseph. *Jewish Literacy: The Most Important Things to Know about the Jewish Religion, Its People, and Its History*, rev. ed. New York: William Morrow, 2008.
Thurman, Robert A. F. *Essential Tibetan Buddhism*. New York: HarperOne, 1996.
★Wilkinson, Philip. *Eyewitness Companions: Religions*. New York: DK, 2008.
Zaehner, R. C. *Hinduism*. Oxford, UK: Oxford University Press, 1983.

CHAPTER 6: HOT BUTTONS

All research was done with newspaper and magazine articles and websites, due to the need for the most current information at time of publication.

CONCLUSION: YOU'VE READ THIS BOOK; NOW WHAT?

Everett, Melissa. *Making a Living While Making a Difference: Conscious Careers for an Era of Interdependence*, rev. ed. Gabriola Island, BC, Canada: New Society Publishers, 2007.
Hitchens, Christopher. *Letters to a Young Contrarian* (Art of Mentoring). New York: Basic Books, 2005.
Krugman, Paul. *The Conscience of a Liberal*. New York: W. W. Norton & Company, 2009.
★Martin, Courtney E. *Do It Anyway: The New Generation of Activists*. Boston: Beacon Press, 2010.
Sharp, Gene. *From Dictatorship to Democracy: A Conceptual Framework for Liberation*. Boston: The Albert Einstein Institution, 2003.
★Shaw, Randy. *The Activist's Handbook: A Primer*. Berkeley: University of California Press, 2001.
Walljasper, Jay. *The Great Neighborhood Book: A Do-It-Yourself Guide to Placemaking*. Gabriola Island, BC, Canada: New Society Publishers, 2007.

NEWS & THE WEB

Al Jazeera English http://english.aljazeera.net
The Angry Arab News Service www.angryarab.blogspot.com
The Atlantic www.theatlantic.com
BBC www.bbc.co.uk
Brainy Quote www.brainyquote.com
CNN www.cnn.com
The Daily Dish http://andrewsullivan.theatlantic.com/
Daily Kos www.dailykos.com
Dictionary.com www.dictionary.reference.com
The Economist www.economist.com
Fox News www.foxnews.com
The Guardian www.guardian.co.uk
Ha'aretz www.haaretz.com
The Huffington Post www.huffingtonpost.com
Human Rights Watch www.hrw.org
Informed Comment www.juancole.com
KCRW's "To the Point" www.kcrw.com/news/programs/tp
Los Angeles Times www.latimes.com
The Nation www.thenation.com

National Geographic www.nationalgeographic.com
National Review www.nationalreview.com
The New Republic www.tnr.com
The New Yorker www.newyorker.com
The New York Review of Books www.nybooks.com
The New York Times www.nytimes.com
NPR www.npr.org
Open Secrets www.opensecrets.org
Pat Robertson www.patrobertson.com
Publishers Weekly www.publishersweekly.com
Rolling Stone www.rollingstone.com
Science www.sciencemag.org
USA Today www.usatoday.com
U.S. Central Intelligence Agency www.cia.gov
U.S. Federal Election Commission www.fec.gov
Vanity Fair www.vanityfair.com
The Wall Street Journal www.wsj.com
The Washington Post www.washingtonpost.com
The White House www.whitehouse.gov

For an extensive list of specific newspaper and magazine articles used to research this book, please visit www.americapediathebook.com.

FURTHER READING AND WATCHING

CHAPTER 1: CIVICS, PIMPED OUT
TO READ

Aronson, Marc. *The Real Revolution: The Global Story of American Independence*. New York: Clarion, 2005.
Freedman, Russell. *In Defense of Liberty: The Story of America's Bill of Rights*. New York: Holiday House, 2003.
Hakim, Joy. *A History of US: Book 1; The First Americans*. New York: Oxford University Press, 2006.
Johnston, Robert D. *The Making of America: The History of the United States from 1492 to the Present*. Washington DC: National Geographic, 2010.
Selzer, Adam. *The Smart Aleck's Guide to American History*. New York: Delacorte, 2009.
Sergis, Diana K. *Bush v. Gore: Controversial Presidential Election Case* (Landmark Supreme Court Cases). Berkeley Heights, NJ: Enslow, 2003.
Zinn, Howard. *A Young People's History of the United States*, Enhanced Omnibus Edition. New York: Seven Stories Press, 2009.

TO WATCH

America: The Story of Us; Revolution. Directed by Nick Green. New York: A&E Home Video, 2010. (Documentary)
Glory. Directed by Edward Zwick. Culver City, CA: Sony, 1989. (Dramatization—the Civil War)
Recount. Directed by Jay Roach. New York: HBO Home Video, 2008. (Dramatization—the 2000 presidential election)
1776: Restored Director's Cut. Directed by Peter H. Hunt. Culver City, CA: Sony, 2002. (Fiction)

CHAPTER 2: DYNASTY
TO READ

Baker, Russ. *Family of Secrets: The Bush Dynasty, America's Invisible Government, and the Hidden History of the Last Fifty Years*. New York: Bloomsbury, 2009.
Bush, George W. *Decision Points*. New York: Crown, 2010.
Cooper, Michael L. *Theodore Roosevelt: A Twentieth-Century Life* (Up Close). New York: Viking, 2009.
Ellis, Joseph J. *First Family: Abigail and John Adams*. New York: Alfred A. Knopf, 2010.
Fleming, Candace. *Our Eleanor: A Scrapbook Look at Eleanor Roosevelt's Remarkable Life*. New York: Atheneum, 2005.
Freedman, Russell. *Franklin Delano Roosevelt*. New York: Sandpiper, 1992.
Gherman, Beverly (author), and Matthew Bird (illustrator). *First Son and President: A Story about John Quincy Adams* (A Creative Minds Biography). Minneapolis: Millbrook, 2005.
Golway, Terry, and Les Krantz. *JFK Day by Day: A Chronicle of the 1,036 Days of John F. Kennedy's Presidency*. Philadelphia: Running Press, 2010.
Hakim, Joy. *A History of US: Book 8; An Age of Extremes 1880–1917*. New York: Oxford University Press, 2007.
Marrin, Albert. *The Great Adventure: Theodore Roosevelt and the Rise of Modern America*. New York: Dutton, 2007.
Sandler, Martin W. *Kennedy Through the Lens: How Photography and Television Revealed and Shaped an Extraordinary Leader*. New York: Walker & Company, 2011.
Sullivan, Robert, ed. *The Kennedys: End of a Dynasty* (Life Books). New York: Time Inc. Home Entertainment, 2009.

TO WATCH

American Experience: FDR. Directed by David Grubin. Arlington, VA: PBS, 1994. (Documentary)
American Experience: George H. W. Bush. Directed by Austin Hoyt. Arlington, VA: PBS, 2008. (Documentary)
American Experience: John and Abigail Adams. Directed by Peter Jones. Arlington, VA: PBS, 2005. (Documentary)
American Experience: The Kennedys. Directed by Phillip Whitehead, Marilyn Mellowes, David Espar, and James A. DeVinney. Arlington, VA: PBS, 1992. (Documentary)
American Experience: TR, the Story of Theodore Roosevelt. Directed by David Grubin. Arlington, VA: PBS, 1996. (Documentary)
Crisis: Behind a Presidential Commitment. Directed by Robert Drew. New York: ABC News, 1963. (Documentary—integration)
John Adams. Directed by Tom Hooper. New York: HBO, 2008. (Dramatization, Miniseries)

CHAPTER 3: ECONOMICS MADE FUN
TO READ

Mayer, David A. *The Everything Economics Book: From Theory to Practice, Your Complete Guide to Understanding Economics Today*. Avon, MA: Adams Media, 2010.
Rodrick, Dani. *The Globalization Paradox: Democracy and the Future of the World Economy*. New York: W. W. Norton & Company, 2011.
Taibbi, Matt. *Griftopia: Bubble Machines, Vampire Squids, and the Long Con That Is Breaking America*. New York: Spiegel & Grau, 2010.

TO WATCH

Capitalism: A Love Story. Directed by Michael Moore. Beverly Hills, CA: Starz/Anchor Bay, 2009. (Documentary)
Collapse. Directed by Chris Smith. Orland Park, IL: MPI Home Video, 2009. (Documentary)
Inside Job. Directed by Charles Ferguson. Culver City, CA: Sony, 2010. (Documentary)

CHAPTER 4: DIPLO-MESSY
TO READ

Barakat, Ibtisam. *Tasting the Sky: A Palestinian Childhood*. New York: Farrar, Straus & Giroux, 2007.
Fasulo, Linda. *An Insider's Guide to the UN*, 2nd ed. New Haven, CT: Yale University Press, 2009.
Hampton, Wilborn. *War in the Middle East: A Reporter's Story; Black September and the Yom Kippur War*. Somerville, MA: Candlewick, 2009.
Junger, Sebastian. *War*. New York: Twelve, 2010.

Luttrell, Marcus. *Lone Survivor: The Eyewitness Account of Operation Redwing and the Lost Heroes of SEAL Team 10*. Boston: Little, Brown, 2009.
Marcovitz, Hal. *The Ottoman and Qajar Empires in the Age of Reform* (The Making of the Middle East). Broomall, PA: Mason Crest, 2007.
Population 1.3 Billion: China Becomes a Super Superpower (24/7: Behind the Headlines Special Edition). New York: Franklin Watts, 2009.
Smithson, Ryan. *Ghosts of War: The True Story of a 19-Year-Old GI*. New York: Collins, 2010.
Watad, Mahmoud, and Leonard Grob. *Teen Voices from the Holy Land: Who Am I to You?* Amherst, NY: Prometheus Books, 2007.

TO WATCH

China: A Century of Revolution. Directed by Sue Williams. New York: Zeitgeist Films, 1997. (Documentary)
The Hurt Locker. Directed by Kathryn Bigelow. Universal City, CA: Summit Entertainment, 2008. (Fiction—Iraq War)
Munich. Directed by Steven Spielberg. Los Angeles: Universal Studios, 2005. (Fiction—terrorism)
No End in Sight. Directed by Charles Ferguson. New York: Magnolia Pictures, 2007. (Documentary—Iraq War)
Restrepo. Directed by Sebastian Junger. New York: Virgil Films and Entertainment, 2010. (Documentary—war in Afghanistan)
Thirteen Days. Directed by Roger Donaldson. Los Angeles: New Line Home Video, 2000. (Dramatization—Cuban Missile Crisis)

CHAPTER 5: GOD BLESS THIS MESS
TO READ

Bowker, John. *World Religions: The Great Faiths Explored and Explained*. New York: DK, 2006.
Dalai Lama. *The Art of Happiness: A Handbook for Living*, 10th anniv. ed. New York: Riverhead Books, 2009.
Esposito, John L., and Dalia Mogahed. *Who Speaks for Islam? What a Billion Muslims Really Think*. New York: Gallup Press, 2007.
Johnsen, Linda. *The Complete Idiot's Guide to Hinduism*, 2nd ed. New York: Alpha, 2009.
Landaw, Jonathan, and Stephan Bodian. *Buddhism for Dummies*. New York: Wiley, 2003.
Schoen, Robert. *What I Wish My Christian Friends Knew about Judaism*. Chicago: Loyola Press, 2004.
Stone, Caroline. *Islam* (Eyewitness Guides). New York: DK, 2003.
Toropov, Brandon, and Father Luke Buckles. *The Complete Idiot's Guide to World Religions*, 3rd ed. New York: Alpha, 2004.
Wagner, Richard. *Christianity for Dummies*. Hoboken, NJ: Wiley, 2004.

TO WATCH

American Experience and Frontline: God in America. Directed by David Belton. Arlington, VA: PBS, 2010. (Documentary, Miniseries)
American Experience and Frontline: The Mormons. Directed by Helen Whitney. Arlington, VA: PBS, 2007. (Documentary)
Religulous. Directed by Larry Charles. Santa Monica, CA: Lion's Gate, 2008. (Documentary)
10 Questions for the Dalai Lama. Directed by Rick Ray. Thousand Oaks, CA: Monterey Video, 2006. (Documentary)

CHAPTER 6: HOT BUTTONS
TO READ

Alsenas, Linas. *Gay America: Struggle for Equality*. New York: Amulet, 2008.
Garden, Nancy. *Hear Us Out! Lesbian and Gay Stories of Struggle, Progress, and Hope, 1950 to the Present*. New York: Farrar, Straus & Giroux, 2007.
Haugen, David, Susan Musser, and Kacy Lovelace, eds. *Abortion* (Opposing Viewpoints). Farmington Hills, MI: Greenhaven Press, 2010.
Hulme, Mike. *Why We Disagree about Climate Change: Understanding Controversy, Inaction and Opportunity*. New York: Cambridge University Press, 2009.
Lanier, Wendy. *Abortion* (Hot Topics). Farmington Hills, MI: Lucent Books, 2009.
Miller, Debra A. *Health Care* (Hot Topics). Farmington Hills, MI: Lucent Books, 2011.
Morrow, Robert. *Immigration: Rich Diversity or Social Burden?* (USA TODAY's Debate: Voices and Perspectives). Minneapolis: Twenty-First Century Books, 2010.
Shiva, Vandana. *Soil Not Oil: Environmental Justice in an Age of Climate Crisis*. Cambridge, MA: South End Press, 2008.
Walker, Sally M. (from the adult book by Tim Flannery). *We Are the Weather Makers: The History of Climate Change*. Somerville, MA: Candlewick, 2009.

TO WATCH

All the President's Men. Directed by Alan J. Pakula. Burbank, CA: Warner, 1976. (Dramatization—Watergate)
American Experience: Stonewall Uprising. Directed by Kate Davis and David Heilbroner. Arlington, VA: PBS, 2011. (Documentary—gay rights)
Dick. Directed by Andrew Fleming. Culver City, CA: Sony, 1999. (Fiction—Watergate)
An Inconvenient Truth. Directed by Davis Guggenheim. Hollywood, CA: Paramount, 2006. (Documentary—climate change)
Milk. Directed by Gus Van Sant. Los Angeles: Universal, 2008. (Dramatization—gay rights/biography)
Sicko. Directed by Michael Moore. New York: Weinstein Company, 2007. (Documentary—health care)

CONCLUSION: YOU'VE READ THIS BOOK; NOW WHAT?
TO READ

Halpin, Mikki. *It's Your World—If You Don't Like It, Change It: Activism for Teenagers*. New York: Simon Pulse, 2004.
Lewis, Barbara A. *The Teen Guide to Global Action: How to Connect with Others (Near and Far) to Create Social Change*. Minneapolis: Free Spirit Publishing, 2008.
Taft, Jessica K. *Rebel Girls: Youth Activism and Social Change across the Americas*. New York: New York University Press, 2011.

TO WATCH—AND BE INSPIRED

Erin Brockovich. Directed by Steven Soderbergh. Los Angeles: Universal, 2000. (Dramatization—environment)
Gandhi. Directed by Richard Attenborough. Culver City, CA: Sony, 1982. (Dramatization—biography)
Silkwood. Directed by Mike Nichols. Los Angeles: MGM, 1983. (Dramatization—nuclear power/environment)

ACKNOWLEDGMENTS

We three thank Emily Easton, Stacy Cantor Abrams, Mary Kate Castellani, John Candell, Jennifer Healey, Melissa Kavonic, and the entire Bloomsbury crew for turning our groceries into a feast; Sarah Burnes for being a smart and devoted champion; and Tara-Lynne Pixley for being the Photo Whisperer. Without their hard work, this book would be blank. Now that we think of it, blank books sell quite well. Those Moleskine things are everywhere! And they're not cheap, either. Seriously, they must be making bank. Nevertheless, it wouldn't have felt the same.

Dan says: Thank you, Jess, Nate, the Ehrenhafts, the Wollmans, the Rankins, and the Dunns for their boundless love and support. For inspiration, thank you (in no particular order): Kurt Vonnegut, Coretta Scott King, Tom Morello, Howard Zinn, Eric Foner, Jim Shenton, Harvey Milk, Elizabeth Blackwell, Neil Young, Dave Eggers, Sarah Vowell (and the entire 826NYC staff and board), all those involved in *The Daily Show* and *The Colbert Report* . . . and pretty much any other person who's ever gotten off their butts to try to understand the world and make it a better place—including Andy and Jodi.

Andy says: Thank you, Christi, for your pride and patience. You're the bestest. Thank you, Mom and Adelaide, for your love and kindness. Thank you, Ken Edelstein, for giving me my career; Matt Gove, for always saying yes when I call to read you something; Jodi and Dan, for inspiring me, making me smile every minute we're together or talking, and carrying me on your shoulders when things got rough. And thank you, Dad. I love you and miss you every day.

Jodi says: Thanks to my parents for instilling in me some of the values we wanted this book to embody, namely: be thoughtful, be kind, and don't yell. Thanks to my smart, passionate, and savvy DC friends who shared their ideas and wisdom as this book was taking shape. Much appreciation to Tryst Coffeehouse in Adams Morgan for selling me all those cappuccinos. Thank you, Mark, for being such a support and inspiration. And finally, thank you to Andy and Dan . . . how did I get so lucky as to work with two people I admire so much *and* who tell such good jokes?

CREDITS

Location key: l—left, r—right, c—center, t—top, b—bottom

Albuquerque Police Department: 21cr, 221br; **Jodi Anderson:** 116t; **Aokettun:** 105tr; **Marius Arnesen:** 125; **Associated Press:** 26l (J. Scott Applewhite), 33br (Cheryl Senter), 53t, 102tr (Shayna Brennan), 134l, 179tr (Manuel Balce Ceneta), 201l (Rich Pedroncelli), 212t, 218 (J. Scott Applewhite, *George W. Bush*); **David Barrie** (under Creative Commons): 114r; **Rosemary Behan:** 77; **Clifford Berryman:** 51bl; **Bettman/CORBIS:** 21tr, 58l, 76r, 192l; **John Candell:** 180br; **CDC:** 107t; **CODE PINK:** 167 (*Mahmoud Ahmadinejad*); **Columbia Pictures:** 209r ("Mr. Smith Goes to Washington" © 1939, renewed 1967 Columbia Pictures Industries, Inc. All Rights Reserved.); **Congressional Pictorial Directory:** 39; **Corbis:** 67c (Deborah Feingold), 105l (CinemaPhoto), 185r (Sara De Boer/Retna Ltd.); **Jose Cruz:** 104 (*Mahmoud Ahmadinejad, Hugo Chavez*); **Joeff Davis:** 30t, 32t, 90l, 171b; **Chris Doelle:** 109r; **The Dolph Briscoe Center for American History/ The University of Texas at Austin:** 22b (Wally McNamee, Reading America's Photos/Presidents [e_wm_0322]); **Eric Draper:** 61b (UPI), 213 (*George W. Bush*); **Daniel Ehrenraft:** 212b; **Elliott Erwitt/ Magnum Photos:** 21bl; **FBI:** 92l, 93t (*Osama bin Laden*), 213 (*John Dillinger*); **FEMA/Mark Wolfe:** 220l (*Mark Foley*); **Fibonacci Blue/Flickr:** 189b; **George Bush Presidential Library and Museum:** 59t; **Getty Images:** 19 (Alex Wong/Getty Images News), 22t (Mark Wilson/Getty Image News), 24 (John Moore), 35r (John G. Mablango), 52 (GAB Archive/Redferns), 62 (Getty Images News), 64bl (Evelyn Floret/Time & Life Pictures), 68 (Bob D'Amico/Disney ABC Television Group), 75c (Bloomberg), 78l (Brad Mangin/Sports Illustrated), 80l (Daniel Boczarski/Redferns), 96 (L. Busacca/WireImage, *NSYNC*), 123b (Charles Hewitt/Hulton Archive), 126t (Keystone/Hulton Archive), 148l (Drew Cunningham/Getty Images News), 149r (Theo Wargo/WireImage), 149c (Bob Thomas/Popperfoto), 154bl (Graham Wood/Hulton Archive), 165 (Johannes Simon/Getty Images News, *Eastern Orthodox clergy*), 175 (Kevin Winter/Getty Images Entertainment, *John Travolta/Kelly Preston*), 175 (Theo Wargo/WireImage, *Kirstie Alley*), 201r (Abid Katib), 211bl (ABC Photo Archives/Disney ABC Television Group), 218 (Tom Williams/CQ-Roll Call Group, *Richard Perle*), 219 (Scott J. Ferrell, *Lawrence Lindsay*); **GfK GeoMarketing/UNAIDS:** 193; **Mark Godfrey/The Image Works:** 204; **The Granger Collection, New York:** 45b, 57tl, 57tr, 90r, 140, 142, 148r, 171t and 223l (ullstein bild); **Steve Grochowsky/Flickr:** 20l; **Julien Harneis:** 198; **Interpol:** 96 (*Lashkar-e-Taiba*); **Edi Israel:** 126b; **Israel News Agency:** 161; **iStockphoto.com:** front cover (Lewis Wright), 9l (Nicholas Monu, *man*; Pavlo Maydikov, *clogs*), 25r (Morgan Lane Studios, *film frames*; Shannon Toth, *Frankenstein*; Anderson & Anderson, *cupid*), 38, 72l (Mlenny Photography), 72br (DNY59), 75r (David H. Lewis), 78r, 81r (Imad Birkholz), 82bl, 83 (Tony Campbell), 89tl (Ljupco), 103br (Aleksas Kvedoras), 110l (Ilya Terentyev), 110br (Mike Wooten), 113l (Soubrette), 138l (Jon Schulte), 139l (Chad Breece), 139br (Elisa Garrido), 141l (Christina Veit), 143 (Torsten Schon), 157 (Andrew Rog), 159t (Evgeny Terentev), 166 (Duncan Walker, *King Henry VIII*), 175t (Marc Fischer), 184r (Kostas Koutsoukos), 186bl (kevdog818), 191tl (Lise Gagne), 195r (David Parsons), 196 (Eric Isselée, *cow*), 196 (Tim McCaig, *traffic*), 197r (AtlasImages), 199l (Terry Katz), 199r (Neil Riehle), 200tl (Beboy_ltd), 200bl (Michelle Hillmer), 200r (Anton Brand), 202l (James Steidl), 202r (cjmckendry), 203l and 203r (Alex Slobodkin), 205r (Tim McAfee), 207r (Ricardo Reitmeyer), 209l (Natalia Klenova), 210t (Ryan Balderas), 224t (Scibak), 224b (Justin Horrocks), 226 (Claude Dagenais); **John F. Kennedy Presidential Library/Cecil Stoughton** 57br, 213 (*Jacqueline Kennedy*); **Patrik Jones/Flickr:** 186tr; **Jorge 11/Flickr:** 9br; **Jupiter Images Corp.:** 26r, 31, 36, 41, 42 (*all*), 43l, 44r, 45tr, 49tr, 54l, 58r (*crowns, sword, rock*), 61t (*crib, oil well*), 86l, 87r, 89r, 92r, 93t, 94l, 95l, 95b, 99l (*bird*), 100l, 102br, 107br, 111br, 112bl, 112br, 113r, 117tr, 119br, 128br, 180t, 182 (*leprechaun*), 187r, 188; **Damian Kettlewell/Flickr:** 34; **Heinrich Klaffs/Flickr:** 73b, 150 (*Dizzy Gillespie*); **Liberty University:** 191r; **Library of Congress:** 10t, 10b, 11, 12t, 12b, 13, 14r, 15l, 16bl, 16bc, 16tr, 23, 27t, 27b, 28, 29l, 46tl, 47tr (*William Henry Harrison*), 49bl (*Daniel Webster*), 50tl, 50tr, 51r, 54r, 63l, 63r, 64tr, 65tl, 74, 86r, 88l, 93b, 97tr, 107bl, 108, 111l, 119tr, 121tr, 121br, 122l, 123t, 124, 129tr, 130l, 138t, 145br, 149l, 155, 156r, 164 (*Orthodox Jews*), 165 (*Billy Graham*), 167 (Ira Rosenberg, *Muhammad Ali*), 167br, 168, 169r, 181 (Warren K. Leffler), 196 (*coal*), 206l, 206r, 211tl, 211r, 213 (*Abigail Adams, John Adams, John Quncy Adams, Muhammad Ali, Franklin Delano Roosevelt, Theodore Roosevelt*), 213 (Marion S. Trikosko, *Henry Kissinger*), 223r; **Alan Light:** 175 (*Tom Cruise*), 219 (*Jay Leno*); **Jim Lo Scalzo:** 21br; **LWY/Flickr:** 9l; **Richard Lyon:** 191bl; **Mangwanani:** 104 (*Robert Mugabe*); **Kat Mereand/WIKI:** 228tr; **Microsoft Archives:** 67l; **mptvimages.com:** 132r (Bud Gray), 160 (Floyd McCarty), 166 (© 2002 Glenn Weiner, *Mel Gibson*), 185l; **NASA:** 76c (*earth*), 99r, 213 (*James Lovell*); **National Archives and Records Administration:** 48 (*all*), 53b, 69t, 103tr; **National Counterterrorism Center:** 94br; **National Park Service:** 46tr (*Thomas Jefferson*); **National Security Archives:** 60; **NATO:** 135r; **The New York Public Library:** 69b (Robert N. Dennis Collection of Stereoscopic Views; Miriam and Ira D. Wallach Division of Art, Prints and Photographs; Astor, Lenox and Tilden Foundations); **North Korea Government:** 104 (*Kim Jong Il*); **Andisheh Nouraee:** 34, 35l, 41, 44r, 47tr, 47br, 49tl, 49tr, 49bl, 49bc, 51tl, 54l, 60, 61t, 75l, 98l, 107br, 116b, 118l, 121l, 127t, 127b, 141r, 147, 150, 151b, 156l, 170, 179tl, 184l, 187l, 195l, 197l, 207l, 208, 214r, 216r; **Charles Opitz:** 73tr; **Paramount Pictures:** 33bl, 205l (all rights reserved); **Picture History:** 196 (*hippies*); **T. Lynne Pixley:** 180bl; **©2011 ProvidenceCollection.com:** 153 (image 00143); **Public Library of Science Journal:** 183; **Richard Nixon Presidential Library:** 213 (*Pat Nixon*); **Alexa Scordato:** 169l; **M.R. Sellars:** 196 (*pudding*); **Susan Sermoneta/Flickr:** 79l; **David Shankbone:** 65tr, 194r, 228br; **Pete Souza/White House:** 57bl; **SplashNews:** 66t; **Sean Sprague:** 194l; **Charles Steinberg/Bead for Life:** 228bl; **Sterling and Francine Clark Art Institute, Williamstown:** 6; **Art Streiber/NBC Universal:** 152; **sxc.hu:** 72b, 76l (Laura Leavell), 76c (Robert Linder), 179b (David Lat); **Sir John Tenniel:** 30b; **Terre Haute City Government:** 117br; **UN Photo:** 128tr (Andrea Brizzi), 131t (Paulo Filgueiras), 131b (Basile Zoma), 133r (Marie Frechon), 134r (H. Arvidsson); **U.S. Army:** 106r; **U.S. Department of Defense:** 94tr, 99l (*bomb*), 109l, 115, 130r, 133l, 213 (*Richard Nixon*), 216 (*Monica Lewinsky*), 218 (*Donald Rumsfeld*); **U.S. Department of Energy:** 102tl, 102bl; **U.S. Department of Homeland Security:** 91; **U.S. Fish and Wildlife Service:** 87l; **U.S. House of Representatives:** 103l; **U.S. Mint:** 43r; **U.S. Navy:** 196 (Emilio Segre Visual Archives, *Roger Revelle*), 219 (L. Paul Bremer III); **U.S. Senate:** 37 (*John McCain*), 56l; **U.S. Supreme Court:** 88r; **Edward Valachovic:** 132l; **Washington DC:** 14l; **White House:** 20r, 37 (*Barack Obama*), 57bc, 59b, 98t; **Wikimedia Commons:** 15r, 16br, 17, 21tl, 21cl, 25l, 29r (Dale Frost/The Port of San Diego), 33tl, 33tr, 43b, 45tl, 49bc (*William Henry Harrison*), 49br, 64tl, 65b, 66b, 67b, 73tl, 75l (Manfred Werner/Tsui, *Richard Fairbrass*; Dan Smith, *Federal Reserve*), 79r, 80r, 81l, 82tl (Elvert Barnes), 82br (Justin McIntosh), 96 (*Osama bin Laden, Farc, Hezbollah*), 97tl, 97bl, 100r, 105br, 106l, 110tr, 112tl, 114l, 117l, 118tr, 118cr, 118br (David Shankbone), 119l, 120, 128l (Glenn Francis/www.PacificProDigital.com), 129tl, 135l, 145bl, 146bl, 151t, 154t (Andrew Bossi), 154bc, 154br, 159b, 164t, 164 (*Joe Lieberman*), 164 (Rubenstein, *Jon Stewart*), 165 (*Pope Benedict*), 166 (*Anabaptists, Pentecostals, Susan B. Anthony*), 173, 174t (Harkanwal Singh), 182 (Manuel González Olaechea, *matador*), 182 (*beret, Queen Elizabeth*; Agencia Brasil, *George W. Bush*), 186tr, 196 (Agencia Brasil, *George W. Bush*), 196 (*Al Gore*), 210b, 213 (Cpl. Wil Acosta, *Jon Voight*; David Shankbone, *Paul Sorvino*; Donna Lou Morgan/U.S. Navy, *Laura Linney*; Elena Torre, *Anthony Hopkins*; Alan Light, *Tom Hanks*; Andre Luis, *Tom Wilkinson*; Chrisa Hickey, *Amy Adams*; watchwithkristin, *Paul Giamatti*; lukeisback.com, *Josh Brolin*; John J. Kruzel/American Forces Press Service, *Robin Williams*; Vanessa Lua, *Will Smith*; nicogenin, *Johnny Depp*; MC1 Chad J. McNeeley/U.S. Navy, *Katie Holmes*; gdcgraphics, *Frank Langella*; Jaared Purdy, *Joan Allen*), 213 (*Amelia Earhart, Benjamin Franklin*), 214l, 216l, 219 (*Kenneth Pollack*), 220r, 221l, 221tr; **Chris Willis/Flickr:** 172r; **World Economic Forum:** 190 (Remy Steinegger), 192r (Philip Schwaib), 218 (Flickr, *Dick Cheney*), 228tl (WIKI); **Daniella Zalcman/Flickr:** 101

Note: *Italic* page numbers indicate illustrations. The letter *n* after a page number refers to a footnote and is followed by the note number.